BRANDAMAJO DIARIES

ANNA CROSS

Cromwell Publishers 405 Kings Road London SW10 0BB
An imprint of First Century Ltd.

Website: www.CromwellPublishers.co.uk

E mail: Info@CromwellPublishers.co.uk

ISBN 1-903930-18-9

DEDICATION

I would like to dedicate this book to Martin, husband, father, skipper and many other things besides, without whom the whole trip would never have taken place.

I would not have done it with anybody else, and the brunt of the responsibility was always on him.

David, Brinsley and John also helped make it a trip of a lifetime.

INTRODUCTION

"Why don't we sell the house, buy a yacht and sail round the world?"

About a year ago, a chance remark led to where we are now.

We had a lovely large white house in rural Cheshire, a garden that I had cherished and developed over the years, children settled in their schools, friends, and a selection of animals. Sailing at weekends down at Budworth Sailing Club, good holidays. Did we really want to give up all of this?

We are a family of five: myself, Anna, Mum, first mate, Bub (family nickname), keen horse rider and gardener and a sailor by default. I was born to one, married one and have given birth to at least one, if not three. Then there is Martin, dad, keen dinghy sailor, corporate man and wage earner, skipper to be.

We have produced three sons: David, 11 years old, good looking, (actually although I may be biased, they all are!) loves outdoor sports. Optimist, sailor, eternal worrier, second mate.

Brinsley, 9 years old, wiry, loves making things and animals; not quite sure if he likes sailing or not, Able Seaman.

John, 7 years old and having two older brothers to contend with, a bruiser, likes his football, and is just beginning to start optimist sailing, but has one hell of a temper on him, Bosun.

Then we have Buchi, Dalmatian, and Peter's elderly highland pony, Scooby Doo, naughty round fat chestnut pony bought for the children to ride. And on permanent loan a mad thoroughbred, Dixie, that has been my provider of adrenaline rushes up till now. They have to be found homes for the duration of our absence.

The decision to sell our house and go was not taken easily; we have lived here in Cheshire on and off for the last ten years and the roots are getting deeper. What happens if we can't sell the yacht when we get back? Why don't we just let the house? What happens if the company won't give Martin a break? What about the children's education?

But there are answers to all of the questions. We can rent or live on the yacht; we can't afford to let the house, we need the capital to buy the yacht and live in not too much poverty for a year. If Martin won't be given a career break, we will go anyway, especially if we manage to sell the house. We can teach the boys, and anyway, what is the worst that can happen? They will go back a year… and by the time they reach further education, who is going to mind if they are seventeen eighteen or nineteen? Once the seed of an idea has taken root it is not that easy to dislodge.

My father always wanted to sail across the Atlantic but he died when he was 48 and never got the chance. We are both forty. If we don't go now, the children will be too old and their schooling will be too important to be able to take them away from it for a year. So it is now or never.

And the final question we must pose to ourselves, "Will we regret it if we don't go? The answer to that is undoubtedly yes, because if we don't go, we will never know what it would have been like.

So, a decision is made. It is a relief. The house is put on the market.

We have never done any ocean sailing, but Martin is an excellent dinghy sailor, and I have done minor yacht sailing all of my life. As a family we have chartered in the Mediterranean, we have sailed off the West Coast of Scotland and Martin has raced yachts in the Solent, so although not experts, neither are we complete novices.

Some questions we can't answer. Will we still be a family at the end of it or will we have discovered that living in such close confines for a year is unbearable and be seeking the divorce courts on our return? But one thing is for sure, if we don't try we will never find out. Until now, he has been working the typical corporate businessman's life, working almost every waking hour, and when he gets home he is too tired to do much with the children. All of a sudden he is realising that they are growing up and he hasn't seen much of them. And, as he says, whoever wants on their epitaph 'I wish I had spent more time in the office'?

Decision made, the house is put on the market, we get ourselves on the mailing list of yacht brokers, and our fingers are crossed. I cannot imagine anybody not wanting our lovely house.

Going to the Boat Show when you are really and truly a potential yacht purchaser is a lovely experience. All of a sudden you are given seats, cups of coffee, ushered onto boats instead of off them and we can fluff up with a little self-importance.

CHAPTER ONE

FROM ENGLAND TO THE CANARIES.

AUGUST 1999

End of May was our deadline. If we hadn't sold the house by then it would be impracticable to go. But here we are in July and tomorrow we exchange contracts. The little pony Scooby Doo is already at the stables where he is going to spend the year and apparently settling in very well. If we don't go then he will just come back here. The mad thoroughbred Dixie, who I'm sure would have killed me in due course anyway, refused to go in the trailer that was to take her to her new home so a lorry came with a confident man and she walked in like a lamb.

The removal men are booked, we have found a boat almost ready to go, we just need to sell the house. Every day somebody asks us "Are you going or aren't you? And we get more and more frustrated as there is nothing more we can do about it.

Tomorrow finally comes and the phone rings, I am on tenterhooks, hopefully it is the solicitors telling me that the sale has gone through and we will have the money to buy the boat with. I rush to the phone full of anticipation.

"Hello?"

"Mrs Cross?"

"Yes, have we exchanged contracts?" I ask eagerly.

"Um, No, I'm sorry but we can't exchange today'.

"Why not?" I ask, exasperated, over the phone, feeling my body slump Outside the birds are singing and the garden is in full bloom. Maybe we are not meant to go.

"The money is not available yet." I am ready to weep, we cannot force them to exchange, but we can pull out of the sale. Another few years added to my life, I already have a few grey hairs, what harm can a few more do?

Faxes, visits to solicitors, deep sighs of 'why are we doing all this anyway?'

We finally exchange the following day, spend the money on the yacht and move out the following week. The lovely garden is somebody else's now. But at least we can get on with the serious planning of the forthcoming year, not that there is much time left to plan in.

Martin formally gets his year off work. Now no longer a corporate man he goes and has his hair cut, number one on the clippers, he has a thick head of black hair, speckled with grey now, and number one is virtually like having your head shaved. "Do you know what this looks like sir?" asks the barber.

"Yes."

"Are you sure you want it?"

"Yes."

Your wife won't like it," but he proceeds to shear Martin's hair off, and with it goes the corporate image. True enough his wife doesn't like the convict look, so I persuade him to wear his leather bush hat from South Africa for the first few days anyway. At least we are unlikely to get mugged down a dark side street. It does have a nice feel to it though!

Two weeks later and we are in Hayling Island with the good yacht *Brandamajo*. Only she isn't called this yet.

She is entered in the ARC (Atlantic Rally for Cruisers) as *If* after the poem of that name by Rudyard Kipling.

"You can't call her *If*, I say.

"Why not?" asks Martin, as we sit in a traffic jam.

"Because I would rather she was called 'When'" so that we have 'when we get there' instead of 'if we get there'."

"So, any suggestions?"

A chorus of suggestions come pouring forth from the back seat where the boys are sitting, the beep, beep, beeping of the Gameboys providing a background noise. "Frobscottle........ Bad to the Bone........ Mid Life Crisis........ Sea Shadow...... Crossfire......."

But none of them are acceptable to our future skipper and we must carry on thinking.

A 46 ft Bavaria, about four years old, she is out of the water, looking ungainly, like a fish out of water, her antifouling ready to be redone and we have a lot of hours work on her. There are several other yachts out of the water, all in different stages of repair or perhaps just there for storage. We are on the front with other Bavaria yachts and as you climb down the ladder onto the concrete there is the marina for the yachts in the water. As the tide goes out, mud flats appear all around, leaving a well-dredged puddle in the middle in which all the pontoons sit. I wonder how long it will be before this gets silted up and has to be redredged.

People walk past us here, on their way to the chandlery or the on site pub, or just wandering to look at the boats. We have to be careful when throwing water out that a bucket of dirty water doesn't inadvertently land on somebody's head.

Two yachts down from her on the hard is an identical yacht, but brand new, belonging to a friendly Aussie Barry. Barry now lives in the Bahamas and has bought his yacht as a new toy, he is also planning to sail her across the Atlantic with the ARC, so she is the one boat we must aim to beat, as she so far is the only other Bavaria 46 entered. Every now and then Barry appears at the top of our ladder "Ready for a beer?" and looking to see where our water maker is, or where the fuel tanks are, as he is still deciding where to put all these accoutrements. His brand new mast still wrapped in bubblewrap is lying in front, balanced on stands; it is difficult not to walk into a spreader every time you walk past.

All five of us, and Buchi the Dalmatian, cram into Kay and Robins tall, narrow house in Haslemere. Kay is pregnant with her third child and waddles around amidst the chaos the other two small children Isabelle and Laurie have created and to which we have considerably added. But she and Robin could not be more welcoming to us.

"Just make yourselves at home." she says as we dump yet another bag into her hallway.

David, Brinsley and John are put to sleep in the living room on a sofa bed and a lilo on the floor. Martin and I are sleeping in a little room with Paddington bear wallpaper and the computer. It is two a.m. and the light is still on, those little bears with their Wellington boots, staring at me from the wall, some of them peering over a wallpaper book, some just staring directly with their wallpaper eyes.

Outside a train thunders past on the main Portsmouth to London line.

"Why on earth are you reading the dictionary?" Martin is lying next to me and is the reason for the visibility of the bears at this time of night.

"Looking for a name for it."

Where have you got up to?" It looks as if he has almost finished the book.

""I'm only on W."

"That's great, not much further to go then?"

" I started on Z."

"Oh."

I choose more relaxing reading of a novel. I don't think that I've ever found the Oxford English dictionary particularly stimulating reading anyway, so I don't feel as if I am losing out.

Martin's thinking beside me is too distracting and I put down my novel and start to think as well. We finally settle on *Brandamajo*, which is an accumulation of all our names. Naff, I know, but we could always invent some great and meaningful meaning for the word.

'What am I going to tell them on the Radio course?' Martin says. 'If would be so much easier to say in a distress call. Indigo, Foxtrot. …Now isn't that easy compared to Bravo, Romeo, Alpha, November, Delta, Alpha, Mike, Alpha, Juliet, Oscar?'

"I suppose so, but I hope that we won't be making any distress calls on this trip." I answer.

Peter, my thirty-year-old pony survives the trip down here where he is going to live with the Pearse family in Petersfield for the year. He even shows enough spirit to kick one of their horses when he is let out of the box. There is still life in him yet. I tell the Pearses not to be too upset if he dies whilst he is with them… though I will be extremely upset and weep buckets, I have had him since he was two. I think they are a bit concerned at the responsibility of taking on such an old faithful.

Martin decides to move out of Kay and Robins house and live on the boat so that he can spend more time working on her. I decline to join him, the thought of climbing down that steep ladder with the boys in the middle of the night if they want a wee, just doesn't bear thinking about, then what if one of them falls overboard onto the concrete all those feet below. The boys and I carry on taking advantage of Kay and Robins hospitality. Besides she has a washing machine.

So we just commute the forty minutes down to Hayling Island every day. The boys then decamp into the boat and watch endless telly (whatever happened to all those parenting thoughts of not using telly as a babysitter?) Buchi is tied to the stands that hold *Brandamajo* up and gets a fine dust of antifouling over her white coat. I decide that perhaps it will be better to move her to the next-door boat. For a break in the work I will gather the children together and take the dog and them for a walk along the gravel muddy beach that adjoins the boatyard, whilst I remind myself what all this work is for.

I spend hours scraping off old anti-fouling, which in many places refuses to come off. Don dust masks, boiler suits and goggles, but still my throat burns and chest stings. At the end of the day when I am packing everything into the plastic boxes and bags that we will leave under the boat for the night I stop to read what it says on the packet of dust masks "Martin!" I yell.

"What?" he yells back, returning from the tap where he has been washing paint brushes.

"Did you read this?"

"Read what?" The packet of dust masks."

"No, a dust mask is a dust mask."

"I say s here 'Does not prevent dust from getting into the lungs." I can feel the layer of toxicity on the bottom of my lungs even as I read the label.

"Well they were the cheapest. What do you suppose they *do* prevent then?"

I don't have a reply for that, and we decide that before we go any further we had better get some better ones.

"Well at least seaweed won't grow in your lungs!" says Martin.

"Or on my hands." I look at where the fine red dust has ingrained every crease, despite gloves. At night the starlings come to roost on the mast and they have been eating blackberries. The deck has purple splodges on it.

Martin keeps dashing off to do VERY IMPORTANT THINGS.

I scrape and sand, and scrape and sand and scrape and sand. The dust gets everywhere, but at least there are good showers here so at the end of the day I can get the worst of it off.

Martin returns with a scraper to help me.

"How's it going?" He asks.

"Awful, even my contact lenses seem to have got a bit of antifouling on them," I answer tackling a particularly difficult piece of paint and knowing that despite the goggles I have got a small piece of antifouling on the bridge of my nose, I can see it every time I look downwards, an enlarged blob of red small to the onlooker but large to the closeness of my own eyes. "Hey where are you off to?" the skipper to be has put down his scraper and is heading off towards the sheds on the boatyard.

"I have something VERY IMPORTANT I have to do."

"What's that?"

"I have to go and see how the rudder repair is getting on."

I vow that I will never scrape off antifouling again. Martin agrees that next time we will pay someone to do it. I haven't agreed that there is going to be a next time yet.

"Mu-um," a voice appears from above me.

"Can I help?" Brinsley is coming down the ladder, I watch him as always my heart slightly in my mouth as it is when I watch any of the children on the ladder.

"No, this stuff is far too poisonous."

"Why are you doing it then?"

"Somebody has to, I smile at him."

"I'm hungry."

I look at my watch, it is only eleven a.m. "Go on then see if you can find something to eat. Behind him John is coming down the ladder. "I'm just going to get some fruit pastilles," he says.

"Wait until Brin is down PLEASE John," I say watching him almost run down the ladder.

There is a little chandlery here where we have set up an account and everything from kitchen roll to new oilskins gets put on it, but not the children's fruit pastilles or ice creams.

There is a total solar eclipse of the sun in Cornwall. We had planned to sail down and see it, but the boat is still high and dry, we still have a lot more scraping of antifouling to do, so we watch the 98% eclipse from the cockpit, with our Tesco's eclipse watching glasses. I stop scraping, Martin stops doing IMPORTANT THINGS, and the starlings come in to roost in the middle of the day. It is an eerie light but what surprises us most is the enormous amount of light even 2% of sun can provide.

We are almost half way there with the scraping.

Friday 13th August, unlucky for some but we finish the scraping. We have done as much as we are going to do; the second half is definitely less well done than the first half.

In comparison to scraping the antifouling off, painting it on is a pleasure, but Sods law has it that this lovely hot weather is having a break and now we are rushing to get coats on between patches of rain.

Friends and family come to visit the boat and have a sail on her, but she is still high and dry so they are given jobs to do instead. "I've even brought my seasickness tablets with me" says Jane as we sit in the cockpit high above the concrete drinking beer as the children whizz around in the rubber dinghy (they have finally got bored of watching unlimited television!)

Wednesday 25th August. In she goes. She has got six coats of antifouling on, the skipper is still doing VERY IMPORTANT THINGS, but our new home is swung in the air on the end of a crane and put in the water, I arrive from picking Granny up from the station just as she is about to touch the water, the boys are all watching importantly, and the skipper is chewing his fingers. Granny is coming to see what her daughter and grandchildren are going to be living on for the next year.

She slowly goes in, remains floating and the chains are removed.

There is a feeling of tense excitement amongst the family. "You'll need to move her from here" says the Marina manager.

"Come on then everybody aboard," says the skipper.

I rush around trying to be important with the warps, the skipper fiddles around with the throttle, Granny tells us how she used to do things when she was a sailing wife and the boys squeal excitedly.

Screeeech…."Whoops." screeching stops.

"This warp's snapped," says Brinsley.

"Whoops."

Luckily we did not crash into the boat aft of us and we had more than one warp attaching us.

"I think the throttle was jammed," says the skipper, "Shall we try again?"

Second time around we are more successful and manage to manoeuvre *Brandamajo* onto a new berth. It is all very new and large to us, despite our previous yachting experience, and it doesn't help when you have an audience.

We all move into our new home, she is certainly a bit smaller than our last one, but in the water she is suddenly alive and comforting. The boys rush around making their cabins personalised for the year, and I sort out provisions into the many different nooks and crannies that a boat has. Our estimated date of departure grows ever nearer and our list of things to do grows ever longer. Stress is still a side effect of our lifestyle, but we keep reassuring ourselves that this is only temporary. We do a couple of day sails from Hayling Island, wincing as the depth alarm goes of as we return over the bar of Chichester harbour. Buchi is cowering in the corner, she is not a sailing dog, just as well she is not coming with us, and Granny enjoys it for a bit, but is glad when we decide to return to the tranquillity of the harbour as she is beginning to feel a bit queasy. Sailing across the Atlantic seems a bit daunting to us at the moment.

Martin goes of on a radio operator's course and comes back with a bread maker. "We can have fresh bread every day when we are sailing across the Atlantic," he says with a grin.

We try to find a space to keep it.

We must go up to Scotland to say goodbye to the families. "Do we have to go up there, why can't they come down here?" asks the skipper, who is still working every available minute.

"I think we should go." I say. They are all planning farewell parties and meals for us." And anyway I am quite looking forward to a little break from all the work. So we drive up to Scotland to say goodbye to our respective families. Arrive late, very late, for my sister Harriet and Alistair's delicious farewell meal, the family have long gone to bed, the food has been put in the oven but still tastes just as good, and we feel guilty that we have not made it in time to eat it with them. Niece Rachel has made a cake with a blue icing boat on it, and we realise that we have got so involved in our preparations that we have forgotten that our families may want to say farewell to us as we sail into the wide blue yonder!

Leave Buchi in Edinburgh with Granny. I am almost in tears as we leave her; she has been a member of the family since she was born, Granny is going to have her for the year. My sisters Harriet and Jessica and their families give the boys little gifts.

"What is it, what is it?" ask the boys ripping off the wrapping as we sit replete after a huge brunch in Jessica and Gordon's walled garden in Portobello.

"Open them and see." But they of course already are opening them.

"A penknife! I've always wanted a penknife!" says Brinsley and the other boys are equally impressed.

Later, John has his present out, and we are in the car on our way up to Aberdeen, and a voice says from the back "I wonder how sharp this is?"

"Very," I say, without turning around. " Don't test it"

"Ow!"

"Mum, there's blood pouring out of John's thumb." This is from Brinsley. I turn around, "Here wrap this around it," I pass him wads of kitchen roll.

"You tested it, didn't you?"

John nods, he is trying not to cry. Luckily the wound is not too bad and a plaster will be enough.

Then up to Aberdeen for another farewell party, this time with the paternal relations and grandparents. "We're only going for a year." We say, but enjoy the parties nonetheless.

But work on the boat is calling us and we cannot stop very long, we must drive back south.

Non-stop from Aberdeen to Hayling Island is a VERY long drive.

At last we are ready to leave Hayling Island, the last bits and bobs have been left with Kay and Robin or with the Pearses who have moved into an enormous house near Petersfield. The cars have been sorted, one to go back to the company and the other with the Pearses for the year.

The weather is very un-British and roasting hot on the day we leave.

"Mum, mum, look what Brendan has given us." The boys run back from the little chandlery bearing purses, each with a pound coin in them.

"It's all those fruit pastilles you bought," I say to John.

Brendan from the chandlery gives us a large bottle of champagne. How very generous of him.

"Well we did spent £5000 there," says Martin.

"We did what!"

"We spent about £5000," he repeats.

"On what?"

"Those lovely ocean-going oilskins, Dubarry boots, paint, paintbrushes, kitchen roll, shoes, and John's fruit pastilles."

"OK well it's no wonder he gave us a bottle of champagne then," I say but nonetheless going down below and putting it in the fridge. I didn't realise quite what good customers we had been.

Decide that we had better fill up with fuel before we leave. All we have to do is move the yacht sideways from her place on the pontoon, across a small space of water to the fuel jetty. Much easier than trying to manoeuvre her, (especially as we haven't exactly had much practise) by engine, is do throw ropes and pull her across the small gap. There is a little crowd of people standing here to wave us off, we have not exactly been an unobtrusive family here, children, raining red antifouling dust on passers by, lunches in the pub, and almost living on site. We are not a quiet family.

The skipper throws the rope...or warp, (I'd better start using the correct terminology) I stand on the fuel jetty catch it and pull....and pull....and pull.. and the rope just keeps on coming. Plop, the boat end falls in the water. It is not attached. But *Brandamajo* comes slowly across anyway. I think she will look after us.

"I had better phone ahead and warn the other places that there is a yacht coming who doesn't secure their warps" the manager of the marina says with a laugh as he stands watching us.

"I think we had better start a 'Bad dad list? Hadn't we boys?" I ask grinning, as we retrieve the rope. The skipper is a perfectionist who rarely gets things wrong. The first mate is not a perfectionist, who often gets things wrong!

As we sail away, over the bar, that is at the entrance to Chichester harbour and we truly feel that we are on our way. Our fuel tanks and food cupboards are full and the sun is shining.

"Champagne?" asks the skipper, standing smiling at the helm.

"Coming up," I answer bringing up Brendan's bottle and some plastic glasses. We sit in the roasting hot sun, looking forward to the adventure ahead of us and drink champagne and eat nuts.....now that really is a great way to decrease stress levels!.... and we throw a small amount on the front of the boat as we had not got any when we launched her, can't waste too much though!

"You want a sip of champagne boys?" I ask.

"Are we allowed?" asks David.

I pour them each a little in an Ikea plastic beaker.

"I like it," declare both David and John. Brinsley is not so sure.

"Mu—um!"

"Yes."

"What's that smell?"

I stick my head down below and take a sniff. It is an unmistakable smell.......diesel.

"Diesel. Now where is that coming from?"

I stick my head up through the companionway "There's a smell of diesel down here." I relay to Martin.

The smile is wiped off his face. "That's all we need."

I decide to finish drinking my glass of champagne before I go and investigate. At least it is not visible swishing around the cabin floor. Well at least not yet!

Champagne downed, and I am crawling along our bunk trying to remove the board of the aft locker behind our bunk. The origin of the diesel perfume is soon apparent. The newly filled reserve tanks are leaking and pink slimy diesel is flowing steadily under our aft bunks into the bilges. Mop it up with acres of kitchen roll. Luckily we have acres of it.

"What is a boat without the smell of diesel anyway?" I say, thinking back to my days sailing on *Goblin*, a friend Antony's 26 ft Colvic Sea Rover. She always smelt of diesel.

"Pleasant," is the skipper's reply. I have to agree with him, but at least we are not mid Atlantic. Martin skilfully manoeuvres into

Lymington marina. I stand on the bow rushing from side to side convinced that we are going to hit every boat in sight.

"Watch that one! Are you OK?" I ask willing us not to hit the yacht close on our starboard bow.

"Stop panicking, I won't hit them," says Martin. But he is chewing his fingernails, a sure sign that he is not all that confident! *Brandamajo* seems such a big boat to us, and the boats we are going to hit are even bigger, and gleaming with wealth and lawsuits.

Amazingly we don't hit any. And manage to berth successfully "Don't get into such a panic says Martin, once we are safely moored" but secretly I think even he is pleased with his abilities.

"Wow look at those yachts "says David, as I am trying to teach the children how to tie fenders on. "we even look small here."

"David, concentrate," I say.

"I am concentrating, how do you do that knot again?"

"What knot?"

"The fender knot."

"You mean a clove hitch?"

"That's what I said."

I show him again. "By the end of this trip, you'll be doing these in your sleep," I say.

September comes and we are in Dartmouth marina. It costs an absolute FORTUNE. Nearly £50 for one nights mooring! But I find not only showers but also a bath in a bathroom. I soak in it as long as possible, goodness knows when I will next have a bath. We have Matt, Kate and Matthew Baldwin on board. Matt Smith was Martin's indispensable Laser Two crew (the last dinghy he sailed) and Kate his lovely South African wife, of about a year. She has yet to become acclimatised to the British weather so this mini heat wave we are having suits her perfectly.

"We have to leave at 0530 tomorrow morning," says the skipper.

I give a little groan.

"Don't worry," says the skipper, the Matthews and I will take her out. You can sleep.

Come morning I of course don't sleep, but enjoy lying listening to the shouts and slapping of ropes and hauling of sails as we get out of the harbour and under way.

The weather is still roasting hot, not at all like the Britain we know and love, so new bimini gets brought into action.

Drink more champagne brought by Matt and Kate. I could quite easily get used to this. Plymouth is our final departure point and in the roasting sun we get final jobs done, buy yet more food and wait for the ships papers to arrive. We cannot leave without them.

I am still hunting for Scopaderm, which I am told is the answer to seasickness, but these stick on patches seem very hard to come by, either GP's are unwilling to prescribe it, or worse still don't know about it! I finally find a very nice GP who is also a sailor. She saves the day, and we have enough to see us across the Atlantic, well almost.

Scopaderm is a prescription only drug that comes in little patches that you stick behind your ear, and they are meant to last for three days before they run out. The few people we have spoken to who have tried them swear by them, so I surely hope that they will work for me.

David writes on a postcard to his best friend Daniel, 'Count Dogular has drowned again, we have a diesel leak and a bomb went off in Plymouth. Love David.'

No sorry, he didn't write love; eleven-year-old boys don't send love to each other, just 'from'.

It wasn't actually a bomb that went off in Plymouth, but there was a bomb scare when we were shopping there and we were evacuated from the city centre.

John's diary for the 7th September reads '*yesterday we went into Plymouth and there was a bomb scare and there was a fire in c and a there was a lot of smoke and mum left Tandy without paying for her batteries.*

We haven't got into punctuation yet, and I did manage to go back and pay for the batteries the following day.

As we decided to change her name, she was called Lone Signature with a not very happy history, we have had to re register her so we are now waiting for the papers to come back from the marine registry, despite repeated phone calls, we still do not have them, and without them we cannot go anywhere. We must sit here and wait in Plymouth until we get them.

While we wait I go shopping, and shopping, and shopping, and I spend hundreds of pounds on school books, at the moment our bank account is full of the money that we are going to live off for the year. I am full of enthusiasm for teaching our sons and they are full of enthusiasm for only having two hours schoolwork a day. Lets hope it lasts.

Between telephone calls and getting the diesel leak fixed, the skipper has also caught the shopping bug and comes back with microwave and a printer for the computer.

"Save the cabin from getting too hot when you are cooking in the Caribbean," he says .

"Where on earth are we going to put those?" I ask,

"It's all right. I know exactly where."

"Where?"

"Wait and see."

He does and it fits. Just. The printer is somehow found a space in a cupboard. The boat is getting more and more crammed with the paraphernalia of living.

Ships papers still have not yet arrived, so we must carry on waiting and we must phone John Chapman to tell him not to come yet. John is going to help us sail across the Bay of Biscay. He is another laser two sailor from Budworth sailing club.

"Could we please get someone to help us sail across the Bay of Biscay?" I had pleaded with Martin, having visions of him trying to cope whilst I was looking after the children and throwing up at the same time.

"Why? Other couples manage to do it on their own."

"But not with three children and on a boat they have hardly had time to get used to."

So John Chapman was asked if he would.

The days in Plymouth pass with no sign of the ship's papers and there is a good weather window to make the crossing of the Bay of Biscay. We are now itching to go. At this time of year, the right weather for crossing the bay is hard to come by.

Eventually the non-results of repeated phone calls and the presence of almost perfect conditions for crossing the Bay get to the skipper.

"I'm going to hire a car and go and get them," he says, fed up of the inadequacies of bureaucracy. So he does and drives up to Cardiff, and manages to collect them that day, ready and sat waiting to be posted, or signed or some equally easy thing, unimportant to bureaucracy but of vital importance to us. At last we can go.

John Chapman is phoned and arrives the following day.

Ring up to check up on round fat chestnut pony Scooby Doo, just to confirm that he has settled in for the year. He hasn't. Could we please find him another home.

"But we're leaving tomorrow, and won't be in the country for a year!" I say. "Don't worry though, I'll sort something out." I have absolutely no idea how I am going to sort something out.

Stress levels skyrocket.

"The children keep falling off him and the parents are complaining," says the girl on the other end of the phone.

Despite my internal stressometer rising, I can't help smiling at the picture of a pony fed up of going round in riding school circles and depositing unwary children on the ground. I can almost see his equine grin as 'another one bites the dust'.

My mind whizzing around various possibilities I wish that I hadn't phoned to check, but I must now come up with a solution within the next few hours!

Phone Judy, whose horse Marty I used to ride in the normal pre-house sale days. She saves the day , and says she can sort something out. Thank goodness for friends. Stress level comes down slightly.

Friday 10th September.

The day has finally come, we have all the papers, we have John Chapman aboard, the weather forecast looks OK for the next few days and there is nothing more we can do now. It is quite windy so dose the children and myself up with Stugeron, I want to save the hard gained Scopaderm patches for the Atlantic crossing.

That is just in case I decide to do it. At the moment I have got flight tickets for myself and the boys to fly over and meet Martin and the rest of the crew out in the Caribbean, I am still not sure if I really want to be sick for three weeks continuously!

It is fairly late in the afternoon when we leave, the weather looks good for the crossing, but I am not without apprehension, both the other times I have crossed it we have been in force nine gales, and seasickness has made me not worry about death, yet here I am again, maybe I am suffering from some sort of masochism!

We progress into the Bay of Biscay and I am glad that John Chapman is with us. Despite the Stugeron, it is not long before that familiar queasy feeling comes over me. The children go all quiet. "I'm not feeling very well mum."

I daren't go down below and help them I don't think that my stomach would stand it. "Nor am I " I answer, trying to sit as still as I possibly can in the hope that I might fool my body into thinking that the motion of the boat is no different from my normal everyday motion. It doesn't work. "Come up here and get some fresh air. "

They crawl up, clipping their harnesses on as they do so and curl up in little balls in corners of the cockpit. At different stages the children and I all throw up, harnessed on as we vomit into the sea, sometimes I hold the children's feet to give them a bit of extra security. Even John C looks a slightly unhealthy colour, only the skipper appears totally unaffected, as we roll along over the large Bay of Biscay swells. Venture down below long enough to put on Scopaderm patches, I hope they work. Swell gets larger but George proves his worth. Now I know you're wondering who the heck George is. Well George is our 7000 series autohelm, named by Simon Barter, another of the friends who joined in the sailing from Portsmouth to Plymouth.

George doesn't get seasick, doesn't get tired, and you can plot a waypoint in and set the autohelm towards it, he will get there on his own, taking into account tides and currents. Now we have GPS (Global positioning system, which with the use of satellites can accurately pinpoint us anywhere on the globe,) gone are the days of dead reckoning and starlight navigation with a sextant. However our George does occasionally throw a wobbly whenever he thinks that we are relying on him too much. That is just when you are far away from the wheel relaxing drinking coffee, he suddenly comes of automatic and goes onto standby, which means he is no longer in control of the helm, which usually results in a complete change of direction. To be fair to him though he does beep as he does this, unfortunately if the noise of the wind and waves are such, then you can't hear the beeps, the only warning in these cases being a sudden swinging of the helm, flapping of canvas and change of motion.

Scopaderm does not seem to be working, not yet anyway. "Well what do you think boys, do you want to sail across the Atlantic?" I ask when I am compos enough to speak.

"Definitely not," says John who is curled up in his life jacket and waterproofs on the cockpit floor. The children are always harnessed on whenever they are on deck and sometimes it is a veritable cobweb of blue lines in the cockpit!

"I still want to," says David, who is looking slightly less green than he was.

Brinsley is not sure.. I try hibernating in my bunk, but the hibernation hole still moves around. Sleeping is OK though. Where has all that nice solid dry land with grass and trees gone?

All three of us adults are later on deck though when there is a loud crack. "What the hell was that?!"

There is a lot of crashing and flapping as the Genoa comes hurtling down. It is dark and raining and windy so we cannot see exactly what has happened, but the skipper and I go up on the foredeck leaving John at the helm (he is a far better sailor than me and there are times when even George cannot manage) and try to lash the billowing sail down with ropes before it gets damaged. It is a huge sail and freed from its constraints it has a life of its own, grab hold of part of it and the wind gets in a pocket of the sail threatening to pull you overboard (though we are also harnessed on)it is all we can do to tame it into submission, but as between us we manage to lash it to the railings, it suddenly seems peaceful as the noise of blowing heavy wet sail is no longer. Now even the wind and the rain seem less. The skipper and I make our way back to the safety of the cockpit, where we can stand out of the wind.

"Bloody sail. I'm sure I've broken my thumb!" says Martin as he cradles his right hand in his left hand, once we are back in the relative calm of the cockpit. We examine the thumb and decide that it is probably not broken, but there is not much we could do about it if it was, except bind it up.

"I don't think that we handled that mini crisis very well," says John Chapman, and we agree, but we are still on a very steep learning curve as far as ocean passages are concerned.

We ascertain that the Genoa halyard has broken and in the daylight things always seem less dramatic and easier so we attach the sail to a spinnaker halyard and hoist it up again.

Stop throwing up, not that the urge isn't there, just the food isn't there! So do the boys though so maybe the Scopaderm is beginning to work. Don't feel much like cooking or eating.

"Anybody want anything to eat?" asks the skipper. John Chapman is at the helm. There is not a very enthusiastic response. The skipper eats something anyway.

Now one of the other small problems we have on the boat at the moment is a leak in the forward hatch. Let me explain. Right at the front underneath the anchor locker there is a collision space which is supposed to be a totally watertight space of air, so that if we hit something the boat won't sink, however when we bought the boat, this space was full of water, stale and stinking, that had to be emptied,(bucket by bucket when we were on the hard at Hayling Island, we threw it over the edge making sure that we did not throw it on passers by.) so the water tight hatch was removed in order to find out how the water was getting in. Unfortunately as a result of moving this hatch any water that comes in does not remain in this small compartment but progresses further into the bowels of the yacht.

The leak is somewhere from above, but as about every third wave is a green one coming over the front, there is a lot of water getting into the boat. (a lot being sixteen gallons every eight hours). Emptying this is one job that George cannot do; only mere mortals can cope with this.

This involves the skipper (as he gets the least seasick) crawling to the end of one of the forward bunks, lying on his stomach and stretching forwards into the dark bowels and filling a bucket by means of a sponge. "Can someone pass me a torch please?" comes a voice from the depths of the forward bunk.

One arrives in my hand. I think that John Chapman has passed it to me and I pass it past the feet that are sticking too close to me, and Martin's hand takes it.

He can now see to fill the bucket. The bucket is then passed back to either John C or myself who then has to try tipping it down the sink. This doesn't work very well as we are still rocking and lurching on big

Bay of Biscay rollers and so most of the water comes out of the sink again, as the boat lurches when it is more than likely to get soaked up by our clothes as it exits the sink.

We will never make it out of the cockpit, with the motion of the boat, so finally tipping it down the heads (toilets) seems the right solution.

Outside though, and with the seasickness death wish abating for a bit, I have to admit that there is an upside to this ocean sailing. Dolphins play in the bow waves and shearwaters skim the waves. These lovely creatures seem actually to ENJOY the wind and the waves. The little brown birds glide close to the waters surface getting lift from the surface winds.

As we get across the Bay, the winds ease and come around behind us. John Chapman wind burned and unshaven sticks his blond head through the companionway "I stink." He declares, washing has not been a priority up until now.

We all do, so we can stink in unison.

By the time we are across the Bay of Biscay the wind has come round behind us and the seas have flattened out a bit, I have survived and am beginning to feel a bit more human, and come up to relieve Martin on watch and he is staring at the rows of very bright lights from sardine boats ahead of us. "I'm sure those lights are not getting any nearer," he says . He hasn't slept for ages and is worried that he might be hallucinating. "What do you think?" I think I agree with him. We are motoring now and both M and John C are in need of sleep and as I am no longer throwing up I take over and watch the bright lights of the sardine boats in the dark night . Their bright lights, are out on long arms from the fishing boats, spotlighting the water and in theory attracting the sardines to the surface so that they can then catch them.

We are getting nearer the brightly lit boats and eventually pass them on our way to land.

We will have to go into Vigo to try and get a pump to sort out our leak, and by daylight we are at the entrance to the river. It is flat calm and sunny, the wind rain and waves from the Bay of Biscay now in our memory banks. We stop for a while and drift. "Who's going to swim then?"

"It's freezing!"

Nonetheless we all have a swim and the skipper goes up the mast and retrieves the broken Genoa halyard.

David's diary on 13th September reads,' *Today we spotted more than 5 dolphins and this time they were playing in the bow waves. At about midnight when me and Dad were on watch, we had more dolphins right next to us and we could tell they were dolphins because every time they came they churned up the edge making it fluorescent and lit up the dolphins body*'

(we must work on David's grammar and spelling, but the dolphins are truly fantastic. Imagine the sea inky black, and all of a sudden almost from nowhere lines of pale blue start coming straight towards you, not totally straight but definitely heading for the bow of the boat, it is only when they arrive that the lines are the phosphorescence they leave in their wake just below the surface of the water.)

John Chapman now clean-shaven and sweet smelling flies home to his wife Mandy and the children. We have now lost our only Spanish speaker but without Spanish we must try and get someone to put a pump in that will sort out our leak., and learn to sail this boat with just us.

Don't speak any Spanish at all but decide to go and have a cup of coffee, and ice cream for the boys.

"You ask for the bill," says Martin.

"No you can do it." I say.

"You're the linguist," he says .

"But not Spanish" I say.

"I'll try speaking in Japanese, do you think that she'll understand that?!" asks the skipper grinning. The boys at a corner table have finished their chocolate ice creams and are ready to go back to the boat.

"You could try, but I don't hold out much hope " I answer. We finally try actions and ask for the bill by miming a scribbling action on a piece of paper. The waitress duly brings us a piece of paper and a pen! We play noughts and crosses before persuading her that what we really want is to pay her for the cups of coffee.

Now if we have difficulty trying to communicate such a simple action, try to imagine the communication problems associated with getting engineers to put a pump in the forward part of *Brandamajo*!

But something happens and we are 36000 potatoes (or pesetas if you'd prefer) poorer, and one bomba (or pump if you'd prefer) richer so maybe we have at least a temporary solution to our problem. Two men have spent the best part of the afternoon in the forward locker fitting a pump that should automatically pump any excess water out.

"What are you doing?" I ask. I am half asleep and am aware of a cold Martin getting back into bed beside me.

"Just checking the navigation lights," he says .

"But we are not at sea!" I say, opening my eyes slightly.

The following morning we fill our tanks with fresh water.

"It's taking a very long time to fill up," we say, both of us leaning over the rails and peering at the overflow which indicates that the fresh water tanks are full. There is nothing coming out of the little hole.

"It must be full up by now." The skipper disappears into the bowels of the boat and returns looking glum. He has discovered that the men putting the pump in have somehow rearranged the piping so that the overflow from the tank now fills the forward compartment.

Skipper is not pleased (to put it mildly). We will not be leaving Vigo today.

I'm not quite sure how but we manage to persuade the pump engineers to return.

"Agua, agua," says Martin pointing and miming the actions of water with his hands "Bomba, no good," he mimes a cut off point with his hands.

The men nod and shake their heads and shrug their shoulders but lots of gesticulation, Bombas, Aguas and *Mananas* later we think the men will be back to repair their bodge tomorrow, or tomorrow or tomorrow.

Brinsley's diary for 16th September reads ' *Our power ran out today because well we don't know why but we didn't have any lights that night except the TV which was alright because it gave a bit of light.*' (must remember to tell Brin about punctuation)

The men have put a new junction into the water pipes so that the overflow now goes out, but we still can't leave the following morning as the engine won't start, our power problem is serious, is there a problem with our battery charger now?

I leave the skipper trying to solve this problem and go on a hunt for camping gas.

After one more day in Vigo we leave. I am sick. Again. The boys just become motionless, their natural exuberance chopped off at its roots for a while. We must try and sail down towards Lisbon, but the weather is getting worse and there is a gale warning. "What do you think?" asks the skipper, "should we call in somewhere?"

I do not hesitate "Yes definitely., especially if we can get in before the gale hits."

So call into Viano do Castello in Portugal to sit out the worst of the weather.

We crawl slowly into the harbour in the pouring rain with the shallow alarm going off all the time, we have only inches under the keel, it seems to be too shallow for us to go on the pontoons where as few other yachts are so we moor against a wall beside a disused disco hall, grey concrete covered in graffiti, and wonder if we will go aground at low tide. We still haven't got much water under the keel. Howling gale and pouring rain lash the boat as we settle in for the night with pasta and a video.

"Pass us a tissue please," comes from the engine compartment as the skipper services it.

Walk around the town in our oilies. Nobody else is around, the locals obviously do not consider this to be the weather to be walking about in, until we spot two other people clad in bright yellow oilskins. "They must be yachties as well" we observe, and we smile at each other in a sort of mutual recognition. Nobody else is stupid enough to be outside in the rain and wind.

There is a British yacht called *Gravitas* in the harbour and I think that they might be off this.

Viano do Castello is a lovely little Portuguese town, quiet and sleepy at the moment, but I'm sure in August it is not so. We walk up to a little church and come down on the funicular railway. "Why can't we go up on the railway and walk down?" ask the children.

Force 9 gale raging just north of us in The Bay of Biscay, we are not going anywhere today. How thankful I am that we are across it.

"Time for school, boys," I say.

"Do we have to Mum?" is their answer. I don't answer; they should know what the answer is without asking. The enthusiasm is waning already.

The next day, go to get a weather forecast from the port master and tell him we are thinking of leaving. "There are 6 metre waves out there" he says .....or rather mimes and points as he is speaking Portuguese and I am speaking English, my Portuguese is as about as good as my Spanish!

Find a place to buy 'camping gaz' without even looking!

But as the wind has died a little we leave anyway, we have now arranged to pick up brother in law Gordon Russell in Lisbon, and he is going to help us on the next leg of our trip to the Canaries. Gordon is Scottish, has never really sailed before, loves to shock and has a great sense of humour, he has always been very good value at parties, and manages to reduce almost every conversation to a lavatorial level! Being self-employed with not much work at the moment he can afford to take some time off.

So we must leave, the wind has eased but the passing gale has left 25 to 30 ft waves in its wake and it is not long before all the crew except for the skipper are comatose on the cockpit floor, oblivious of the rain washing over them and Martin manfully steps over all the wet prone bodies as he deals with the sails. Finally the crew deteriorates so much that we turn around and head into Leixos (John is hanging over the side shouting "I am going to die" I am hanging onto his feet trying not to move too much. A school of dolphins leap clear of the high waves ahead of us and the crew noticeably cheers up upon this decision.

Two hours after this, "I can't see anything, can you see any lights?" asks Martin. I peer through the appalling visibility and try to look when we are on top of a wave. All I can see is a little fishing boat heading in the same direction as us, then as we go back down into a trough we lose sight of it. "No, what should I be able to see?" I ask.

"We should be able to see the lights of the harbour now."

I peer forward again shielding my face against the rain, but still no lights.

We try the radar and on the radar can see that we are very close to the harbour, this is also borne out by the fact that the waves are getting bigger as they mount over the shallowing ground.

All of a sudden there are the harbour walls, exactly where we are expecting to see them and in the dark and the rain we get into Leixos harbour ,. We have radioed ahead and there is the dim figure of a man through the dark and the rain gesticulating to us and beckoning us to fit in beside a German boat. "The wind is in quite the wrong direction for me to be able to get in there!" shouts the skipper, but we slowly edge towards the gap and his shouts go unheard. "It means that you cannot fail on your rope throwing," he says, as I prepare the warps "We will get no second chance." I nod through the rain.

But guess who fails at their rope throwing? My first throw does not make the man standing ashore and the wind catches us broadside and we swing into the German boat, hitting an edge of her wind vane and earning us a torrent of abuse.

The figure is still beckoning us in. "I'm not going in there again," says the skipper and we settle for a space at the end of the pontoon. Once safely secured Martin goes and makes his peace with the German yacht and we will stay the night here and move to a more sheltered berth in the morning.

The following day the marina fills up with yachts seeking shelter from the storm and we move to one of the innermost berths, secure against the wall, and phone Gordon telling him that we will not make it to Lisbon and can he find his way to Leixos?

"Ahoy there, are you there!" A voice permeates the noise of the cabin. Gordon turns up, having made his own way from Lisbon by train, and we open up the hatches and haul him inside away from the horrible weather. We drink whiskey and listen to the wind and rain buffeting us through the night. One of our warps breaks and further out in the marina a pontoon breaks away . Our anemometer reads 54 knots that night.

We discover later that a Danish boat got rolled coming into Leixos and further down the Portuguese coast a French yacht is found with both its crew lost and drowned.

We are not going to be able to go anywhere for a few days.

"Time for school," I say.

"Oh Mu—um, do we have to?"

Big party ashore with all the storm bound boats. 29 yachts from 9 nations. Very cosmopolitan. Everybody has a story to tell about the stormy weather and we hold a minute's silence for the crew of the French yacht. suddenly amongst all these yachts we are no longer that strange family who has decided to sell up and go off, we are just normal and amongst like-minded people.

I hunt for Camping Gaz the next day, it does not seem to be the easiest thing to find.

"Well what do you think, are we ready to leave?" asks the skipper, the weather forecast is for light winds that although in the wrong direction are no longer gale force.

"I suppose we'd better," I say. We don't have Gordon with us indefinitely.

Gordon fills up the water tanks, I pay the marina and Martin starts taking sail covers off and starts the engine, we are squashed inside of a French yacht so he must move before we can.

At last we are clear of the harbour, there is a light swell and the wind is not dead against us so we can sail.

"Is it possible to bauf in bed, while you are asleep? Asks Gordon who is rolling a cigarette in the cockpit. He is still deciding whether he is a landlubber or not.

"No " I say encouragingly, "At least I never have so far, although sometimes you might have to be a quick mover!"

Stop for one night in Cascais to stock up and go out for a meal with Alberto. Alberto is the General Manager for Martin's company in Portugal and used to work with Martin. When I am asked if I like shellfish, I reply "No" (Well I don't like cockles, mussels etc.)

The meal turns out to be lobster, which I would have thoroughly enjoyed. Never again will I say I don't like shellfish without first ascertaining exactly which kind of shellfish are on offer.

Gordon's bright red sunburnt face contrasts nicely with his brand new white sweater.

"Come on boys come and help us cast off!" yells the skipper, the boys are down below making the most of having power before we come away from the shore.

"You're not planning to leave in this?" ask the people on the yacht in front of us,

"Why not?"

"No wind and it's in the wrong direction."

"We'll be alright, says the skipper, "Can't stay here for ever."

"You do fore, and I'll do aft," I say to Gordon. The boys haven't appeared yet, they might appear in time to coil the warps.

It is dark when we leave and we motor out of the harbour. There is no wind, not even wind in the wrong direction! But my stomach is much happier about this state of affairs.

We are not long out when the waves begin to ripple and the breeze begins across our faces.

"Come on then let's get that mainsail up."

"Pull!"

"I am pulling!"

"Pull harder.....No it's jammed ......Stop pulling now."

We peer through the dark at where the mainsail is jammed. It is almost up, but something seems to be caught.

"I'll go head to wind and then see if you can do anything about it!" says the skipper who is needed on the helm so Gordon and I must sort it out ourselves.

The boat is rolling around in the dark, but we are harnessed on, and finally we manage to get it sorted, and set course for the Canaries with a North Easterly wind, it couldn't be in a more perfect direction.

Sun, following wind and a gentle hiss alerting us to a minke whale spouting just off our stern, we see its long black body before it once more spouts, spitting a spray of fine droplets upwards into the air before it veers away from us having satisfied its curiosity about the invader of its space, and it swims of on some other pursuit. What more could you ask for?

Gordon is examining our fishing line. "You can't catch any fish with this. Have you got any silver paper?"

I ferret about down below. "Will this do?" I ask handing him a piece of shiny biscuit wrapper.

"Perfect."

A few hours later we catch our first fish.

"What is it? " I ask, peering over the boys' heads as they watch Gordon hauling it in.

"No idea."

The boys go down below and come up with what books we have, none of which are a fish identification book, but some mention different types of fish. We decide that it is some sort of tuna and eat it for tea. There is nothing quite so delicious as a very fresh fish that you have caught yourself.

Now I am getting more used to this sailing and at last I believe that the scopaderm patches are actually working so I can fully participate in the watch taking. They do give your mouth a dry feeling and there is still an element of queasiness, but that is better than a death wish! We do two hours on and four hours off, only if the weather is bad will we call upon someone else to come and help.

Between about midnight and four am is quite the loneliest time of night, the hours seem longer and sleep more pressing, but there I am, the others are all sound asleep in their bunks and there is the light of half a moon. We are sailing gently, the only sound apart from some gentle snoring coming from down below is the lapping of the water and the sound of the boat cutting through the waves.

The green display on the binnacle, showing windspeed, boat speed, direction etc. is strangely hypnotising.

I must look around to check that we are not about to be run down by a boat, it can take fifteen minutes for a large container ship to get from the horizon to hitting us. At the moment there is nobody but us on the black ocean but as I am looking around something catches my eye, it is a small unidentifiable object on the sprayhood, and thinking that it might be some vital bolt or screw from the rigging I put my fingers out to pick it up.

Ugh! It is revolting and slimy. No sooner than I have touched it than I withdraw my fingers, definitely not a bolt or nut but something completely different, it needs torch investigation.

I go down below and rummage around for a torch beneath the chart table and the snoring tone changes but doesn't stop.

Under the torchlight a solitary eye stares up at me, not at all what I was expecting. I stare back at it before flicking it back into the sea. Where on earth can a loose eye have come from, the imagination runs riot. It is quite a relief to pass the watch over to Gordon "Look out for stray eyes." I say.

Still in the trance of one woken from a deep sleep, Gordon takes this comment in his stride. "OK I'll do that."

I slither into my bunk beside the gently snoring Martin and images of eyes hesitantly float before my eyes as I go to sleep.

Daylight reveals the owner of the eye, an eyeless flying fish that has landed on the deck. Martin finds the eye on the side deck. My flick was obviously not strong enough to get it back into the sea.

"Come and see this fish boys" They examine it in fascination pulling its winged fins this way and that, and then we lay it on the deck and we draw it for art.

As the day progresses the wind increases. We are racing along but as the wind gets up she becomes more difficult to handle, so we reef mainsail and Genoa, and with the lessened sail area she immediately becomes more manageable.

"Pass us a tissue please" says Martin, he is sitting in the cockpit cleaning something.

A loud reverberating belch emanates from the depths of Gordon's stomach. "Barney!" we all say in unison (if you watch the Simpsons you will realise where that comes from.) The skipper holds up a nest of long black hairs that have accumulated in the corner of the cockpit.

"Come and sit here with your feet in the water" says Gordon, the skipper is down below at the chart table plotting courses and working our when we will arrive at the canaries, and leaving George at the helm I search the horizon for any sign of ships and join Gordon at the stern of the boat where we sit dangling our feet in the water, the boys are drawing endless ships on pieces of paper down below.

'Beep, beep, beep,' whoosh, we don't even hear Georges warning and we have rapidly altered course.

"Whoa, what's happening!" the skipper leaps out through the companionway. George obviously disagrees with this kind of inattentive sailing and has thrown a wobbly, throwing the boat around.

"Whoops, sorry," I say, duly chastised.

The wind is still increasing. "We don't really want to get there in the dark," says the skipper, looking at the boat speed, the wind and the chart, and giving his fingers a chew. "so lets drop everything except the staysail." We do, tying the mainsail securely to the boom and furling the Genoa until it is a neat red line round the forestay. We are still racing along at about five and a half knots but now the waves are travelling faster than us. Gordon is trying to catch up on sleep down below.

"Mum, watch us!"

"I'm watching!"

John and Brinsley have discovered a great new game, they sit on the seat at the aft end of the cockpit and as the boat rolls from side to side, they use it as a slide, the angle of the slide altering with each roll of the boat.

" WHAT was that!"

Gordon has suddenly appeared out of the companionway like a cork out of a bottle."

"You a bit wet, Gord?" asks the skipper smiling, completely unruffled. "We just got pooped." Getting pooped is when a wave comes over the boat from astern rather than from forward, which is more normal. A result of the fact that the waves are travelling faster than us.

"We saw it coming Mum," say the boys still sitting on their slide, but now watching the water filled cockpit. They get the best view of the following wave that overtakes us and poops us, pouring into the cockpit, swirling around and through the open window onto a sleeping Gordon, before what is left of it trickles slowly back into the ocean.

"Wondered if we were going down," says Gordon, now bringing his wet sleeping bag up to dry.

Another flying fish lands on deck and a turtle floats by waving its flipper in the air. Gordon is nearly out of cigarettes.

"What do you think boys?" he asks trying to light a cigarette bent in half and is contemplating smoking tealeaves.

"You can't really smoke tealeaves can you?" ask the boys watching their uncle clowning around.

"You can smoke anything if you try hard enough." He attempts to straighten the bent cigarette but it immediately resumes its bent shape, to the boys' roars of laughter.

The SSB (single side band) radio is the gossip centre for yachties and in the mornings we chat with Pat of Aldebaran. The skipper is sitting at the chart table, black microphone in hand.

'Aldebaran, Aldebaran, Aldebaran, this is *Brandamajo*, *Brandamajo*, Over'

'This is Aldebaran, HOW do you spell that? Over'

'Bravo, Romeo, Alpha, Delta, Alpha, Mike, Alpha, Juliet, Oscar. And how are you this morning Pat?'

'Fine, thank you, Martin. And yourselves?'

'Rolling along nicely Pat. Got pooped this morning.'

"Did you now, well that's a strange thing because we got rolled this morning, funny thing that!"

"Yes, and we caught a shark."

"A shark did you say? Well a what was on our boat, but we just had to let it go, it moight have sunk us otherwise!" And so the cock and bull stories continue.

We met Pat and Olivia from Ireland in Leixos, along with, Dave and Emma the yellow clad yachties from Viano do Castelo, on a yacht called *Gravitas*.

We are nearly at the Canaries and from there I will send a newsletter to all our friends.

A colleague of Martin's, Ashley Cooper, replies to our newsletter, summarising our trip so far very succinctly thus:

Martin,

I must count as the most landlubberly of all your readers but I think that I have now got the hang of deep water sailing, as least as far as the theory goes;

❑   Things work fine in port.

❑   On leaving port, things go wrong immediately you have covered 20% of the distance to the next port. This is an exquisitely chosen point and the crew's decision is nearly always to accept the hardship of the onward voyage rather than to turn back.

❑   A pump doesn't.

❑   sometimes it might seem to, but only if it can circulate the water back to where it is pumping.

- ❏ Spanish pumps go wrong bombastically.
- ❏ Boats leak.
- ❏ this applies particularly if you don't shut the doors on them in rough weather.
- ❏ Ropes break.
- ❏ Attempts to confuse ropes by referring to them as warps or sheets, only makes them break at even more awkward places.
- ❏ Fishing lines are sort of ropes too.
- ❏ For a sailor to describe something nasty happening around his rear end as mildly as "being pooped" came as a surprise to me too.

CHAPTER TWO

THE CANARIES

"Land! I can see land!" The day has dawned and with it the sight of La Graciosa, just off Lanzarote.

"Are you not coming up to watch us come into the land?" asks Gordon, looking down through the cockpit window. I am trying to catch up on some last vestiges of sleep before I know that I will have to get up.

"In a minute, in a minute," I say, keeping my eyes firmly shut.

We radio ahead to see if there is space on the marina "Yes, that is no problem *Brandamajo*, you will find a space about half way along the pontoon, you can dive down and moor a rope to a concrete block." We are not sure if we have heard correctly, DIVE down and secure a rope, is that what he said?

Sure enough we get into this tiny little harbour with no signs of life, and we edge into the only gap available, moor our bowlines and then Martin has to dive down to attach a stern line onto a lump of concrete on the bottom. Nobody offers to do this for him.

He is exhausted after five days at sea, and I am thankful it is not me having to do this.

There is a tatty boat next to us with an angry war relic aboard, grey hair, grizzled chin, brown weather beaten leathery skin from years in the sun and clad in faded blue jeans a hole at either knee and oil stains mingling with other stains on the denim. A brown shirt with rolled up sleeves and you can just see where the dark brown skin suddenly goes white beneath the sleeves. He comes out as Martin prepares to dive in. "You watch my anchors,!" He has three out at different angles from his stern it is difficult not to watch them, we had to manoeuvre our way through the ropes to get our bow to the pontoon.

Martin reappears at toe surface of the water, snorting water through the end of his snorkel.

"Have you done it?"

"No not yet, but I've found what we have to attach the rope to, just had to come up for some air".

He next surfaces with the end of the rope in hand having successfully threaded it through the metal ring on the concrete block that is lying on the bottom of the harbour. Not a conventional way of mooring I think. has successfully attached our warp and is drying himself. The little man growls at us, "You have moved my anchor! It gets very windy in here," he says , "you must go down and re lay my anchor."

His little yacht is streaked with rust and the windows look less than waterproof, a dirty pair of jeans and a towel are hung over the boom, and the wind vane at the stern of his yacht is held together with string.

Our skipper smiles and pacifies him as best as he can. "Don't worry, if your boat moves I will go down and re lay your anchor, but I have not moved it right now."

"Yes, now it is here…. Before it was there!" he points at two points not far apart, his voice still seems to be growling.

I think he just doesn't want us here as we are disturbing his peace in one of the few free marinas left. - It does have no water, no electricity, and what pass for showers and toilets would also be a serious health hazard. You walk across the sandy street to a breeze block enclosure where there is a hole high up from which water in theory should come, and from which a distinctly unpleasant odour emanates. But we have no intention of moving right now. Gordon is ashore and kissing the ground, pleased to be on dry stationary land and the boys have jumped in to swim.

"Black pudding, sausage, egg and chips, let's go and see if we can find some!" says Gordon, who has been pining for some black pudding ever since the seasickness wore off.

No cars, no black puddings, no 'camping gaz' here, but the streets are made from sand and we find cigarettes for Gordon and a restaurant serving delicious Spanish omelette and chips. The skipper falls asleep at the table before his food arrives, his unshaven wind blown head dropping on his chest and jerking back up again. The boys laugh and I take a photograph, but we have now done the first leg of our trip and have six weeks to enjoy the Canaries and prepare for the Atlantic crossing.

"Let us do some school work," I say to the boys but without much enthusiasm.

"But Mu-um!" They say. It doesn't take me much persuading to give in and let them swim and play instead. I am developing a '*manana*' personality.

Customs office seems to be permanently closed here, but at least we have tried to check in.

Take the storm boards off the windows, these are thick pieces of Perspex, screwed over each window, giving us extra protection against storms and should we get rolled. Hopefully it will be along time before we will need those on again.

Walk along the sandy street and onto the beach with the children while Gordon and the Skipper sleep. There are tents full of bohemian Spaniards, rousing from drugged filled sleep to lie naked on the beach . Brin comes running back to me "Mum, guess what I have just seen, it is disgusting!"

"What?" I reply avoiding stepping on a discarded condom on the beach.

"A NAKED LADY, Yuck!"

"You've seen me naked," I reply.

"Yes but not in public!" He says in the shock of naiveté. He rushes on with his brothers looking whilst trying hard not to appear to be looking at this new novelty.

Past this small temporary encampment, the island is deserted and barren, with ash cones making hills of hard lava that later we climb and picnic at the top of.

More like the lovely deserted island we remember visiting with Martin's parents some years ago. Gordon leaves us here, he is going back to Jessica and his boys James and Calum who he has sorely missed, and has been with us longer than he expected, we will miss his humour and sense of fun.

Once he is gone we find a little shop from which you can hire bikes. "Here David, I think this is for you" A middle sized pink bicycle is leaning against a white washed wall.

"I'm not having that one!"

"Why not, what is wrong with it?"

"It's PINK!"

"Well I'm not having it," says Brinsley , firmly sitting astride that one he has been given.

"I don't think that my brakes work very well," says John, screeching to a halt with his feet beside us. It turns out that none of their brakes work very well and they all look as if they could do with a good dose of oil, but we set out under a cloudy sky to explore the island. There are no roads except for sandy tracks and not really any traffic except for incongruously occasionally a large truck thunders past, maybe carrying gravel from quarries that will be used for building either here or on Lanzarote.

I forget to take hats or sun cream, and the sun comes out at about eleven a.m. (Just as well we don't have a bad mum list!) I watch our children's bare skin and pray for clouds. There are no trees, no shade - just one large desert island that we are trying to cycle around. Find a few palm trees in a village of mostly holiday homes powered by a field of solar panels, so we fight for the shade under which to eat our sandwiches.

We cycle round the desert island occasionally having to walk the bikes when the sand gets too deep, until we come across a windward beach full of golden Sahara sand and rollers that we will try to match for the rest of the year.

"Look at those waves!" exclaim the boys, dumping their bikes and racing down to the water's edge, stripping of and discarding their clothes as they go. There is not a soul in sight except for us, and soon the skipper and the boys are getting thrown around in the breakers, I look on anxiously as one son after another disappears under an enormous wave before reappearing, sometimes feet first. As their trunks fill up with sand they strip them off and play naked in these huge waves, which I am sure is not truly sensible but is great fun--- for the male contingent of the family anyway.

By the evening we have reached the leeward side of the island and here I swim more sedately, tall dark cliffs of the northern end of Lanzarote stare down at us from across the channel and here the sea is calm , but it is full of hidden stings. "Ow….Ouch….Oooh…." and we soon enough leap out of it and I have weal's on my arms that will take weeks to disappear.

Cooler and more slowly now we cycle back in the evening sun, the nude bohemian Spaniards have returned to their tents.

Back on board, "Has anybody seen my breadmaker recipe book?"

Nobody answers. I rummage through cupboard after cupboard, and even in the bin, but by now we have already got rid of several bags of rubbish.

"Anybody volunteering to help me find my recipe book?" I ask. Silence.

I take all the books off the bookshelf in an effort to locate it. "500 pesetas to anybody who can find it." All of a sudden there is a flurry of activity and I have three helpers, but it has totally disappeared. George must have stolen it, or at the very least hidden it.

Crash, bang, clatter, the saucepan cupboard is fighting back, you put one saucepan away in it and it spits all the rest out at you. However I can get the upper hand by pulling the whole contents onto the floor, making as much noise as possible (so that everybody can know that there is an ongoing battle between the saucepan cupboard and the first mate), then restacking them slowly whilst holding its mouth wide open.

We leave La Graciosa and sail down the coast of Lanzarote, becoming adept tourists. Battery charger that has been getting sicker and sicker, finally stops working., so unless we are motoring or plugged into mains we have virtually no power. That means warm beer, as the fridge and the autohelm are the two most power hungry things on board, and guess which has to get sacrificed first?

Boys decide that they prefer riding camels to doing schoolwork. On Mount Timanfaya you can take a camel ride across the moonscape of lava, as well as a bus trip, we do both, the camel ride gets the biggest popularity vote. It is a desolate landscape of broken fields of lava, with little except a few lichens growing on it despite it having erupted 700 years ago.,

Puerto Calero towards the southern end of Lanzarote is a concrete walled marina, clean and clinical and guarded by 'The Fat Controller' a balding large power hungry man sweating in his uniform, who sits in his little guard house watching everybody who comes and goes. There is a rule that you may not hang washing out on the railings to dry, in case it spoils the look of the place, and at the weekend bronzed sailors and sport fishermen and their wives or mistresses come down and work on their boats, working in their swimming trunks or bikinis getting their skins even more bronzed and leathery, round buttocks sticking out and sunglasses worn as headbands.

"You can't do that here!" The Fat Controller yells at Martin who has got the canoe out and is canoeing out of the harbour entrance, to try and watch the start of the Transatlantic race. This is a single handed race across the Atlantic in little 26 foot yachts, many of them have no engines aboard as they do not want to add to the weight and they are getting towed out. Rather them than me, they have already had several casualties across the Bay of Biscay.

"Why not?" answers Martin, never one to give up without a fight.

"You must go back, go back!" shouts the Fat Controller waving his arms fiercely . Sometimes overt disobedience is not wise and we are not ready to be chucked out of here just yet, so Martin does and carries his canoe over the breakwater and rocks and launches it in a much more dangerous place before canoeing out and joining all the other support boats at the start of this race. He is the only canoe there though! and once out there is nothing the Fat Controller can do about it.

The children and I sit on the breakwater with our binoculars and nervously watch as he bobs among the waves and the washes of all the support boats.

John's diary reads 'wo burt clips'

"What does that mean John?" we ask.

"What do you mean, what does it mean?"

"Well I don't quite understand what this says ?"

"Mum, can't you READ what it says …?"

"Well you read it to me then?"

"WE BOUGHT CLIPPERS" He tells me as if I am stupid.

"Oh of course I say. Feeling well put down.

We had, of course, bought a pair of hair clippers that day, as the hair of the entire male contingent is getting a seventies look about it.

Skipper is still asking for a tissue for whatever bit of maintenance he is doing and the boys reluctantly catch up on some schoolwork.

New battery charger and batteries are finally bought, at vast expense, that is most of our emergency fund gone already! We are suffering from port rot and are ready to leave so set sail for Fuerteventura, we will have to return later to collect the new batteries.

43

Fuerteventura is a large desert island South West of Lanzarote that has nothing much on it except sand and tourists.

The sail from Puerto Calero on Lanzarote should be a walk in the park; the sun is shining, we are all relaxed, the wind is only force two to three and we start off with a good broad reach. "Feels a bit thundery," says the skipper as we leave, we haven't managed to get a forecast today, but following the previous long term forecast, and knowing that it should only be a couple of hours , we are happy to go.

"No" I say, "Don't worry, the forecast is fine."

Just as well I don't do weather prediction for a living.

The skipper stands at the helm the wind has died, we furl the limp Genoa and we are having to motor now, he sticks his hands out palms up . "It's raining."

I look up, the sky is black. Down below the table is spread with school books each child at a different stage in maths. "OK, boys we will finish schoolwork for the day, you can put the books away."

"Hooray. Can we go on the computer? We are motoring." There is not even a glimmer of hesitation in putting down their pencils, and shoving the books haphazardly back into the cupboard.

I nod and pass the skipper's oilskins up to him and then put mine on before joining him. A few drops of rain soon become a torrent.. The thunder starts, growling rumbling and crackling all around us..

The thunder gets louder, the rain gets harder and the lightning flashes get ever closer. The skipper is looking at the weather, "That's most peculiar," he says , chewing his fingers.

"What is?" I am sheltering from the worst of the rain crouched in the companionway under the spay hood.

"The wind is blowing away from us, but the thunderstorm seems to be coming nearer. It doesn't make much sense."

I have no doubt there is a meteorological explanation for this!

We can no longer see land, and there is nothing like being apparently the only yacht in the middle of a thunderstorm. The rain is so heavy that the small waves have been flattened out and it is pouring in a spout of water from the end of the boom,

Flash...."Mississippi one,..... Mississippi two.....Mississippi three ...missi...." Crash.

"Three miles," we say simultaneously.

The lightning is beautifully forked and the next flash and thunder don't give us time to start counting, the water boils and fizzes a few feet from us where the lightning hits and the boys come out, the crash has almost shaken the boat with it's intensity.

You can feel the electricity in the air and all around us but mercifully we haven't been hit, yet.

"Are we going to die?" Asks David, his big blue eyes worried as he sticks his head up. Another inch gets chewed off the skipper's fingers.

"Don't touch any metal and you'll be fine" we say encouragingly.

Somehow this edict makes the children stand still as if statues so they stand poised in their positions, hands in the air, so as mot to touch anything.

"It's all right, you can move," I say.

And the thunderstorm passes almost as quickly as it has arrived, the land becomes visible and the rain stops. We go into Fuerteventura, feeling like we have been in a washing machine. Skipper finishes tying up the boat and walks slowly backwards off the pontoon, stepping sedately into the sea, still fully clothed in all his foul weather gear. As if he wasn't wet enough already. As he surfaces the boys are roaring with laughter, even I am having trouble keeping a straight face.

"Just watch it, it might be one of you next time," he says clambering back onto the pontoon, water pouring out of his sleeves.

"Who is this Sod who makes up such a silly law?" asks Brinsley as we explain yet another happening to "Sods Law"

The harbour here is lovely, in complete contrast to the one we have just left, here the boat owners seem to party on the pontoon all day long, drinking wine and gutting their fish, just moving their chairs out of the way so that we can get past, and greeting us in a variety of European languages until they hit upon the right one. There is an outdoor swimming pool close by to the marina which we are free to use whenever we want to so the boys spend hours there and we book them onto a windsurfing course. However no wind, too much wind and a broken down rescue dinghy means that they only really have one day's effective windsurfing! With no Fat Controller they can canoe to their hearts content. Skipper windsurfs and I decide to get my exercise, by running, but discover one of the disadvantages of living in confined space and not having the luxury of a carpeted living room floor. There is no space to do sit-ups. You try doing them on the pontoon......it is full of ridges and hard bits just designed to hit each bit of your spine like a knuckle (or spinal) duster.

So try the floor of the public showers on shore,(they are clean here) you have to be very resistant to funny looks.

So try the beach, then get all those grains of sand out of your hair and ears where they have managed to worm their way in. But that done, running along the beach is lovely especially early in the morning before anybody is about, though one morning I do get a bit of a shock when a naked man pops out from behind a bush. I decide to take a different route back that day, and don't let my thoughts delve too deeply into what he might have been doing this early in the morning with no clothes on behind a bush.

The children don't like paella very much. "What IS that Mum?!"........ "I CAN'T eat that!"......they examine minutely a small octopus nestled in the yellow rice. "Can we have some chips please?"

Fuerteventura is full of tourists. And words to the rhythm of the worm song leap unbidden to my mind.

Bodies from England,
Bodies from France(actually more Germans)
I think they'll come and get burnt.
Long thin slimy ones,
Short fat squashy ones,
See how they wriggle and squirm.
They lie on their deckchairs,
They suck in their cold beers,
See how they wobble and flop.
Pizzas and ice creams
Children and suncreams,
Toast them from bottom to top.

.........and we were one of them!

Back on Lanzarote. Skipper cooks tea.
"I didn't know Dad could cook, Mum"

"Of course he can, he used to cook me tomato soup followed by kedgeree, when we were courting."

"What's courting mum?"

"Before we got married."

John digests this bit of information, you can see him having difficulty envisioning his parents as anything but married.

Back in Lanzarote briefly to get our new batteries fitted it pours with rain...who says it only rains seventeen days every year in Lanzarote? "The computer's wet" David is wiping the rain off the computer and attempting to plug it in.

"Why is it wet?"

"It was under the hatch, and the hatch was open."

"Who left the hatch open?"

I have a sneaking suspicion that it might have been me, so at this point I remain silent. Computers of course are not very happy with this sort of treatment, so it decides to give up functioning completely. Nonetheless we lay it out in the sun to dry...when the sun makes an appearance.....

"Probably won't work again," says the skipper, "Never mind you'll just have to spend the year without a computer, won't do you any harm."

"Oh no, oh no!" wail the boys "Are you very cross?"

Sod is obviously having a day off because the computer decides to start working again after a good sunbathe.

Ashore the skipper has laid the huge red and yellow spinnaker out and is unpicking some of the sponsorship (the previous owner of the boat was heavily sponsored and we have slowly been removing all the sponsorship from the sails). Busy unpicking letter after letter he is half way through one of the larger letters when he holds it up and realises that there is now a substantial hole in the sail. "Oh ----" Another thing for the 'Bad Dad list! The larger letters are right through the sail and removing them will leave letter shaped holes. Oh dear now a bit of needlework is needed.

Sail overnight from Lanzarote to Tenerife.

"Dolphins!" the cry always guarantees that everybody will come rushing out onto deck.

"Don't forget to clip on!" as a child in his eagerness, is half way out of the cockpit before he has clipped his safety harness on.

A school of Atlantic Spotted dolphins come and play in the bow wave, some pale and some dark but all well spotted, like a skin that is covered in freckles, one leaps clear of the water revealing a bright pink belly. "Wow look at that one, and that.......here's one coming underneath the boat..."

I am seasick, the boys suddenly become subdued a sure sign that they too are feeling the effects of the sea, but it is not that rough and by the morning when we are once more in the shelter of the islands, life looks bright once more.

"Another dolphin!"...... "No it's a whale, ...no several whales......." And once again we abandon chores and watch the black shapes, much less exuberant than dolphins and larger, as we sail through a pod of pilot whales on the way into Santa Cruz harbour in Tenerife

Inside the walls the contrast to the wind and wildlife out side almost couldn't be more marked, past huge container ships, a dead rat floats by and we tie up alongside a quay where dead cockroaches abound., squashed on the quayside by wheels or feet.

"I don't want to stay here Mum " says David "we might get diseases".

But away from then quayside the town is clean, civilised and full of tubs of brightly coloured chrysanthemums.

Decide that we will climb Mount Teide, at 14000 feet, the highest mountain in Spain. The cable car is not working so it will be a long climb. Of course we haven't bought any walking footwear so we go out and buy some.(at this stage in our trip our bank account is still very healthy, even if we are already over budget.)

Where is the 'Camping Gaz' here? My usual problem to be solved at almost each new port, but I eventually find some at a garage.

Sunday 31st October, the day we are climbing the mountain.

The alarm goes off. It seems like we have only just gone to bed (we have!) I look at my watch 2.45 am. "Did you really mean to set the alarm for this early?!" I ask my still dozy husband beside me. "Yes, a quarter to three, you know that we needed to get up at this time."

But even as I am complaining we are getting up, not difficult as the children had gone to bed in their clothes and the rucksacks are all packed, we take only minutes to be ready.

"Shh now, remember that most people are still asleep." We creep over the decks of the neighbouring yacht to get to the quayside, trying not to wake anybody up, the tide is low so it is a climb using rusty metal rings and to get up, then we can haul the children up. We forget that the hire car has an alarm that promptly goes off when we open it, screeching loudly thereby cancelling out our attempts at silence.

Make a quick getaway, before we are discovered.

El Teide is 3718m, and we start at about 2200 m, so we still have higher than Ben Nevis to climb. I never thought we would be wearing our thermal underwear again for a while, but here we are, fully togged up and climbing a mountain by moonlight, and in the freezing cold. It is not long before the novelty of our night climb starts wearing off and for a while we all plod in our own thoughts, but the children doing remarkably well in keeping up.

"Snow!" calls out John, who at this point is in front and we all get excited at this little patch of frozen white winter.

"Ice, watch you don't slip!" calls out Brinsley.

The sky is lightning as dawn creeps across from the east and enthusiasm for the walk quickens a bit as we encounter these small patches of ice and snow. But then.....

"You've got a clear bit here!" says David. It is now with some relief that we can walk without slipping and sliding for a few feet, or if we are lucky a few hundred feet before we are once more slipping and sliding (in our trainers!) once more on frozen ice or snow.

The sun comes up, bouncing off the snow and ice giving the landscape a surreal like glitter. We stop and eat egg and bacon butties for breakfast. Sheltering behind the stone walls of a shelter that is undoubtedly used during the season, but now is deserted and has snow drifting up its edges. We don't stop for too long, it is all too easy to get cold. We now are walking from rock to rock on the path, to avoid the melting ice.

"Mum....it's too slippery!"

"Mum.....how much further?"

"Mum.....lets go back, I'm sure this is far too dangerous!"

"Tell Dad."

"Dad can we go back now?"

"What after coming this far, what are you, men or mice?"

"Boys Dad, just boys."

But us cruel parents persuade them to push on, stopping for rests or brief medical stops when one of the crew needs a plaster after a piece of rock jumps up and hits him in the knee (well so he says).

Reach the deserted top of the cable car, and a little chain across what there is of a path, saying in both Spanish and English "You are prohibited to go pass this sign, without permission for further information and permission please contact......" and there is a name and a telephone number. How do they expect us to contact them once we have got this far.

"Do as I say, boys, not as I do," says the skipper, as we duck under the chain and carry on walking the little extra we have to go to the top.

The snow and ice have disappeared right up here. It is barren and dry, but a bitterly cold wind is blowing and we fight against it, leaning into it as we walk the last bit up to the summit. Now on a very well marked path, which no doubt in the season, with a functional cable car has had its fair share of tourists.

We reach the top and whiffs of sulphur greet us, the children forget that they ever even mentioned that they wanted to go down, or that it was too slippery, or too cold or too much like hard work.

"Is this volcano live?…Will it erupt?"

"Feel this stone ….it's HOT!"

We sit on rocks warmed by the Earth's central heating system, that is the heat of the volcano, roast our frozen feet in little sulphur vents and eat the remainder of our butties plus hard boiled quails eggs whilst we take out the mobile phone and make phone calls!

The boys have carried raw jelly up the mountain to eat for instant energy.

"Hey this is NOT jelly!" says Brinsley in disbelief opening the cardboard packet and peering dispiritedly into the contents..

"What is it then?" I say, collecting the last little bits of eggshell and putting them back in our rucksacks.

"I don't know, it's a kind of powder." The three boys each in turn peer disappointedly at the packet of powdered flavoured gelatine. I would never have believed that such a simple thing could cause so much disappointment.

All too soon we must begin our descent as we have a long way to go.

The sun has begun to melt the surface of the snow and ice and the descent is slightly easier, the icy surfaces having turned to slush. Come to landscape that we had walked through in the dark, it is strangely Martian, reds, oranges, ochres of barrenness, with just the occasional tuft of grass that has managed to get a roothold. It seems to go on and on and on and on and on........., but lava flows of pumice are plainly visible and large boulders or 'volcanic bombs' litter the Martian landscape.

The children get second winds though and collect pieces of black shiny obsidian, the volcanic glass, from amongst the pumice and Brinsley wonders why his rucksack is getting so heavy, John disappears into his imaginary planet of Wig Wog using two pieces of stone in his hands for spaceships or aliens ,which takes him down the rest of the mountain and finally eleven hours after we had left it, we are back at the car again, footweary but satisfied.

The following day the alarm goes off at three am. Far too early but having realised that we have put the clock back two hours instead of one, we decide that as we are up we might as well leave so we quietly cast off and leave, for Gomera, a small and relatively unknown one of the Canaries.

Have you ever heard of acceleration zones? Well they are when the wind accelerates round the ends of islands, and this trip we certainly discovered about them. From 20 to 30 knots of wind to flat calms. Like a washing machine, violently whirled around then it pauses whilst it fills up for the next cycle.

One minute you are quietly having lunch and then the next the plates are hastily thrown down below as you reef the sails for the sudden increase in wind as it comes round the corner of the land.

Gomera is a haven, it has no airport, so as yet still has more locals than tourists.

The saucepans have obviously not enjoyed the washing machine motion of the boat as they jump out and attack me with renewed vigour when I try to take one out.

"There is a big chunk of hair here!" Martin holds up a nest of black hair in which bits of crisp, biscuit and other oddments have come to rest.

Guess who the only one in the boat with long black hair is?

"Sorry," I say trying to push the saucepans back into the cupboard.

"And there's more here!" The skipper is cleaning the cockpit, thank goodness he is not doing the bilge yet, I am sure there will be a few black hair nests there.

"I'm going to go and find some 'camping Gaz'," I say, "any of you boys coming with me?"

"And more!" the skipper is still scooping things out of the cockpit.

They all come, a new place is always exciting to explore.. Gomera doesn't seem to have any camping Gaz, but Ferreteria Pepe says that he might get some '*Manana* tardes'…. And we all know what *Manana* means!

Gomera is green and lush and exciting for the boys they have never seen banana plantations, here in the valleys there are plenty. The hills are so steep that the locals had developed a whistling language as a way of communication across the mountain tops. We drive our hired car along lethal roads, my heart is in my mouth at times and later we are told that one of the roads(one of the better ones) is known as the screaming route.

"Why?" I ask

"Because when the bus with tourists in comes down here, they scream as we go round the bends."

Guy Fawkes night is spent here. Ask the man in charge of the marina if we may hold a bonfire, and the following day he comes back with permission from the police, the army, the coastguard and anybody else who could possibly give us permission. He also gives us six home made rockets. The boys make a guy, using their old clothes and stuffing him with dead palm fronds collected from the beach, and adding an external penis made from a stick for good measure. Well boys will be boys.

We stand around the bonfire with people from other British yachts, and local Spanish children watch as we celebrate this truly British of festivals. Someone has even made some treacle toffee, and there is plenty of beer flowing. John has found a friend and is of exploring the breakwater, we keep an eye on him from where we are. Suddenly there is a piercing scream, and we turn towards the breakwater, John has tumbled off onto the sharp chunks of concrete below, we are not the only parents who run. It is with some relief that when we haul him back onto the top, he can actually move. There is blood pouring down his face, but nothing seems to be broken, and for once it is quite nice to here his screams as it means that he is still very much alive. I leave the revellers and go back to the boat with John.

"It hurts, it hurts." But John is very stoical and after we clean him up he has a nasty cut on his chin which requires me delving into the big green first aid kit....the one that has sutures, blood plasma, lots of dressings etc..... We in fact patch him up with steristrips and he is soon recovered enough to go back to playing on the beach, this time well away from the breakwater. We still have a few 'guilty bad parent' thoughts and are thankful that it wasn't worse.

"What are you celebrating?" ask a Dutch couple we have invited.

"We are burning an effigy of somebody who tried to burn down the houses of parliament, but he failed."

She is totally mystified, but joins in watching anyway, we have a few out of date flares and the harbour masters home made rockets, and when we leave the Spanish children run and jump over the embers of the fire, as dares.

Las Palmas, Gran Canaria. The start of the ARC is drawing ever nearer, boats are now collecting here. We need some time to stock up and get ready for our transatlantic crossing.

'Pass us a tissue please' The engine cover is off, the skipper's head is in the small engine compartment, sweat dripping off him. To get out into the cockpit you have to step three feet up or pull yourself up like a monkey being careful not to kick the skipper crouched over the engine hoping that it will still be reliable when we reach St Lucia.

'Mum is it a break time yet? Why do we still have to do schoolwork, it must be holidays by now"

'Is that more supplies you are bringing on board?'

'Why aren't you bald yet? This boat is FULL of your hairs'

And the time passes. I would never have believed we could have got so many provisions on board, but there will be nine of us on board.......'HOW MANY...?'

'nine'.

We are next to a Danish boat *Flyer,* with Kel, Ingar and their very good looking son Morton. Ingar is not planning to sail across the Atlantic, she will fly out and meet them at the other end, one of Morton's friends will help them sail the boat across.

Ingar is sitting relaxing reading the paper when she suddenly shrieks and leap up, Martin has been washing our decks and has inadvertently sprayed the hose directly on her!

We have tins of beans, vegetables, tuna, tuna, corned beef, stored in every available nook and cranny. And then of course there is the beer. We'll need at least four cans each a day. So we have cases of beer on top of every water and fuel tank, tucked down the sides of lockers, squeezed in wherever I can.

"Ahoy there!"

I raise my head from where I am trying to fit another case of beer.

"Hello Barry! When did you get here?"

."Just yesterday, Every time I come and visit, you are stocking up your boat, with all the floorboards up and food and drink everywhere!" It is true. Australian Barry from our sister yacht *Lady Penelope*, first met in Hayling Island. "Hello Barry, come and have a drink." The skipper appears from the generator locker which is up forward.

"Barry sits on the step, there is nowhere else to sit at the moment, and a cold beer is put in his hands.

"I don't think you'll starve," he says .

Then just when I think the boat will not fit any thing else in, doubt appears from somewhere and visions of a hungry crew wanting to know what there was to eat dances in my head so another trip to the supermarket was in order. Food for nine people for three weeks is a hefty amount.

Martin's dad phones up to say that the tax man is investigating us. Martin has never been investigated before.

"Just tell him that all our documents are in storage and they can look through as much paperwork as they want when we return, but meanwhile tell them to contact the company.....they know exactly how much tax I have paid."

I suppose as we have just left the country and he has stopped a well-paid job, some people cannot conceive that there just might not be an ulterior motive.

Anyway nothing further comes of it. Except that same night when we get back from a seminar Kel from *Flyer,* sticks his head up. "The police were here looking for you earlier, they knocked and knocked on your boat."

I feel the adrenaline pumping, but the skipper seems much less ruffled. "Did they say what they wanted?"

"No, but there were here in force, blue flashing lights and everything."

We decide to ring both sets of parents up to make sure that they are not dead, and then stop worrying about it, if it is very important they will come back.

We do not sleep well that night. But the police never return and no disaster seems to have befallen anybody at home..

"I need to do a final check on the rigging," says the skipper, are you ready to haul me up the mast?"

I suppose so, I say taking off my rubber gloves and coming out onto deck. To haul him up the mast he sits in a boson's chair, which is basically a piece of canvas attached to a halyard, and the rope comes back and round a winch. It is hard work winding eleven stone up sixty-five feet!

"Can I go up?" asks Brinsley. And so one by one our children are hauled right to the top of the mast, none of them showing any fear but I cannot watch. I feel distinctly ill looking up and seeing a child so small and so high up, and knowing that I wouldn't be able to do it myself. I have to shut my eyes as they get nearer the top.

We go to seminars on provisioning, seminars on rigging, seminars on navigation and there are several seminars that we don't go to. Chay Blyth comes to talk to us, and the yachts are dressed overall, this means that we hoist lots of flags up the rigging, their fluttering sounding like pattering raindrops. At least twice we get up during the night to shut the hatches, only to discover that it is not raining at all.

Our pontoon sinks under the weight of a pontoon party and we eat and drink whilst paddling ankle deep in water, before moving to another party on the next pontoon on board *Gravitas.*

Nikki off *Alice Ambler* starts an aerobic class in the car park. "Are you coming?" She asks full of bounce and enthusiasm as she leaves her son Toby to play with John.

So we go, the skipper included. There are about three men in total doing aerobics with the women in the car park and as the day starts up this little group are sashaying and doing other things to the sound of music from a cassette player on the ground beside Nikki . They stretch up and down and side to side, sweating by the end." I never knew aerobics was so strenuous" ignoring the looks of the dustbin lorry as it passes or the other not quite so energetic yachtsmen as they pass by on their way to the showers.

I only go once. "Wimp!" but am running along the concrete seafront instead.

"Morning boys!"

"Morning!"

"Who is going to go in Don Pedros boat race today then?"

Don Pedro runs the garage on the marina, provides camping gaz, collects washing to be sent to the laundry and every year arranges a dinghy race, in the rubber dinghies for whoever wants to enter and doesn't mind getting wet. I don't fancy ending up in a water fight, so leave the male contingent to go and walk around to watch them from the quayside.

A slightly wet bedraggled figure finds me in the crowds "Mum."

"John, what happened? Why aren't you with the others?"

"I didn't like it, they were throwing water bombs and gofio balls." Gofio is a glutinous maize flour, a staple of the Canarian diet, but mixed with water and thrown makes a horrible gluey mass, which when combined with children's hair, apparently becomes even more glutinous. We go and watch the rest of the race.

Water bombs, some with coloured water, gofio balls, tomatoes etc. are flying through he air. Little boats filled to sinking level and one turned turtle with loads of people on its upturned bottom are frantically trying to race up and down the 'course'. We spot the *Brandamajo* tender, are they winning?

14th November Brinsley's diary reads: '*Today was a very exciting day because it was the* dinghy *race but it doesn't normally turn out as a race more like a water fight because there was gofio being thrown and someone who had a whole bucket full poured it all over my head that was when we went to get some tee-shirts when we were near shore trying to get them John jumped out'* We are still working on punctuation!

But with no discernible start and no discernible finish, everybody gets a cup, it is truly a race where winning or losing is not part of the vocabulary.

The crew begins to arrive. Paul and Paola are first, Paul is amenable, enthusiastic, untidy and going through a painful divorce. Paola from Italy is the new love in his life and practises aromatherapy, she will stay until we leave and then be there to meet us when we arrive at the other end, she goes and chats to the Italian participating boats to give her own country some support.

They go off to stay in an hotel, living on a boat with three noisy boys and us, is not exactly the most romantic of situations!

David, Rebecca and Antony all arrive on the same day, weighed down with luggage.

David was at school with Martin, they were each others best men, and almost have a language unique to them as people do who have known each other for so long that there are lots of shared past experiences and jokes which mean nothing to the outsider.

We have climbed Kilimanjaro with them, camped in Africa and now left my old pony Peter with them. They have left their four children behind, and I can feel Rebecca already beginning to miss them.,

"Are you scared about the crossing?" asks Big David as we sit and drink bottles of beer.

"No not any more," I say, having now been through our Portuguese experience and spoken to lots of old hands, this crossing of the Atlantic is supposed to be so easy that it is known as the 'milk run.''

Antony, my mothers ex lover, and family friend is in theory bringing some experience of years at sea on board, he is a deep sea pilot and has skippered the sail training tall ships. Also he always gets on well with all sorts of people, but how will this little group of people survive for three weeks in each other's company with nowhere to escape to?

Martin and my ten days of preparation we think have paid off, but the crew are not so sure. "Have you got enough toilet rolls?'

"Yes even if we all have diarrhoea"

'Are you sure there is enough water?'

"We have a water maker, but we have enough to drink even if the water maker breaks down."

"What about the beer?'

"That's going to be rationed!"

So we go back to the supermarket again. Then somehow we have to fit all the fresh stuff on board. Mountains of potatoes, a stem of bananas, big chunks of ham (Pork seems to be our main form of preserved meat....... And Paul is Jewish! Sometimes even the first mates provisioning can be a bit short sighted.

David and Rebecca P. buy lots of tomato juice and little extra provisions. "They will have to go in your cabin" I say, there is nowhere else to put anything, but I don't think that we will starve.

"Have we got to go in there?!" they exclaim, looking at trying to fit all of their gear into their cabin, but they pile everything in heaps around the edges and on the floor and still find a place to sleep amongst it all.

"How do you get into bed?"

"Well like a bear." Answers the skipper.

"And how does a bear get into bed?"

"You crawl in until you are on the bed and then you turn around. But you could of course sleep with your head at the other end, it just means that you will not be able to sit up in bed." One more problem solved.

Only one day to go, after a Japanese meal ashore where the skipper had a chance to practise his Japanese, it is dark the children are full of high spirits and running, cavorting through the car park, now empty of aerobics, and David sticks his hand into a car headlight... a broken one...

'Stop fussing David, it'll be all right!' we say as he drips blood in the dark along the road, along the pontoon and back to the boat.

'But it's bleeding Mum! Look!" and under the lights on the boat we could see that it indeed is, blood is pouring out, onto the yellow and white striped cushions we have bought to give us a bit of bottom protection against endless days sitting on the hard wooden seats of the cockpit.. We have one more day to go before setting off across the Atlantic.

"Let's have a look David." And we wash the cut which is deep, and pouring out blood as fast as we wash it. The crew members all look and give advice, before we decide to put our fantastically well equipped medical kit into practice at once, so once again the Steristrips are brought into action, and applied with a big white bandage. The thought of queues in a Spanish hospital, trying to communicate and being held overnight are banished. The big green medical kit is opened once again, and I thought that we wouldn't have to use it at all. We decide not to use any of our precious stocks of antibiotics just yet, hopefully the wound is clean enough that it won't get infected.

We leave tomorrow. Quick better buy just a little bit more food in case we run out. We must also buy all our perishables: onions, tomatoes, apples, potatoes, pineapples, etc and wash them of any traces of cockroaches. The skipper walks past carrying a whole stem of green bananas, which we strap on the railings at the stern of the boat, cutting some off to store down below in the hope that they will ripen at different times.

CHAPTER THREE

THE ATLANTIC

"You won't get too het up about making a good start?" I plead.

"Of course not, what do a few minutes matter when we are starting a two or three week race?" but nonetheless the skipper cannot resist making a good start to the longest race he has ever done and we are almost the first boat out of 200 to cross the line at the start of 2700 miles.

"I don't know what they're all doing over there?" says the skipper looking at the bulk of the yachts all chivvying for space at the far end of the starting line. "This is definitely the best end of the line to be."

There are one or two other yachts here including Pat and Olivia from Ireland, he is also an ex dinghy sailor.

"Let the sails flap!"

"Get ready!" He looks at his watch, the crew are all ready to pull a rope at a moments notice.

"One minute to go." we wait in silence as the seconds tick away.

"Ten…..nine…..eight   …….seven…..six……five……   start grinding in those sails…NOW!………..three, two …..Go on get them in!"…..

"BANG" a puff of smoke from the starting boat indicates that the race has started, the sails are in, the wind is blowing and all of a sudden we sit down not sure if we are going to have to change the sail position today or tomorrow, or even the next day or the one after that….who knows?

We are all drugged up with scopaderm patches…. Well not quite all, the skipper, Antony and big David (in order to distinguish him from little David) are not planning to get seasick so are patchless. Little almost skin coloured patches stuck behind the ear, and ashore we had seen others with patches to whom you nod in sympathy as if a member of some secret cult, but in reality knowing that we all have that same masochistic bent to go and throw up, out of choice, for days on end.

Nobody goes below much, we just dive down to do what ever we have to do and then return on deck for the fresh air. Nobody sleeps very much the first night, and we wonder how we are going to get by for three weeks with a cushionless cockpit!.

A full moon on the first night, gives us plenty of light to see by , and we can just sit and enjoy it, watching a turtle float by in the water and a school of dolphins graces us with their presence. We are not relaxed yet, more full of apprehension as to what the Atlantic may bring.

The first two days are uneventful, the skipper has written up a rota for which watch is cooking and when, we are divided into three watches, named port, starboard, and larboard, and each watch has one child with them to help keep them in order.

"How do you get these saucepans back into the cupboard." Asks Rebecca who has braved her queasiness to wash up.

"Just push them all hard !" I answer from above in the cockpit. Clatter clatter clatter bang........thump.......Silence. The saucepan cupboard is closed.

We are heading south with good strong trade winds and as most of the crew are new to the boat the skipper decides against the spinnaker, I am relieved, we need a little time to get used to each other and let the others get used to the boat.

Paul is standing stretching in the cockpit, arms out sideways, then upwards, bending his whole body from side to side, then his legs..

"What are you doing?" I ask, from my recumbent position on the hard wooden cockpit seat.

"I have been given an exercise regime of simple exercises to keep me fit, I'll show you if you want."

Nobody leaps to take him up on his offer, but we are all happy to watch and comment.

Seasickness is beginning to abate, maybe the patches really do work, and we are lulling ourselves into a timeless routine.

Finished stretching, Paul is down below, he reappears, cracking his head on the hatch as he does so. "You know what I fancy?" .

"What?" several people ask in unison.

"Some ice cream."

You've got a long wait." We have no freezer, and the space in the fridge is limited.

George starts stealing things, or is he just a useful scapegoat?!

Then on day three the water maker breaks down.

"Can we fix it?" asks Antony.

"I don't know." answers the skipper, kneeling down and lifting the cushions off the seat. The water maker takes up the whole of the space underneath one of the seats by the table in the saloon. Antony leans over beside him and they look into the cylinders and hoses that constitute the water maker. The water maker in essence works by forcing sea water at high pressure across a membrane through which the salt molecules don't fit, so you end up with water so pure that it is tasteless.

A switch has burnt out. We don't have a spare…….. for all our preparation, it is impossible to carry spares for everything on the boat..

"You could short circuit it," says Antony, the most electrically and engineering minded one of us on the boat.

"I don't know what that might do," says the skipper, "But I suppose we haven't got much to lose. Let's have a beer whilst we think about it." He is chewing his fingernails, his responsibility for the crew lying heavy on his shoulders.

"Anybody else for a beer?" asks Antony, opening the fridge.

"No thank you." answers Paul, "I didn't spend all these past months getting fit for this sailing trip just to sit still and drink beer!"

"No thank you," I answer, "my stomach is not quite ready to accept alcohol yet." Rebecca, like me is feeling queasy, it is day three of the scopy patch and it is beginning to wear off, definitely not a good night to be on cooking duty. I manage to cook a complex curry but by the time it comes to eat it, all I can do is collapse and lie horizontal in my bunk and leave the rest of the crew to help themselves. But Dave P, Antony and the skipper neither feel sick nor feels the need to remain alcohol free.

(On his arrival Antony had handed me some scopaderm patches, "I hope you appreciate these, I had to go into the doctor and tell him that I suffered from seasickness. I am never seasick!") I was of course very appreciative of the means to keep my drug habit going!

"So what now?"

"No more showers, we wash up in salt water, only a mugful for washing and brushing teeth in, and if you want to wash your clothes you wash them in seawater."

There is silence for a bit.

"Should we go and fill up or try and get it repaired at the Cape Verdes?" someone asks hopefully.

"No."

"We won't die of thirst will we?" asks our David, a worried frown creasing his forehead.

"Don't worry, we wouldn't let that happen," I say, ruffling his short hair.

Two days later the skipper and Antony manage to theoretically fix the water maker.

"OK let's start that generator , we can have fresh water again!"

"Hooray!"

"Nothing's happening!"

"What do you mean, nothings happening?"

"The generator is not going."

"The generator's not going, are you sure?"

Silence and absence of that comforting hum from up forward confirm the non-working of the generator..

"Come on lads, let's solve the problem," says Antony, realising that just listening to a silent generator is not going to solve anything.

The skipper has had it with the failing mechanics so Dave P and Antony harness on and lie up with the generator for a few hours and finally decide there is a problem with the starter motor or the battery.

No generator equates to no water maker. But in addition to no water maker, also limited telly, limited computer, no breadmaker and we will have to run the engine to charge the batteries!"

"I thought you said this was going to be luxurious this sort of sailing?" says Rebecca who has never done any yacht sailing before. "Showers every day and all that?"

"It's all relative!" says the skipper smiling.

However after a day of thinking and deducing by those crew members with a mechanical bent, a semi solution is worked out, by carrying the heavy generator battery aft we can recharge it. The battery is very heavy, and the first thing you have to do is haul it out of the hole on the foredeck that is the generator locker, then carry it down the deck, which, don't forget, is moving. It is a slow laborious process, then it has to be lifted into the cabin and connected where the other batteries are in order that when we run the engine we can charge it up. The whole process then has to be done in reverse and then run the generator enough to make bread, and run the television, and even recharge the batteries to a certain extent, but unfortunately there is some underlying problem and there is not enough power to run the water maker.

So every couple of days Antony sets out on this strenuous bit of exercise, and his humour never falters.

Catch a fish, but just as it is tantalisingly close it disappears together with the lure and the hook. Never mind, we have plenty of spare hooks and lures and Big D reassembles the line and we try again.

We are in luck (little do we know it but this will be the only fish of the whole crossing)

"I think I've caught a fish," says David Pearse,

"Yeah, yeah, we'll believe it when it is on board," answer an unbelieving crew.

"Come on boys, there's a fish!" I stick my head down below. "Yay, a fish! Come on let's go and see," says Brinsley and the boys come up, clipping on their safety harnesses as they clamber out of the cockpit..

"What is it, what is it?"

"Don't know, can someone pass me the rock hammer and the gaff?"

"Come on David, you don't need the gaff for that!"

It is a dorado, often called dolphin fish, beautifully coloured with a strange blunt head, and thrashing around.

"I'll use the gaff." He hauls it out into the cockpit, fish in one hand, rockhammer in the other.

"Shall we pour some vodka over it?"

"Why?"

"Calm it down a bit so that you can hit it on its head."

"Hey watch my cockpit, you're getting blood everywhere," says the skipper as the fish now well battered and dead but still flailing around is spraying blood everywhere.

"Stop fussing, it'll clean off. Can somebody get me something to put it in."

The shoes are tipped out of the shoebox and the fish is put in that until teatime. So dorado steaks for tea, the best meal so far and we look forward to more of the same..

Washing up after mealtimes is in a bucket of sea water, which having no sea water tap you have to haul in from over the side, into the cockpit, This seems a great idea until a wave gives the bucket a life of its own and it slides across the cockpit when it comes suddenly to rest against our cabin window when it neatly empties all the dirty salty washing up water into our cabin on the bed before righting itself and returning with the next roll to its original position! Only empty.

I go down to investigate the damage, first removing the bucket well away from the window.

"How wet?" comes a voice from the cockpit.

I am squelching on all fours.

"Very."

We can pull the mattress out to air, and put on a new sheet, but with no way of washing out the salt, the bed remains very damp. We eventually overcome the problem by piling towels on top of the mattress and under the sheet, now it is only damp instead of wet.

And so the days and the nights roll by. The night watches (although the midnight until four one seems to go on for ever,) give us time to see the sky like we never see it at home. There is no light pollution at all, and on the nights where there is no moon, there is just an inky blackness, the only light to see by provided by the stars, which in the absence of all other light provide a surprising amount of light. We feel small and vulnerable in the middle of this huge expanse of water.

As the rest of the crew sleep, the lapping of the waves and gentle sound of the wind in the sails mask the hum of the self-steering. Houses, beds and England are a world away.

The skipper is learning to navigate by the stars, and so far has got as far as being able to tell the time by Orion.(surprisingly accurately).

The favourite watch for us all is the morning watch, from four a.m. until eight a.m., First we still have the stars and then we can watch the sunrise, it is never not beautiful, and is always different.

The sunsets too, we are usually all on deck for the evening light show, and almost without fail, conversation stops as the sun starts sinking below the horizon in the west, and we remain in silence until the last speck has oozed away.

"What was that?" Rebecca is standing down below drying up. It is now dark, our evening light show over.

"What was what?"

"There's something wet dripping on my head"

Now we keep most of our fresh fruit and vegetables in net hammocks that are slung off the ceiling of the cabin. Rebecca is standing underneath the tomatoes.

Paul stretches his hand up, "I think that the tomatoes are ripe!"

"Mum, something is dripping on my head too!" There is another hammock of tomatoes above where the boys are sitting, they are also underneath some ripe tomatoes.

"Come on boys , what shall we do today? Maths, English? Have you done your diaries?"

"Maths mum," says John, who is going to finish his maths books long before the year is out, unless he gets bored or it gets too difficult.

"What can I write in my diary?" says David, "Nothing different happened today than yesterday?!"

"Well you can say the tomatoes are ripe?" I say hopefully.

"Who wants to know whether the tomatoes are ripe or not, THAT is not interesting!" he says . He does have a point.

"Well draw a really nice picture then"

"What of?"

"The boat?" the teacher is definitely fighting a losing battle.

"Again?!"

"Well draw a tomato then." I am not sure who has got the best end of today's diary writing. The pupil I suspect.

The days start to join into one another, watches of four hours on eight hours off, the best day being when you finish at midnight then have a full nights sleep before your next watch at eight o'clock the next morning. The ocean seems endless, here we are a small boat with mile and miles of sea around us. If we all fall out with one another well there is nothing for it but to jump in, or perhaps alternatively just lump it until we reach that inconceivable piece of land we are aiming for in the Caribbean. Luckily so far there have been no signs of a mutiny.

Each day has its highlight, be it the tomatoes going ripe all at once....don't believe what they say about separating the green ones and the red ones, they still all got ripe almost simultaneously.

Or the almost daily loss of a lure and hook to another fish, there must be a lot of prickly-mouthed fish out there now. We shift around uncomfortably in the cockpit, the hard wooden seats digging into our buttocks, only the helmsman having the privilege of sitting on the cheap Spanish cushions we had bought in the canaries before we left.

Gopher three, John pops his head up and looks around, moving his head slowly from side to side. "We have zero visibility," and pops back down into the cabin. We later find out that this comment comes from Independence Day which is one of the few videos we have on board.

Sit eating tea with the sun going down.

"A fish a fish!"

Big D starts reeling the line, he suddenly stops, or rather the line jerks to a stop and he finds it twice as hard to reel in as it was before. "Hey I think I've got his big brother now."

"What is it, what is it?" we all crowd around eagerly, except for the skipper who is finishing off his potatoes, with Canarian mojo sauce on.

"Wow!"

Aaah!"

. A big, and I mean BIG blue marlin (or is it a sailfish?)leaps and thrashes around, I am sure that it is going to leap onto the boat, and I step back away from that fearsome jaw. I am not the only one losing interest in hauling it in.

But then as quickly as it has come, it has broken the line and is gone, and the skipper didn't even manage to see it. Then all is quiet and we have lost another lure and hook, only this time we have lost half the line with it.(500lb breaking strain, so that gives an indication of how big the fish was!)

That little episode certainly got the adrenaline going, for all except the skipper who was so busy eating his Canarian potatoes that he missed the whole thing.

George is helming magnificently, the Atlantic fish are stealing our equipment the saucepan cupboard is still spitting and the verruccas are still active, the Athletes foot is dying.

The skipper comes on watch and puts on some music, Gilbert and Sullivan...."I am the captain of the *Brandamajo*...o....And a fine good captain too..oo!" he sings along, altering the words slightly. So infectious is his singing that we cannot help but sing along with our skipper, apart from the boys.

"Oh Da-ad not again!"

"And I'm never ever sick at se-ea!" he carries on singing.

The children pop out from down below from time to time like little gophers, look around to see what the adults are up to and then pop back down into their burrow to continue with their computer game or drawing.

"Pass us a drink out boys please?" the weather is getting hotter as we go south and west, and even tepid drinks are better than none at all. If we have managed to have the fridge on at all, everybody is after the drinks that have been at the back of the fridge, they are the only ones that are likely to have a temperature resembling cool.

David C (gopher one) opens the fridge to collect cans for the thirsty crew.

"What IS that smell?" he backs rapidly away from the offending fridge.

"CLOSE THAT FRIDGE!" several adults shout in unison watching their beers warm up.

"It stinks in there" says David gingerly stretching his hand in to get the drinks out.

I know that there is fillet steak in there, that was once frozen and vacuum packed, but now is probably alive, and trying to crawl out.
It is the Pearses' turn to cook and they manage to make a surprisingly edible stew out of the offending article, and none of us are any the worse for it he following day. That was the last of our fresh meat, it never quite made the thousand miles that it was being saved for.

The Atlantic waters move by beneath us, the winds have eased, the crew have got used to the boat so the spinnaker is put into use, but it is not long before that big yellow and red spinnaker puts my back out putting up a fight as I haul it up.

"*Brandamajo, Brandamajo*, this is *Accolade, Accolade*, over?"

"Morning *Accolade, Brandamajo*, reading you loud and clear." Antony is in his position at the chart table, to give our daily noon position, which will be relayed by the yacht named *Accolade* back to the ARC headquarters..

We wonder where Barry's boat *Lady Penelope* is,(our sister ship); she does not have an SSB so we do not get her position.

"I could always ring up Portsmouth and see if they have got any record of where she is?" says the skipper.

He does and we discover that she is somewhat North of us, and still a little behind.

"Hey, Hey, we might beat us yet, despite all Barry's go faster gear he put on," says the skipper.

Sunday 28th November....we hit 1000 miles. Cannot believe that there are still 1800 to go, it seems like we have been at sea, forever.

"Pass us a tissue please!" calls the skipper from a recess.

Antony switches off the music.

"I really could do with an ice cream" says Paul to no one in particular as he sups on another warm drink, whilst stretching his legs for some form of exercise. His exercise regime has deteriorated somewhat as the wind has died and the weather got hotter.

The Pearses are on watch, the bimini comes down and they soak up the nearly tropical sun. Fair skinned Paul smears himself in factor twenty and looks for some non-existent shade.

"Are those bananas ripe yet?"

"No" The bananas are just beginning to show a glimmer of yellow, maybe they'll ripen before we get to the other side of the Atlantic.

The phone rings, we have a satellite phone, which came with the boat. It is quite uncanny how a telephone can ring on this little boat in the middle of the Atlantic. It does cost three dollars a minute though.

"Rebecca it's for you!" Rebecca is sunbathing in up forward in "The Garden" that is the foredeck.

It is her children. " Hello........I know, I'm missing you too, but it won't be all that long........... That sounds great Ruthie,.......... well done Martin.........No we're not having much luck with catching fish at the moment........... Oh Katie that's fantastic............. Well give Phil my love when he comes back in."

She wipes away a tear as she puts the phone down.

David and Rebecca roast in the sun, Paul, Antony and I try to avoid roasting and the skipper does both. (Antony does occasionally escape up into the garden and have a quick sunbathe though) The gophers of course seem to spend most of their time below except when they pop up for meals or the tennis tournament.

In a polite and civilised manner Antony switches the music off.

In a polite and civilised manner the skipper switches the music on.

It's getting hotter. The skipper tries to rig up a seawater shower with a pump, but after a lot of effort it proves easier to use a bucket. You sit at the stern of the boat, well harnessed on and either get someone to throw buckets of seawater over you or attempt to do it yourself. Plus a bit of soap. Hey Presto you feel clean and refreshed, if a little salty.

Salt is permeating all corners of the boat, the stainless steel cutlery has got rust spots on and even the clothes seem to be going rusty!

"Don't worry, when we get a squall, we will all be able to have a fresh water shower," says the skipper, busy keeping crew morale up, as we move south and west the weather is becoming more and more typical of squally weather.

"Well I'm going to try and wash some clothes in sea water," says Paul, "after all you did tell us that we only need bring a couple of tee shirts and a couple of pairs of shorts!"

"I'm going to wear this same pair of shorts until we get to the other side " says Brinsley. The children are revelling in the fact that their parents have gone from one extreme to the other, from telling them to wash and change their underwear, to telling them that they won't die if they don't wash too thoroughly and don't change their underwear.

It's funny how priorities change when there is no water!

John goes and helps Big David haul the line in.

"What no fish!"

The bananas decide to ripen almost simultaneously so we have bananas for breakfast lunch and tea, they are certainly very tasty, but there does come a stage when you have had enough bananas!

The skipper puts some music on.

Gopher number three, alias John , pops his head up, looks around and says "We have zero visibility," and pops down again. I know they have seen Independence day too many times!

"A squall, a squall!" the cry goes out as the telltale black line of cloud appears on the horizon.

"A shower, a shower,!"

"Get the soap, get the soap!"

Now in normal sailing you do everything you can to avoid squalls, the increase in wind can be quite dangerous, but we have little wind and everybody would love a good dousing of fresh water, so we turn the boat and head towards the threatening black line of cloud, getting ready to reef in the sails should it be necessary.

Gopher one David is actually on deck, "Go on Dad, make this boat a Go Faster boat and see if you can catch the squall, remember the Laser Two Nationals?"

"I'm trying, I'm trying , says the skipper who has temporarily taken over from George.(If I don't do some sailing I might forget how to he has said)

"I don't think you're catching it," says David looking in the direction of the long heavy line of black cloud that is just beginning to discharge rain.

We all stand in the cockpit clutching our bottles of shampoo or bars of soap.

None of this trying to avoid squalls that the books all tell us we should be doing!

No luck though, Sod is in action again and we do not get our showers, the soap goes away and we resign ourselves to remaining salty for a little while longer, though we do manage to get some wind as we run along beside the cloud.

Shoals of flying fish are becoming much more abundant now and it is not uncommon for one to land on the deck, especially at night. The unfortunate fish we can use as lures to try and catch us some supper. Not with a lot of success.......actually not with any success at all.

It is dusk and the one time of day when the whole crew, boys included, is on deck to talk and eat our fishless evening meal, for once we are not struggling to get speed, and nobody is feeling seasick, I could almost see me spending some more time doing this. We have just had our silent revering of the sunset, each one is different from the last.

"What was that?" says Paul.

"Oh look!"

We all look and swimming alongside us, is a pod of pilot whales, blowing and looking at us in the fading light with there beady eyes, a baby swims close to its mother.

"Fantastic."

Big David and Rebecca have been scanning the ocean for whales ever since we have started, and it's surprising how many whale spouts you can imagine you see when there are lots of white horses on the waves.

They swim with us for a while, then their curiosity satisfied they move as one and go off on their own way.

Wednesday 1st December.

Half way. The Atlantic stretches endlessly behind us and in front of us, it has taken us longer to get to this point than it should have and the Pearses are beginning to worry that they might not catch their plane home again. The skipper does not want to use the engine. The trade winds do not want to set in, so it seems we are at a bit of an impasse.

We celebrate our half way status with champagne, smoked salmon and lumpfish caviar.

Paul's' divorce also comes through today. We are not sure if this is cause for celebration or commiseration, but we enjoy the champagne anyway.

"Gopher two, alias Brinsley, pops up and says "What's for pud?"

"I don't know, tinned fruit, rotten banana, biscuit?"

"Biscuit please Mum"

The last rotten banana is consigned to the deep. It is a soggy brown mass., and quite slimy.

Paul takes his trousers off the line "these are solid, I think they were better off before they were washed!" he says .

John, Gopher three, pops his head up through the companionway looks around at the water, mutters " we have zero visibility" and disappears back down below to his drawings of more and more elaborate yachts.

Paul and Antony are on watch, the bimini is put up, we huddle under its shade. The sun beats down. We are now at a latitude of about 15 degrees North and heading slowly but surely westwards. We hold a tennis tournament......(aren't these days of technology great?.. yes we actually played Gameboy tennis; not exactly very physically demanding, but it passes the time and it is surprising how excited a close match can get.) Not much of a spectator sport though.

"I DO need an ice cream" says Paul.

The wind is getting less and less, the sun is getting hotter and hotter, and we struggle to keep the spinnaker filled and persuading the boat to move along. It is harder work when there is no wind than when there is some!

The skipper and I on watch during the night, he takes the helm and has me sitting on the side deck playing with the spinnaker to keep it filled, he is trying to get every ounce of speed he can out of the boat.

"*Brandamajo, Brandamajo, Brandamajo*, this is *Mainframe, Mainframe*, do you read me?"

"*Mainframe, Mainframe*, this is *Brandamajo*, you are a bit broken up but I can read you"

"Could you give me your noon position please."

"15. 52 North, 38.57 West. Wind East 10 knots.

Accolade is obviously out of our range, but Antony dutifully relays our position back to the yacht *Mainframe*. It will be interesting putting faces to voices when we get ashore

Our flight is booked for the twelfth of December," says Rebecca, "what are the chances of us getting there on time? The inactivity is beginning to get to her, the daily walk up to the bow of the boat, all 46ft, is not proving to be enough, so she whiles away quite a lot of time sleeping and reading.

"Don't worry," says the skipper, we will make your flight, If I have to use the motor I will." But every ounce of him is willing the wind to come up so that he doesn't have to engine, There is something nice about using only the power of nature to get across the Atlantic.

Rebecca has a another fight with the saucepan cupboard, I hear a yell and think that she has got the better of the cupboard. The cupboard is certainly putting up a good fight, maybe tidying it would get a better result?

"Pass us a tissue please?" says the skipper, fiddling around with something mechanical, lying prone on the floor, the engine hatch off.

Schoolwork.

Well yes, schoolwork. The novelty of home schooling is definitely beginning to wear off. We are sitting doing maths, the books spread around the table, and the children each working at their own level.

"Squall coming!" the shout comes from the cockpit. Sounds of the sails being reefed, and winches grinding coming from up above. But it is too late for us to stow everything before the wind hits..

"Quick grab those books!…….. and the Marmite!"

We grab what we can, but the Marmite joins the bread and some paper on the floor, where it slides noisily to come to rest in the galley beneath the cooker and the sink." (I KNEW you should always stow everything when it wasn't being used)

We give up school for the day, much to the delight of the pupils.

"Quick David, get the soap and get on deck we may get a shower!" yells Brinsley Gopher two. The children join the adults on deck shampoo hopefully in hand, and we watch the rain head towards us, a few forlorn drops land on the sun baked teak of the decks, evaporating as it lands.

"It's raining, it's raining!" But the drops amount to no more and the squall veers off away from us. Oh well no shower again today.

The skipper puts the music on.

5th December. The wind is back. We are off watch in the small hours, and sleeping the sound sleep that sailors know so well.

"What was that!" the skipper is bolt upright in bed , and on deck there is the sound of flapping and clattering sails, in particular the spinnaker.

He is out of bed like a shot, "You all right up there?" he asks Antony and Paul who are on watch.

Antony is on deck trying unsuccessfully to snuff the spinnaker (this involves pulling a rope which in effect pulls a large sock down over the spinnaker thereby 'snuffing' it). The large sail is trying to wrap itself around the forestay, and if that happens more often than not, you have to cut the sail to free it.

"I think the guy has broken" says Antony. (the guy being one of the controlling ropes of the spinnaker coming back into the cockpit.)

However, on further investigation it is revealed that the guy has come uncleated from the winch and once this is rectified calm is restored,

Antony suffering quite a bad rope burn on his hand though as the sail bursts out of it's 'sock' in it's partially snuffed state.

Big David's clean salty drying tee shirt gets blown of the guard rails and lies spread-eagled on the surface of the sea as we move away from it.

"Oh no! that's one of my better tee shirts!" we watch it as it floats away.

"Hey we've caught it!" says David, Gopher one who is sitting in a dream watching the water float by(and tee shirts!)

And so we have, our fishing line has hooked the best catch so far. We may not be able to catch fish, but tee shirts... easy!

Rebecca and David are sleeping curled up together in their bear pit, Martin and I are on the morning watch.

"What do you think, had we better charge up the batteries?"

The battery power is getting very low. "Yes."

So the engine goes on, although resolutely not putting her in gear(we must SAIL all the way) Not much later, David and Rebecca emerge sweating from their cabin.

"See we've managed to steam you out again?" we say grinning. The combined heat of the engine and the ambient temperature make sleeping in the aft cabins almost impossible.

"It's like a bear pit in there," says David. We only have 791 miles to go.

'*Brandamajo, Brandamajo*, this is *Accolade Accolade*, do you have your position?'

Accolade, Brandamajo, we are hearing you loud and clear, our noon position is 16.19.N, 49.25W, wind ESE 18 knots.' Antony is our radio man and the voice of *Brandamajo* for the trip.

Our daily position reporting is done. Back home those who are tracking us on the internet will be able to see where we are.

As *Brandamajo* rocks her way across the Atlantic, the sound of 'pabbajackas, pabbajackas,' can periodically be heard from down below in the gopher hole. (If you want to know what that is, get a computer game called 'Age of Empires' and listen to it , then you'll know.

"Where IS my pencil?!" the skipper quietly roars from his chart table. Everybody looks innocent.

"George must have it"

"George, does not have it. This is my pencil and must not be removed from the chart table.

The skipper chooses a CD 'sounds of the seventies' and puts it on.

John and Big D are hauling in the fishing line.

"Fish for tea tonight?"

"No. I'm going to put this mega lure on."

A huge lure is attached to the line, we are fast running out of lures.

"That'll slow us down" says the skipper.

"Take it off then" says Rebecca returning from the foredeck where she has been sunbathing.

Monday 6th December. The SSB radio brings us news of a man overboard off a Norwegian boat. We were only having drinks with them just before we left Gran Canaria. All boats anywhere in the vicinity are asked to join in the search, we work out that we probably passed that point sometime during the middle of the night, it will take us a long time to get back there now, luckily there are three or four other boats there. We shudder to think of this poor man floating around in the middle of this huge ocean, probably not believing but none the less hoping he will be rescued….or maybe he is already dead.

He has already been in the water for four hours and none of us can believe that he will be found. The *Brandamajo* crew are suddenly more vigilant about clipping on their harnesses when they are out of the cockpit.(he was not clipped on), and our vulnerability and mortality in this vast ocean are brought home to us.

18 hours after he has fallen overboard he is found. Alive. It just goes to show that it is worth searching and searching. He had been able to see the searching boats but unable to make them see him.

7th December and we are totally becalmed, The sails crash and bang in the lack of wind, the spinnaker is hanging like a limp rag and the anemometer (instrument that measures wind speed and direction) is spinning at random in the still air. The skipper is at the helm trying to coax some speed out of her but I think that we are going backwards.

"Come on Martin, why don't we just drop the sails for a minute and go for a swim?" suggests Antony.

"Yes lets!"

"Please"

"Can we Mum?"

And so the mainsail is dropped with a flop and lazily tied up, the spinnaker snuffed and we tie a fender out on a long piece of rope so that we have something to swim to should the yacht start to drift. The water is a phenomenal blue and we can see the shafts of sunlight reaching down into the depths. It is the biggest swimming pool we have ever had the privilege of swimming in the middle of.

The adults are in first, the children next, but the experience of swimming, half way across the Atlantic with three miles of water underneath him and hundreds of miles to the nearest land, is altogether too much for John, gopher three.

"Help!........Help me! ....the boat is moving.......I can't get back...." In utter panic we help him back to the boat, which is indeed drifting in a current, and he is relieved to get back on board, I think even for us adults it is a slightly unnerving experience.

We are allowed fifteen seconds of fresh water shower, which is just bliss. Water and power are luxuries I will never take for granted again! "Who's on cooking watch tonight then?" asks a voice.

"I think its us" says Rebecca, idly scooping a handful of black hair from the corner of the cockpit floor. She throws it overboard.

"So what's it to be tonight then, "Mush variety one two or three.... Or even a new variety of mush?" asks David P.

We are now reduced to making delicious(or not quite so delicious) mushes out of our dried and tinned stuff, the fresh fish being remarkably unforthcoming.

"What's for pud?" asks Brinsley gopher two.

"Tinned fruit, or chocolate."

"What no ice cream?!" says Paul., as always with a good-natured smile on his face.

There are lots of flying fish now, and every now and then one lands on the deck, we try using these as lures on our fishing lines, but have no more luck than with the plastic ones. The children are struggling to find things to write in their diaries, for example John's diary for the 2nd December reads *We played on the computer watched Flubber and it was sunny.*

3rd December *We sailed. We had a nice tea. Sunny.*

4th December *We had a boring day and it was sunny*

And so on and so on, but they are remarkably content despite it all.

Eventually the wind comes back and with it the waves. The sails fill and we start heading with a vengeance towards our destination, it looks as if the Pearses might catch their flight home after all.

When the sun has gone down and we have enough power we can occasionally watch a video, and except for David and Rebecca who are on watch snuggled up together at the wheel, we are sitting watching a video of Absolutely Fabulous, dinner is washed up, and another two hours until I am on watch again.

"What was that!" I stand up, I am soaked. A wave has come through the open hatch and deposited half of its bulk into my lap, and my lap only, somehow avoiding everybody else who is sitting down below, around me.

"A wave I think, say the others who seem to have remained dry. The other half of the wave goes into our cabin and soaks our already wet fetid damp cabin. Just pile a few more towels on top of the mattress. The yacht is developing its own aroma.

"Can I turn this music down?" says Antony.

"I'm sure this is off" says David Gopher one, sniffing at the milk only opened a short while ago. "It honks!"

"The milk is NOT off, the smell of the fridge may be, but the milk is not, it just doesn't smell like milk at home," I say sounding like a mother.

Then the next day the wind drops again and once more we are becalmed for a few hours. The spirits of the crew now rise and fall with the wind strength

David and Rebecca are getting fidgety again as we are still a long way from St Lucia, and their flights home. Skipper draws up a chart, and shows it to them. " I promise that as soon as we get to the point at which we will only get back if we motor all the way, I will switch on the engine," he says . The chart joins the other pieces of information on the chart table, including a very complex record of our journey drawn up by Antony.

We squash up into the little bit of shade at the end of the cockpit, the sun is burning hot now.

"We have zero visibility" Gopher three is popped out and looking around. The boys are relaxed and happy in their routine of sleeping and waking whenever they want to, playing most of the time, mainly with paper and pens, doing schoolwork etc, it feels like we have been living this life for ever.

"A bird, a bird!"

It is early in the morning and sure enough wheeling around high above us are two tropic birds, white, bright red bills and delicate very long tails. Apart from the occasional petrel, they are the first birds we have seen for a long time. Land cannot be all that far away, these birds need land to sleep.

Fifty hours to go to David and Rebecca's' flight and the trade winds finally set in, the winds that should have carried us all the way across the Atlantic. We can broad reach with the spinnaker up, we race along at eight or nine knots, the spinnaker every now and then scooping up water and letting it pour off. The sea rushing past, the yacht is alive again, and as for helming, George doesn't get a look in, everybody wants to have a go at this real sailing, the skipper is in his kind of heaven and it looks as if we will not have to motor. None of this faffing around trying to get the spinnaker down over night, we are old hands at this now and so it stays up as we roar along the final two days. Anyway it might be harder to take it down than leave it up.

Saturday 11th December 0645 The whole Cross family is on deck. "LAND! LAND! I see land!"

Is this what the old sailors felt like? And they wouldn't have known which piece of and they were going to hit. At least thanks to GPS we knew exactly what piece of land we were looking at.

"Where's the land?" asks Brinsley.

"There." Pointing at a small grey triangle that looks like an enlarged stationary wave.

"Where?"

"There."

"That! That is land?"

We are all up by now, forget trying to get some sleep in, soon there will be a full nights sleep.

"I've forgotten what land looks like Mum . " says John, but the excitement is catching and sleep is forgotten, we might get a full nights sleep tonight anyway.

The little grey wave materialises quickly into more recognisable land with trees and houses and we eat tinned fruit salad, slightly gooey After Eight Mints with Bucks Fizz for breakfast.

And now that we know that we are going to get some more fresh water, there is enough left for everyone to have a quick shower!

We cross the finish line at about noon, full of euphoria and emotion. Hundreds of boats may cross the Atlantic each year but right now we feel like we are the first ones who have ever done it. Before we can go into the marina in St Lucia, David P and Paul jump in and scrape goose barnacles off the bottom that have begun to accumulate on those many becalmed days we had sitting in the Atlantic ocean.

We are given a rousing welcome in, from the yachts already in, and we all cheer and shout as the skipper tries to manoeuvre *Brandamajo* into the marina in front of the onlookers. It's a long time since he's done this. No Problems.

The land rolls as we eat ashore......or is it the rum punch? , David and Rebecca decamp to an hotel for a night of a stationary bed into which they do not have to crawl into like bears and a loo with leg room before they have to fly home.

Paul gets his ice cream.

Oh the feel of a shower, with the fresh water just running and running down my back. Bliss. Even can watch it run down the drain with the pleasure of breaking rules!

The boys run around, excited to be on land, excited to have sailed across the Atlantic but there are too many grown ups and not enough children, and where the adults celebrate with alcohol, food and camaraderie, the boys suddenly feel anticlimactic, we must get out and explore the island.

A rotund black lady, Maud, or Mavis or was it Mary? I can't remember, appears and takes a sackful of washing promising faithfully to deliver it next day. I don't know if it will ever reappear, but it doesn't matter. It stinks.

It does come back,. clean and folded.

I later see these laundry ladies appearing at each new boat trying to get their custom and their loyalty. The keenest lady is up and around before 0630, to catch the new arrivals.

The yacht *Ocean Drive*, on the slip next to us examine their bottom, they got hit by a whale on their way in.

"What kind was it? " asks our enthusiastic children.

"No idea, big, though"

Their sail drive is damaged.

Paola arrives and whisks Paul off to enjoy sheets, showers and romance in an apartment for a week, we have time to clean the boat change the sheets and Grandma and Grandad arrive for a holiday, our family time alone will just have to wait for a bit.

'Knock.......knock,knock,knock.....Up you get you layabouts!" No we are not on watch, it is Dave and Emma inviting us to their party. 6am, and we don our yukatas(cotton Japanese dressing gowns......we can't very well go down the pontoon naked!) and join them on *Gravitas* for the earliest beer I have had since my student days, they arrived in at 4 am and have been partying ever since.

Monday 13th December is St Lucia day. No chance of even thinking about getting the generator fixed today, as everything ashore is shut ,but at least we have a hose with mains water attached to the yacht.

St Lucia is English speaking,(though the locals speak a kind of pidgin French called patois), but it has had a mixed history with the French and English fighting over its possession in the past, it became fully independent in 1974.

Green, lush and mountainous, they are trying hard to develop tourism as a major industry.

"Do we have to do school today Mum?"

"When's he coming then?" The skipper looks up from the generator where he is working, I have just returned from the office to find out when *Lady Penelope* is due to arrive.

"About two hours." I answer.

We give Barry and *Lady Penelope* a rousing welcome. "How did you get in here before us?" Barry asks.

"Just sailed," says the skipper, "Did you manage to sail all the way?"

"Hell no, we used all our fuel! I don't believe you didn't use your engine at all?"

"We didn't!" all three boys chime in unison. Champagne is opened, hooters hooted and Barry is given a true welcome. More parties. More alcohol.

The beach at Gros Islet with its pieces of coral mixed with pieces of litter is filled with holidaying St Lucians their barbecues and their loud stereos. A pig crosses the road through the scrub and golden cows wander munching as they walk.

But go to the bits of St Lucia on show for the tourists, here the beaches are golden clean sand, bordered by holiday apartments and hotels their sharp edges softened by palm trees, these are the beaches the children prefer playing on.

Antony is the last of our crew left on board, but the time comes when he to must fly back to his home and reality. All of a sudden our little group of people that for three weeks has been just us must disperse and go our own separate ways, we at least still have another eight months of our dream to live and experience.

We hire a car to take Antony to the airport, stopping in a bit of jungle on the way where a Rastafarian guide takes us for a walk, imitating bird song so that the birds fly down to branches by us.

"Is this a real jungle mum?"

"Yes of course, you know that Dad and I studied tropical biology at university?"

"Of course we know, you keep on telling us, " I suspect that the parents lives BC (before children) are as uninteresting as so many other non immediate things are to children.

Our guide however, knows everything there is to know about the forest, explaining how he learned as a child how it was detrimental to swing on lianas until they broke at the base, because then they would rot and die. Then he could no longer reach the mangoes from high up in the trees. He would like to spend several hours with us, but Antony has a plane to catch.

"Don't you think he's clever Mum? I wish I could whistle for birds like that," says David.

Stop for a drink, we sit on plastic chairs by the roadside, we are almost at the airport having driven along very bumpy twisted roads through banana plantations. Bougainvillaea is growing over the tin shack from where the drinks are served. There is no beer. Antony has to drink his from a bottle. "That's the second time in two days I've had a soft drink ,not beer, AND had to drink it from a bottle he says with a smile.

Back down at Rodney Bay Father Christmas has arrived for the children of the ARC boats. No he is not black, he is white and very un-Caribbean sounding!. A steel band plays Christmas carols and although the temperature is quite wrong, we begin to feel festive. The adults stand around gyrating to the rhythm of the steel band whilst the children excitedly wait their turns to go up and receive a gift from the Father Christmas and his sack.

The days are passing, we are tied up alongside, the skipper sweating with his head in the generator locker, Grandma and Grandad are getting hot in the cockpit and a local in a wooden boat is trying to sell us fruit and conch shells. We buy some fruit and he goes away happy.

After three weeks at sea there is a lot of work to catch up on.

"Come on, let's stop for at least one day," I say, handing the skipper a whole roll of kitchen roll.

So we do and go and explore another jungle, this time driving up a long rutted track before we park, grounding our hired minibus several times.

I have a bottle of water and suncream in my bag and nothing else so by the time we have finished walking everybody is hungry.

"I could really go a cold beer!" says Joe wiping sweat from his brow, with an already sodden handkerchief.

"Pass us one out then, ship's provisioner," says the skipper, only half joking.

I smile at him and pick up windfall grapefruit and offer him one.

They are delicious "But not quite cold beer!"

Back in the hired minibus and we still have the long rutted track to negotiate.

"Look there's some more grapefruit.....and bananas.....how about some oranges?...."

The bananas are completely inedible, but for Des and I the fruit is lovely. Joe and Martin look on resignedly.

"Hey stop a minute please." I implore. "Come on boys come and look at all these cocoa pods."

"If we eat one will it taste of chocolate?" asks Brinsley.

"No."

The pods are bright red and growing from the trunk of the trees, they are quite beautiful. "It IS educational " I justify as the men's faces get glummer and glummer with each stop. We start hunting for beer trees. Unsuccessfully, finding only the harvested product in a little café attached to a filling station, where we drink and John spends his pocket money on several hard boiled eggs, I hope he is not sick.

"Is it the Christmas holidays yet?" the children ask hopefully as we lay the books out on the table.

"No"

The generator doesn't get fixed again, I think we are beginning to learn a little bit about Caribbean timing and work ethos......sort of non existent!

We have read about port rot, that is in sailors terms when you have been in a port long enough and are ready to leave, and the longer you stay the harder it is to leave, as all sorts of little things keep on cropping up that need doing.

Here in Rodney bay we are getting port rot.

"When are we going to go and find a real island with nothing but sand and palm trees on it?" asks David.

"As soon as possible." I answer.

But first we have the prize giving even though all the boats are still not in yet, those poor things have now been at sea for four weeks.

We come second in the largest yacht class, Class A (despite being the smallest yacht in the class) in the race across the Atlantic, and we stand proudly as a team in our red *Brandamajo* tee-shirts(except for John who has lost his!) to receive a rather pathetic looking trophy and a years subscription to Yachting World. The non use of the motor definitely paid off and it's certainly the longest race I have ever taken part in.

CHAPTER FOUR

CHRISTMAS IN THE CARIBBEAN

Sunday 19th December.

The generator is still not fixed, but we have lasted for four weeks without it so what difference will a few more make?

We have decided to leave Rodney Bay, we don't want to spend Christmas here and it looks as if we could be here until next year if we wait for the parts to arrive for the generator.. Marigot Bay is not far down the St Lucia coast and a nice short sail. Everybody is keen to be on the move again, and it is a lovely sunny day with strong trade winds blowing. It only takes us about two hours to get there "Where's the entrance?" asks Joe.

"See that red roof over there?" I point

"There's more than one red roof. "Says the skipper.

"I know," I say, squinting against the sun, "try and look for the brightest."

One roof does eventually become distinguishable from the rest, bright poppy red instead of russet red amongst the green tropical trees.

.

"Aim towards that and then the channel in should be obvious." I am reading from what is to become our navigating bible, 'The sailors Guide to the Windward Islands ' by Chris Doyle, as I give these instructions.

We negotiate our way through a narrow palm clad entrance, past a long tongue of sand stretching out to allow us only a narrow channel to get in, and find ourselves in Marigot bay which is a beautiful if crowded anchorage, and where during one of the many French/English battles out here the British used to hide their battleships by putting palm fronds on them and coming into this bay. One side is palm trees and the other two sides are surrounded by mangrove swamps.

"Shout when you're ready," I say, heading up forward to the anchor. Where on earth will we find a space amongst all these yachts?

The skipper carefully manoeuvres between two yachts. "OK DROP IT NOW!" he yells, holding his arm in the air to give me a visual signal. I let the anchor run out and at about forty feet of chain I stop and hope for the anchor to bite. The skipper puts the boat slowly in reverse and I sit with my foot on the anchor chain feeling for the telltale vibrations that tell us the anchor is not holding.

I don't hear a question from astern, just a mumble of words jumbled in the wind.

"He says is it holding?" says Joe who has come up and is half way along the side deck.

"No I don't think so," I say, and indeed we can tell that we are moving slowly backwards. People safely anchored on their yachts watch carefully in case we encroach on their space and run the risk of swinging into them.

"OK try again!" comes a yelled order from the stern.

So up comes the anchor, and we slowly motor ahead to try again.

Once more carefully positioned. "OK NOW!"

I let it down and repeat the process. This time I think it is holding. Joe stands half way along relaying the conversation between the skipper and myself.

"Is it holding?"

"Is it holding?"

"I don't know. Yes I think so"

"She thinks so"

But then we begin to slowly move backwards. "No you're dragging again!"

"No you're dragging."

"I thought as much. Get it up again." People are sitting in the cockpits of their safely anchored yachts, watching us warily, especially if we look as if we are going to anchor too close to their bit of personal space.

This time the winch really struggles to get the anchor up and I cannot believe that we are not pulling the whole of the ocean floor up with it. I lean over and watch as it comes up. Joe is with me. "Hey looks like you have a whole chunk on that!" he says

"Ready?" asks the skipper from astern. He cannot see what is going on and is trying to keep the yacht still in quite a strong breeze.

"No, hang on a minute, there's something on it." I yell, trying to push the mud off with the boat hook. The mud turns out to be a large piece of dead coral or rock or something, encased in thick black gooey mud. It will not come off the anchor. Being totally stuck fast, the anchor embedded as if fossilised in it. Joe tries to help. No luck. A huge lump of dead coral or rock is wedged fast in the anchor.

"Can I help?" I look to where the voice is coming from, my face and hands spattered in stinking mud. An angel and his mate, all dressed in white have appeared in a little wooden dinghy and offer to help. I leap at the chance. The skipper has to remain at the helm to prevent us from hitting the rum punch drinkers on the other yachts, or us going aground.

"Oh yes please," I say, "We seem to have something large stuck in our anchor."

The gentleman in his long brilliant white kaftan stands up as his dinghy wobbles from side to side(I have come to the conclusion that these angels are not actually a figment of my imagination but real human beings). He hammers at the immovable piece of wood with his wooden oar, with a split in it, whilst his mate holds tight onto the edge of *Brandamajo* to prevent their little craft from capsizing. The rock doesn't move and the split in the oar gets bigger, and the white angel garb gets splattered in thick black mud, big globules sticking like glue over both of the angels, who after an initial disgusted look and attempt to avoid the mud they give up and accept the dirt.

"I think it is not very good for my oar" he says pointing to his rapidly disintegrating oar, he speaks in heavily accented English.

"No," I agree, and rush back aft to get Dave P's geology rock hammer, (the one we use to kill fish with) "Try this"

They take the rock hammer and pass me their passports and paperwork as the little wooden dinghy rocks precariously, I gather that they have just been to check into Customs and have a shower ashore,. They whack at the object with as much force as they can muster without capsizing and they manage to break some more of the rock/mud off, and spray some more of the mud onto themselves, completely transforming themselves into brown smelly angels.

"I don't think this is working very well" says the muddiest, smelliest angel.

A new approach is needed.

We stop for a thinking spell, waving at the questioning shouts from the skipper at the stern. A new plan of attack is worked out.

"OK, lets try this, pass this around it if you can and then pass the end back up here." I pass them a rope end.

Meanwhile the skipper is working hard at keeping the boat still and more and more people are sitting on their decks watching the spectacle. When you are a yachty there's something naughtily satisfying about being safely anchored and watching someone else making a fool of themselves.

Finally with a rope tied around the rock and fastened to a cleat, we manage to free the anchor., the huge piece of sea floor falls back in completely ridding any bit of cleanliness our angels had left. We pass them their passports back, "Thank you so very much," I say, full of gratitude, "Where do you come from?"

They point to a Belgian wooden ketch lying at anchor only yards from where we are.

"No problem!" they grin and row back to their yacht and then jump in fully clothed before getting back on their yacht.

"Let's try again, says the skipper, still unperturbed. This time we are lucky, the anchor chain goes rigid and taut as the skipper gently puts *Brandamajo* in reverse.

"Are we anchored yet?"

"Can we swim, can we swim?" The boys are ready in their trunks waiting for the go ahead.

Once anchored we all jump in, and visit the neighbouring yachts by means of swimming instead of walking along a pontoon, this includes delivering a bottle of wine to our friendly Belgian Angels. Swimming carrying a bottle of wine is a new experience for me!. As soon as we are anchored little boats rush out to us trying to sell us hats made from palm leaves....we have already bought those in St Lucia, trinkets made from coconut husk....we don't want any more junk aboard.. and delivering restaurant menus, one of which offers to deliver out to the boat, but the idea is a novelty to us so we order a Caribbean takeaway that is delivered to the boat along with rum punches and a high price tag. But very nice and civilised. And it IS nearly Christmas. That night the mosquitoes emerge from the mangroves and attack, the wind has dropped and there is not enough to blow them away.

"Can you get malaria here Mum?" Asks David, looking up from the book he is reading.

"No, but you can get dengue fever."

"Oh, do you die?"

"You'll be fine." I say.

"What are the symptoms?"

I am not going to tell him because he will immediately get them. We have on board a very good medical book called 'the Ships Captains Medical Guide' which we have banned David from reading, just in case he suddenly develops the symptoms of the deadliest disease in the book!

We spray the cabins and ourselves with repellent and wish we had got round to getting some mosquito netting. As darkness falls, the mosquitoes disappear except for some hungry ones trapped in the cabin.

"Aldebaran, Aldebaran, Aldebaran, This is *Brandamajo*, *Brandamajo*, over" It is eight thirty a.m. and the skipper is calling on the gossip net.

"Hallo there Martin! How are you today?"

"Fine Pat, we have just caught the biggest fish you could ever imagine, almost as big as the boat!"

"Well fancy that! As big as the boat did you say? Would that be a toy boat? I don't suppose you've heard of the snow fall we've been having over here? We've just finished shovelling the snow out of the cockpit." Pat replies in his broad Irish brogue

This is standard riposte, each contriving to come up with a bigger story than the other.

And after the gossip net, we have the 'Kiddy net' for the children.

"Can I call Lazy Duck?"

"No Brinsley, It's my turn "

"No it's not, you did it yesterday, didn't he Mum?"

Of course I can't remember. I can never remember whose turn it is to do what amongst the children. Finally David gives in gracefully and Brin picks up the microphone "Lazy Duck, Lazy Duck, Lazy Duck, this is *Brandamajo*, *Brandamajo*. Over."

"*Brandamajo*, Lazy Duck" Sarah has answered, "Where are you?

"Marigot Bay. Where are you?"

"Bequia, Marigot Bay is lovely isn't it? "

"Yes we went swimming last night., what is Bequia like?"

"We went to a whaling museum here."

"Are you ready for a new riddle?" The children are all leaning over the chart table around the SSB adding comments when they can get a word in edgeways.

"Go on then" says Sarah. Sarah on *Lazy Duck* is the oldest of two daughters and is the same age as Brinsley.

"What have I got to say Dad?" Brin hurriedly whispers back to his father.

"Thirty two horses upon a red hill, first they chomp, then they stomp, then they stand still. What are they?"

"OK" Brin returns to the microphone and repeats the riddle to Sarah.

"Do you know that?" he says .

"No, now here is one for you. What is in sweets but not in sugar, What is in sitting but not in standing, what is in hammer but not in nail?"

"I've no idea."

"We'll give you another clue tomorrow then, *Lazy Duck* standing by."

"*Brandamajo* standing by" Brinsley hooks the microphone back on the hook.

"Have you written all that down then?" we ask the boys.

"No, but we'll remember, do you know what that is Mum?"

"Haven't a clue," I reply. Grandma is writing down the questions to see if we can come up with an answer by tomorrow,

And so it goes on, the children exchanging riddles, especially as they often can't think of anything else to say. *Lazy Duck* are much better at their riddles than we are, as the boys usually only start thinking about them when it is time to call them up in the morning.

Monday 20th December. We up anchor and leave Marigot Bay to go a few miles down the coast to Soufriere. The wind is still blowing the sun is still shining, and we can see ourselves easily getting used to this sort of weather.

"Do you think that this is where we go?" I ask pointing to a bay beneath a tall pointed mountain, known as the 'Petit Piton'

There is nobody else here, nobody else at all, can it really be the right place? It looks fantastic. I am reading from the book. "It says here go as close to the shore as you can and if there is a blue and white buoy, pick that up and then take a line ashore and tie it to a palm tree."

A little wooden boat with a large Yamaha outboard is coming our to us. A broad white grin flashes out at us from the black face. "You want to stay here?"

"Yes please." I say.

"Follow me." We do and he points us to a buoy. "I help you," he says .

"I will give you ten E.C," I say, handing him the note. We have been warned that if they help us and then charge us we might end up paying an exorbitant price. He pockets the note and leaves me to catch onto the buoy whilst he chugs ashore to pick up a rope that is lying attached to the tree, on the beach.

With our bow secured to the buoy he takes passes the stern line to us and then says "It will cost you another 10 E.C. for the hire of this rope."

We smile back to his smile, are we already learning the ways of the Caribbean people. The skipper bends down to start untying the rope. "That's OK then you can have this one back, we will use one of our own."

The lad shrugs his shoulders and gives a resigned look. "This time I will let you have it as a favour, but remember me if you want anything at all from the shore, maybe you want to arrange a tour somewhere?"

"Don't worry we will!" we say waving him off, as we finish tying the sails up and relaxing in the cockpit for a while.. Within minutes three fairly small black boys have swum out and full of smiles and giggles they are using the stern of *Brandamajo* as a diving platform. No question of them asking permission, we are obviously put here for their entertainment, they just climb up and jump off repeatedly. Friendly and smiling they encourage our boys to join them. Brin is the only one brave enough to do so. John having decided to swim ashore, and is struggling on the way back to the boat, finally accepts a piggy back from one of them.

"OK let's go snorkelling!"

Newly bought masks and goggles and I am about to enter the underwater world, I am 40 and have never worn a mask and snorkel before, I am as excited as a child with a new toy.

"Mum, can you help me tighten my goggles?"

"Mum, are you coming in with us?"

"Come ON!"

Grandma and Grandad sit sheltering from the sun watching us all start to get acquainted with the snorkel gear.

"Gob on the mask" says the skipper, "then rinse it in the water, it stops it misting up." The boys and I vigorously spit on our masks, then with a great deal of fuss and palaver we have to get our masks on, put the snorkel in our mouths, remember not to breathe through our noses and we are ready to go.

Wow! What other word to describe a new experience, we are swimming in an aquarium, the noise of our breathing the loudest noise around.

"Mum, eeeee eeeee eeeee," I hear through the water as one or other boy shrieks at me to come and see something else.

What is that fish, and that, and that? We have not got a fish identification guide, another thing on our shopping list. Bright red ones with huge eyes (we later learn that they are squirrel fish),blue and yellow ones, green and blue ones with two black stripes, black and white striped ones. All colours all shapes and all sizes.

Sea Life Centres will never be the same again.

"OK we'd better get out now."

"I'm hungry."

"Mum can I have something to drink now?"

"Have ANY of you written your diaries yet?"

"I will in a minute."

"Do I have to write it today, can't it wait until tomorrow?"

"Have a beer" Joe calls out from down below. I accept gratefully and realise that the diary writing may be postponed for an hour at least.

Now maybe this is what it is all about, sitting on deck, turquoise blue seas beneath, sun shining above, palm trees on the beach, the boys playing in the water and a cold beer in our hands. Perhaps the stress relief is at last working.

Forget bills, forget mortgages, forget cars. Even for a short while forget that the generator isn't working, and that we are falling behind with the boys' education.

Just sit and soak up our privilege and the smell of salt and hot teak decks (that is a lovely smell, if you lie face down on the decks that are hot in the sun you can just BREATHE it in.)

We move on to Wallibalou, on the neighbouring island, St Vincent the following day.

Once more there is a brisk 20 knot wind blowing, the sun is shining and we should be able to broad reach all the way down to the next island.

Soon we are out from the shelter of the harbour. "Get that mainsail up! Come on pull!" I stand at the mast giving some leverage to the sail whilst the skipper pulls on the halyard in the cockpit.

"I'm sorry I can't be of any more help" says Joe, who has a bad back, he would dearly love to help, the inactivity more galling to him than to us.

We leave one reef in the sail and let out the Genoa, *Brandamajo* comes alive once more, and we race through the water, sun keeping us warm, wind keeping us cool, Des sits in the cockpit smiling and happy, thoroughly enjoying the experience.

Six hours later we are ready to drop anchor at Wallibalou, where we should be able to clear in customs.

St Vincent and the Grenadines is another political country and so we must clear customs and immigration again. It is a poor country but nonetheless they have strict controls over their coral reefs and fish, fish is only allowed to be caught for your own consumption and there are no jet skis or aquascooters or any such thing allowed.(Thank goodness, I hate the things!).

As we arrive in Wallibalou several young boys come rushing out to meet us, paddling on white plastic remains of windsurfers, lying down on them and using their hands as paddles as fast as they possibly can, looking like large water insects. Again we have to anchor taking a line to the shore as the shore goes down so very steeply. The boys on the boards, (boat boys) are gagging to help us, each knowing that they will get a little pocket money from us for his efforts. We choose one to help us, this time we supply our own warp and he takes the end in his little boat, ashore where he makes it fast to a piece of rock.

"I think that I will check that!" says the skipper eyeing up the casual way the rope is flung over a rock. The shore has been completely ripped apart by hurricane Lenny which hit here about four weeks ago and the one time jetty is now a pile of concrete and twisted metal, guaranteed to snap our shore warps as surely as anything as they chafe against the sharp edges.

The skipper and I leave Grandma, Grandad and the boys onboard, the boat is rocking and rolling in a large swell, but we must clear in customs here. There is no way we can even attempt to land on the pile of rocks that was once a jetty so we aim for the beach. Timing the dinghy to land on the beach through the surf is a skill in itself. "Don't worry" says the skipper, I know what I'm doing....I'm a doctor! As soon as I say 'now', jump out and pull the dinghy up the sand as fast as you can.........NOW." We leap out simultaneously into the surf, grabbing the dinghy and running up the beach with it before the next wave hits .We get on shore, only wet up to our knees.

Wallibalou consists of a few huts and a restaurant. One of the huts is the customs office, but it is shut and boarded up, the customs man is not here, so we wait around outside a hut along with a few other yachties. We sit on a bit of broken concrete wall, an uprooted dead palm tree lies on the beach and at anchor, warps to the shore *Brandamajo* and a couple of other yachts are rocking and rolling in the swell. We sit and wait and give Joe a wave. He is anxiously peering out from under the bimini to see where we have got to. We are just learning about Caribbean timing. Punctuality is not in their vocabulary.

"Here he comes!" We turn around. The customs officer, looking quite incongruous dressed in a full suit and tie and bearing a briefcase full of papers, he is swelling with importance. Inside the hut there is one table and a chair and he spreads his papers around before giving us lengthy forms to fill in and a fee to pay for entering the country. "What about immigration?" we ask.

"Oh I don't deal with immigration, only customs. You will have to find someone on Bequia when you get there to deal with immigration.

Back to the dinghy. To get it out through the surf, you have to wait for a lull in the waves, and then push, run and jump. Then quickly start the outboard, or row before you get washed back in.

We did it perfectly.

A young lad on his battered plastic windsurfer stands at the edge of the yacht, hands paw like over the gunwale, "What you give me? I can get you bananas, You give me money, I help with rope, What you got for me?"

"Sorry," I say, "I will give you money for something, but not money for nothing, you bring me some bread tomorrow morning, or an avocado, or some bananas, and I will pay you."

"I help with rope, I help with rope," he insists.

I look at our mooring lines knowing very well that he did not help with it and we have already dished out some money for that. But I am now wondering if he might untie us and then charge us for tying us back up again.

"You come back with something I would like and I might buy it off you" I repeat.

He sulks of muttering "I got your number, I got you name. Just you wait"

I smile at him.

He scowls at me.

I wonder if he will turn up with bread the following morning, or if they all will, I have made the same offer to more than one of them. Maybe we will be eating bread pudding for a week. Yuck.

Back on board, Grandma and Grandad have had enough of the motion, they are not finding it soothing. I am astonished, maybe I am getting used to the motion for at the moment I don't feel at all sick, perhaps the Atlantic crossing has given me some immunity? Because she surely is rocking and rolling with vigour.

"We could eat ashore," says the skipper, "that large hut, is also a restaurant."

"Yes please!" the enthusiasm is unanimous.

Our little dinghy is not designed to carry seven people in increasing surf and get us there dry so we decide to do the shore trip in two loads, the surf is definitely building up.

Children ashore safely, only slightly wet, then Martin goes back for Grandma and Grandad. Just as they are climbing out of the little rubber dinghy, a wave approaches from behind and grabs Grandmas bottom, helping her up the beach rather more quickly than she was intending. The wave recedes leaving her still standing like flotsam. She is wet, no soaked from the waist down.

"Are you all right?" I hasten down the beach to help her, trying not to laugh .

She is very game. "Just wet." She says wringing out the bottom of her tee shirt.

"You're supposed to get out when the wave is receding!" says Joe.

"I did, or I tried to. It's not that easy you know." She answers.

We pad barefoot into the restaurant where we sit at a table outside. We can keep an eye on the boat, we are none too happy about her security in these rocking and rolling waves, it would take only minutes for her to smash on the rocks should she become untethered. Also we needn't drip water and sand inside.

"Rum punch anybody?" Steve the owner of the restaurant asks?

"Yes please, Boys what'll you have?"

"Coke, or a virgin pina colada (without the rum)."

The rum punches are strong. Optics don't seem to exist and the tall glasses must be at leas fifty-fifty rum and punch. On an empty stomach it is not long before the effects make themselves felt. Grandma has stood up.

"What are you doing!" Joe is looking at his wife. The rest of us do too.

"What does it look like I'm doing? I'm taking off my trousers of course!"

"You can't take of your trousers in the middle of a restaurant."

"They're soaking, and my legs are cold with them on. And anyway nobody will know because I will remain sitting down!"

I spring to her defence. "Of course she can, after all she has got a most beautiful long tee-shirt on" The trousers come off and are neatly folded on the back of her chair.

The boys think that this is hilarious, and the tale of Grandma in her knickers will be dined out on and embellished for many years to come.

Two rum punches is more than enough and the food must have been good, because we ate all of it and I can't remember what we had.

Back to the boat, it doesn't matter if we get wet on the way back, but of course we don't. We roll into the dinghy and through the breakers with the utmost ease. We sit in the cockpit under the brightest full moon for fifty years so they say, and listen first to Christmas carols Caribbean style on the radio, then from Kings College Cambridge on a C.D.

It is almost a surreal experience and by now the rocking and rolling of the boat is such that it is difficult to do much, we can only move about the boat holding on at all times.

"Mum, mum, look at that!" David points across the sky, "It's a rainbow!" And sure enough a moon rainbow shows in the sky, which says something about how bright the moon must be I have never seen a moon rainbow before......And it's not the rum punches talking, the boys haven't been drinking alcohol. The colours are all there, but pale and diluted with white moonbeams.

Next morning the swell has lessened somewhat. 'Knock, knock.' Someone is knocking on the hull, and I am still asleep. Wait and see if they will continue knocking. 'knock, knock, knock, knock,'. They are not going to go away. Maybe there is a retinue of white plastic windsurfers outside each bearing a loaf of bread or some bananas, I hope there are not too many.

'Knock, knock, knock "anybody there, I got bread for you missee."

"I think someone's got bread for you" Joe says , sticking his head in our cabin.

I get up, don my yukata and look outside. Am quite relieved when I can't see a line of little white tatty surfboards each bearing a loaf of bread , stretching into the distance. Instead there is one wooden boat, the lad bearing two loaves of bread, which I buy off him for twice what I might buy it for from anywhere else , but he is happy, and we have bread for lunch.

"Thank you very much," I say, buying a couple of huge, football sized, round avocados off him as well, they come off the tree in his mother's garden. He gives me a broad grin.

We up anchor and leave, the bucking bronco living is not proving very popular with the crew.

20 to 30 knots of wind makes for another good brisk sail. 35 knots and a downpour makes for not very easy anchoring, or in this case picking up a buoy. We have come into Bequia, a Mecca for yachtsmen and as we come into the huge sheltered harbour, the waves disappear but the heavens open and a squall hits. The lad who has appeared in a boat to help us, disappears as the rain gets harder. I am the anchor lady or buoy picker upper depending on which we are doing. I just get wet.

Bequia is much calmer. Full of yachts from all over the world, but there is still room for more, and it is only a couple of days until Christmas.

Christmas in hot tropical climes is a novelty for all of us, doesn't seem like Christmas somehow, but we decorate the boat with tinsel, fake holly berries and a miniature Christmas tree that we had bought in the Canaries.

Other yachts have fairy lights all up their rigging and in the dark they are Christmas trees in themselves.

The skipper is at the chart table tuning in the SSB "Good morning and welcome to the safety and security net, any callers?"

"Yes?.... we have reports of another dinghy that has gone missing, it is a grey Carib inflatable, 10 horse power Yamaha outboard, and there are two oars inside it."

"Daisy Dee, Daisy Dee, this is Second Millennium."

"Hallo Melody, what have you got for me?"

""I have just heard that the dinghy has been recovered."

"This Carib dinghy, is that correct?"

"Ro-oger, ro-oger, ro-oger,"

"Thank you for that Melody, anything from up north?"

"Negative, but talks are continuing with the people on St Vincent with regard to the harassment by boat boys."

Here in the Caribbean we can tune into the safety and security net on 8194 MHz every morning. It is supposed to keep us alert to the dangers of sailing in these foreign waters, though the worst is usually something like a stolen dinghy. Goodness knows what a safety and Security net in Los Angeles would be like!

Following on from this is David Jones with the weather.

"Good morning this is David Jones with the Caribbean weather, any security matters not dealt with by the safety and security net, come now?"

Silence

"OK, then let's deal with the weather."

The weather forecast at this time of year is fairly predictable. north-easterly winds, about 20 knots, sometimes some rain, sometimes a bit of a swell.

The skipper is routing around under his chart table. "Anybody seen my pencil?"

"No Dad, we haven't got it. Maybe you're just untidy?"

"I'm a tidy person by nature."

"No dad, you're not, you're a toaster." This from John, who is very busy at the table not doing any schoolwork, while his mother hunts on all fours for the missing pencil.

All I find is a nest of dark hairs, missed by the brush and dustpan in the corner of the cabin floor.

Two days to go until Christmas. Joe, Des and I go ashore to see what we can find with which to make the Christmas dinner. Some frozen chicken, some frozen smoked salmon and plenty of fresh fruit and vegetables at the market. The fruit and vegetable market is just where you step off the dinghy and as we enter it we are besieged by hopeful Rastafarian stallholders trying to sell us something, their dreadlocks scooped up on their heads in crocheted bright yellow, red and green hats.

"You want mangoes, I got mangoes, come and taste a bit." He hurries back to his stall, me following, and I dutifully taste a bit of a small mango that is more stone than fruit. It is delicious, so I buy some from him.

A woman is tugging at my sleeve, I turn round, "What you like, come and see what I've got?" She smiles her toothless grin.

"Potatoes," I say, envisioning the roast.

"I've got potatoes." I follow her leaving the mango man looking after me dolefully.

"What's your name, I say.

"Princess"

"You look like a princess," I say.

Her floral print dress must have been bright and clean once, but now you are hard put to see the flowers.

Her toothless grin gets even wider. "Here, have a potato for free, she throws one in the bag.

The bag has Eastern Caribbean feeds written on it, and looks like a recycled grain bag. The one I bought bananas from handed it to me. "Here is a present" he said, "It will cost you ten dollars."

"That means it isn't a present" I say.

"OK, for you I give it free, but don't forget me anytime you need anything."

"I won't, " I say, feeling sure that the ten dollars has been paid in the cost of what I have bought. (10 Eastern Caribbean dollars, or EC, there are about 4.25 EC to the pound.) Ah well EC, come EC go.

Des by now has escaped and joined the menfolk, who are waiting for us. "I hope you remembered to get something from the man who gave Martin and I some mango this morning?" says Joe.

"I'm sure I did." I say. After all I bought something from almost every stall, in order to keep them all happy.

Bequia has very little traffic, streets of sand, and about half of the shops are geared to the winter influx of yachtsmen and women (maybe I should say yachtspeople). The local people must milk as much money off us before the hurricane season starts and we all disappear to other places with our money. To the islanders we must seem unimaginably rich, even if our boat is our only home.

But they are entrepreneurial in doing so. Here in Admiralty Bay, water and diesel are delivered to the boat by barge, laundry is collected, washed and dried and then delivered back, and if you want some ice, they will deliver ice as well. There are also water taxis, wooden boats with large outboards.

Skipper decides that it is time he did some windsurfing and spends some time devising a way to rig up his surfboard off the back of the boat. It all has to be lugged up from David's cabin where it is stored along with the canoe. He drops his foot overboard. "----!, I've lost my foot." Brinsley looks at his fathers' all too evident feet on the ends of his legs.

"No, my windsurfer foot you fool, from the bottom of the mast."

"Haven't you got another one?" I say hopefully.

We rummage around in the brown bag that has sailing spares. But no black plastic foot.

"We'll have to buy another one." Now that IS an interesting thought.

"Where from do you think?" I sigh. I can't possibly begin to imagine where on this island we might find a bit of a windsurfer mast, for despite the near perfect conditions for this sport, most of these Caribbean countries are nowhere near rich enough to have many extra leisure activities.

"I'm sure I read somewhere that there is a windsurf school on this island," says the skipper hopefully. There is hope yet.

Christmas Eve.

Grandma and Grandad take the children to the beach whilst we set off in search of the elusive foot. Walk across the island to Friendship bay, the roads away from the town are concrete and steep, occasionally a mini bus blaring religious music and crammed to the gills trundles by.

We look down on this bay from above and it is a postcard bay. Long white coral sandy beaches, palm trees. Waves breaking on a coral reef and only two yachts anchored here. If there is a windsurfing school, they are certainly not doing any windsurfing today.

"It's got to be down there somewhere," says the skipper pointing at the vast expanse of beach, where there under the palm trees are a few houses. We eventually find the windsurfing expert. A Rastafarian lying in the shade with about three very tatty old surfboards piled up beside him.

"Hallo" says the skipper.

"Cool" says the Rastafarian, he makes no move.

"I don't suppose you have a part that would fit this?" asks Martin.

The Rastafarian moves himself in slow motion and looks and then shakes his head. "You might get one on Martinique," he says .

It is obvious that we are not going to find the requisite part here. In the 'shop' a couple of young girls and a not so young girl, are lounging around chatting up a beach bum in his forties. The not so young and the bum are weather beaten and wrinkled from so much exposure to Caribbean sun.

"OK I give up, lets have a drink." Go and have a drink overlooking the beach. A few plastic signs saying Merry Christmas adorn the bar, but it almost doesn't seem right to celebrate Christmas here. Sort of incongruous. How lovely though not to get drawn into the materialistic mayhem that I know is going on back home right now.

"Well I suppose I will just have to dive for my foot" says Martin. We are going to go on a diving course here as our Christmas present to each other.

Back aboard, Carol singers Caribbean style come round in the ubiquitous wooden boat, water is delivered, our water maker and generator are still not working , the skipper has lost his pencil, the saucepan cupboard is spitting, and I must make some bread for tomorrow as there is none ashore and no generator means no breadmaker. So I begin kneading, while drinking beer and listening to the sound of 'Pabajackas' over the noisier sound of the engine which is running in order to charge up the batteries. Never again will we take water and power for granted.

Christmas Day.

Knock knock....... Look at my watch,(or rather Martin's, I haven't worn one for a long time) It is four thirty a.m.

"Go back to bed, it's too early."

"Can we open our presents yet?"

"Seven o'clock!" we answer. "You have another two and a half hours to go yet."

Knock, knock,....pull Martin's arm from under him and peer at the dial. "No! it's not yet six o'clock" the footsteps disappear.

As the light seeps into the cabin I can hear the children getting up and feeling their presents that have been left in their stockings (Yes, we hoisted letters to Father Christmas up the mast. Of course he visits boats in the Caribbean, and he's very good at shinning up and down masts.)

"Happy Christmas everyone."

'Knock, knock........ this does not sound like the knock of a small fist. Joe's voice outside our cabin, "Cup of tea?"

"Yes please," stretching our arms out and retrieving mugs full of hot sweet tea laced liberally with whiskey. Joe's speciality on Christmas morning.

A windless day. That means even less power, as the wind generator cannot generate without the necessary molecular movement!

Brinsley's diary for Christmas day reads *25TH December 99 HAPPY CHRISTMAS It was Christmas and our stockings were full there were lots of presents under the Christmas tree I got lots in my stocking I got some magic tricks, clothes and lots of other things in the evening we had a lovely Christmas dinner on the boat. Oh yeah I got a chemistry set.* (I don't seem to be getting very far with the punctuation!) "Brinsley what would Mrs Barrington say if she read this?" I ask, I can't help myself even if it is Christmas Day.

Apart from having a snack lunch on an almost empty beach, Christmas day is spent much like many others, eating, drinking, and socialising, all to excess.

Despite the heat and the fact that the gas cooker seems to be giving up, you have to hold the knob in to keep a flame going on one of the rings, but I get a boy to hold the knob in whilst I stir and cook and sweat. We manage top roast the frozen chicken pieces, which we serve with roast mango, roast potatoes, some sort of greens and even stuffing and gravy.

We eat in the dusk in the cockpit, the sweat has stopped running down my back. The washing up will be done by the men, and we even have Christmas pudding brought over by Joe and Des.

CHAPTER FIVE

THIS IS WHAT IT'S ALL ABOUT.

We're still in Bequia, Christmas is over, Mr Fixit is coming to try and fix the generator and Martin and myself have started on a scuba diving course. That cold damp place called Great Britain is filed away in our memories to be taken out when necessary.

"Pass us a tissue please?"

No response.

"I said, will somebody pass me a tissue?!" says the skipper's voice from in the engine, only his feet and body are visible across the cabin floor."

"Alright, alright, I'm not a slave you know," says David, echoing those very words of guess who? But nonetheless passing his father the required piece of kitchen roll.

"Can we go swimming now?"

"Yes." I say, trying to push a reluctant saucepan back into the cupboard. Splash.....splash....splash...... one for each boy as they jump in. All John's' fear of swimming in deep waters has gone.

"Yuck what IS that?" the boys are out of the water fast.

"What is what? "Des and I lean over the guard rails to see what has caused the rapid exit .

We have the grey canvas bimini, they sun awning and the spray hood up. This encases the cockpit in a sort of grey cocoon, which does indeed keep the burning sun out, but it means that in order to get onto deck you have to perform an ungainly worm like crawl.

"That!" the three boys point in unison as something gruesome floats past. A piece of fish guts or something whitish and slimy, marring the otherwise usually clean water. Not what you want brushing against your face as you dive down through the water.

Des hangs out some washing on the railings. "Why does my yacht always have to look like a wash house?" says the skipper, emerging from the engine sweat glistening on his back, fiddling around with engines is not good for the skipper's sense of humour.

"So that you can have clean clothes."

"I don't wear knickers, and that is all I can see on the line at the moment."

"Hey I'm trying to sleep here," says Grandad from under a book, he is lying on the cockpit seat, which is very uncomfortable as we still don't have any cockpit cushions.

Another day in Bequia and it is raining. Solid wet drizzle, but warm drizzle and we motor in the dinghy over to the shore for our next diving lesson. Diving is not as easy as I thought it would be. We sit under the water doing exercises, on the sandy bottom of the harbour, following what our young blond instructor Sara is telling us to do. We have done some theory and are now sitting under water in the sand, trying to kneel down whilst watching Sara. We keep bobbing up and down and to and fro with the motion of the water, except for Sara who manages to remain totally stationary. The water is murky, the rain and our movements making it so. We communicate under water with a series of hand signals that we have learned in the little corrugated iron cabin on the shore.

Panic grips me. 'help help I can't breathe' I think, it is not possible to speak under water Luckily the surface is only feet away and I know that I must get some air so shoot up, take the air hose out of my mouth and gulp some real air. Phew.

But not for long, I feel a tug on my legs and I am gently persuaded to go back under water and that really and truly the air in my tanks is fine for me to breathe and I won't drown.

Of course back in the underwater classroom the pupils are taking their masks off and replacing them to show that they can!. I follow them and perform the necessary tasks with absolutely no ease at all. We finally surface. I wonder if I should give up.

"No you can't do that" says Martin, "Listen if you want I'll stay and have extra lessons with you." Sara has agreed to give me(and one other nervous wreck) an extra day of lessons before taking us out on a real dive.

Our heads out of the water, rain pouring down and for the first time since we have reached the Caribbean, I am cold. A dinghy passes by, it has David, Emma and Richard from *Gravitas* going ashore for a drink.

"Hi there!"

We wave . I am happy, my head is out of the water and I am breathing real air, not out of a bottle! The rain is still pitting the water, but we hardly notice it.

"You can't get much wetter!" They shout above the noise of their outboard. "Are you going to join us later?"

We didn't know that they were here in Bequia, but they have the uncanny knack of turning up at many of the same places as we are.

"OK " says Sara, bringing us back to our lesson, "Now we must do the snorkel dive" I hate snorkelling under water, so how on earth am I going to do the snorkel dive?

Sara looks at my face. "You'll be fine." She says . I am, and surprisingly manage to do the required distance without too much trouble..

Out of the water and I realise that I am actually still cold. I know that the wet suit that is a hand me down from Joe, is a little on the large side. 'It should fit snugly' say the books. This one is far from snug, but I am sure that it is better than no wet suit at all.

More theory in the little cabin on shore. ..... Bang! What was that? Only Sara carries on unperturbed. The rest of us leap up ready to evacuate or dive under the nearest table. "Only a coconut falling on the roof" she says drawing pressure gradients on the blackboard. Her long blond hair is straggly and wet over her shoulders. Top half of her wetsuit folded down at her waist the empty arms dangling limply from her hips,

Back on the boat "How was the diving?"

"Great" says the skipper,

"OK" says the first mate.

"Why only OK?" asks David,

"I had to keep coming up for air," I explain.

"I KNOW." I say, "But it was scary"

"You weren't scared, were you Mum?!" asks Brinsley with incredulity in his voice, after all his mother has done a lot more scary things than just sit under water with a bottle of air strapped to her back.

I just smile at him.

"What's for tea?" the children change the subject to something far closer to their hearts.

"What's for pud?" asks Brin before I have even thought of what we are having for the first course. The children are brown and muscular, they are beginning to look as if they have never lived indoors.

Friday 31st December.

Not only the last day of the year but also the last day of the millennium, and I can't think of a better place to be. I do two open water dives, having at last overcome my voluntary rises to the surface, though I do sometimes involuntarily start floating upwards, finding it incredibly difficult to sink, despite the fact that in air I can hardly stand up, I am carrying so much weight.

"It's all a matter of breathing" says Sara, demonstrating that she can control her buoyancy by how she is breathing. It looks so easy.

I try breathing at different rates, but only seem to go up. So yet another lump of lead is added to my weight belt, to help me keep down.

"OK, so when do you guys want to do your next dives?" asks Sara, shrugging off her tank as she stands shoulder deep in the water.

We copy her and take off the heavy tanks in the water so that the water can take their weight.

"Tomorrow?"

"Fine by me"

In true Caribbean fashion, the timing of our diving course is very haphazard, not helped by the fact that we are trying to fit in the requisite hours around Christmas and new Year.

Grandma and Grandad take us out for a meal to send off the old year, the boys play with sparklers on the beach whilst we eat lobster and drink champagne. We are looking out onto all the yachts, some of which are decorated in fairy lights, and all the masthead lights look like very high up candles.

Back on the boat we drink more champagne and watch fireworks, Caribbean style (half size and a bit phutty).

"Wow look at that Mum" a pink parachute flare has gone up, from a boat in the harbour, it curves in a graceful arc across the sky and floats to land downwind, it lands harmlessly in the water. Another and then another soon follows it.

The skipper goes down below and gets out some of our almost out of date flares and soon our bright pink lights are shooting across the sky with the others.

"Just as well we are anchored upwind of almost everybody else" says the skipper as another flare narrowly misses landing on an empty yacht. The little fireworks display on the promontory has run out of fireworks. The new millennium rolls in and the old millennium rolls out, and we are all in bed not long after midnight.

"I only hope that there is not someone genuinely in distress tonight," says Grandad who is a survival expert having spent most of his working life running sur*viva*l courses for all sorts.

"Mum, can we call Lazy Duck?"

"Yes , No wait until eight forty, they won't be listening now."

"What channel are they on?"

"6230, It should be already set." The skipper looks up from the chart table, from where he is planning our next step.

"Lazy Duck, *Lazy Duck* Lazy Duck, this is *Brandamajo*, *Brandamajo*, over."

"*Brandamajo, Brandamajo, Lazy Duck*"

"Hallo Sara, this is Brin here. Happy New Year. "

Hallo Brinsley, happy New Year, are you going to come over to Friendship Bay to have lunch with us today?"

I nod at Brin's raised eyebrows.

"Yes, what time shall we come?"

And so we join the Lazy Ducks for a big lunch, only poor David is not well so doesn't enjoy himself very much. We think that despite permanent entreaties to drink enough he is probably suffering from dehydration, a common sailing malady.

David's diary for the first of January 2000 reads '*I slept and we went to a beach where we body surfed the waves before I was sick*'.

The Lazy ducks are leaving and heading North on Monday, and thence towards Australia. It makes our Atlantic circuit seem a short distance by comparison.

Joe and Des leave to go back to Scotland, the cold and wet British climate. We are a nuclear family once more.

The fridge seems to be getting warmer, I have a feeling that the tropical climate doesn't agree with it. Take the door off in front of the refrigeration unit to help it along a bit. The beer is definitely tepid instead of cold.

Sand is infiltrating the yacht, however careful we are to keep it off. Each night a new generation of sand grains seems to have found its way down our bed and the floor has a permanently gritty feeling.

"*Brandamajo, Brandamajo, Brandamajo*, this is *Alice Ambler, Alice Ambler*, over."

The radio hums into life, and the skipper who is nearest gets the receiver.

"Morning Nikki, how are you this morning?"

"Hello Martin, are you still all on for a barbecue this evening?"

"Yes, Dad!" shout the boys from the table where they are doing some school work."

"Over the radio, Nikki laughs. "I heard that I take it that you're coming?"

""We'll see you late then." *Brandamajo* standing by."

"*Alice Ambler* standing by."

And so we load chicken pieces and salads into Tupperware boxes, and before dark is anywhere near we load ourselves into the dinghy and row ashore. We will no doubt come back at the end of the evening with yet more sand to add to the grit in our beds.

The Lazy Ducks (Jonathan, Caroline, Sarah and Hannah) join us and we build sandcastles, swim and play football until dusk falls. By this time we have got a great fire going and are able to cook out food, even if we can't see it very well.

Fireflies flash brightly all around us and a dark figure appears from the woods behind.

"I'm Willy," he says .

"Hallo Willy,"

White teeth shine out of the dark. "I live just behind here and just want to check that you are not burning the machineel tree."
"Are we?" asks Simon, Nikki's husband.

"No," says the skipper, "At least I don't think so."

The Machineel tree is so poisonous that even burning it can burn the eyes and irritate the skin.

Willy peers at the branches we have lying around and smiles his satisfaction that we will be alright. "

"Would you like a sausage?" asks Nikki, pronging one with her fork, they are getting fairly blackened by now.

"No thank you." And with that he disappears back into the bushes from whence he came.

"Is this rain I feel?" asks the skipper holding out his hand.

"Of course, we always have rain when we have barbecues with the *Brandamajo* crowd," says Nikki.

We laugh and start packing our boxes by torchlight, most of the salad uneaten as the sand got into it early on in the proceedings. We scoop wet food, wet towels a whole heap of sand into the dinghies and set of back to our respective boats.

My camera has broken. Not a chance of getting it repaired here, they don't even develop films or sell cameras!

"I'll sort it," says the skipper, and soon has the camera in pieces on the table. They are small and intricate. He puts it all back together again, there is still a piece sitting on the table.

"Whoops."

We give up and I shall be cameraless until we find an island with a town on.

Mr Fixit thinks that we need a new capacitor for the generator.

"Have you got one?" asks Martin

Mr Fixit wipes his brow, which has sweat dripping off it. "No."

"Can you get one?"

"Well we could possibly get one Fed Exd from Florida?"

"We'll do that," says the skipper. Will the generator get fixed before we return to the U.K?

Meanwhile Mr Fixit and Martin put two smaller capacitors in series to give us some method of producing power other than the engine and the wind generator. It works surprisingly well.

Spend an hour queuing at the bank to get some money and then go to the post office to get stamps. Today the post office aren't selling stamps.

"Do you have any stamps?" I ask.

"Yes." Answers the attendant busy doing something with some forms, she hardly looks up.

"Could I have some please?" I ask.

She gives me a quick dead pan look.

"We aren't selling stamps today.

"Oh I say slightly deflated. "Why not?"

"Not today." She answers, you can come back and try on Monday.

I am baffled. Yesterday they didn't have any. Tomorrow we are leaving. Well the post can wait.

Back on the boat. "Pabbajackas, pabbajackas," greets me.

"Guess what, boys?"

"Oh No" they groan in unison

"Yes, Christmas and New Year are over, computer off, it's time for school!" I open the cupboard and take out a pile of school books dumping them noisily on the table.

I think that we'll do English today. The thought of Mrs Barrington back at their old school spurs me on.

Wednesday 5th January and we are still in Bequia. Probably suffering from Port rot. That is for the uninitiated, when you've been somewhere far too long and feel the need, but every day finds you something else to do, yet another excuse not to leave.

However the very act of leaving will cure the lethargy and 'ailment ' of Port Rot.

There is a little whaling museum on Bequia. What it actually is, is a little wooden house where an old whaler has collected artefacts. He still kills whales in the traditional fashion, with a harpoon from a 26ft wooden boat. They are allowed a quota of two whales (Humpback) a year, (which they very rarely fill), and therefore when one gets caught the whole of Bequia turns up to share in the spoils and have a party.

We Europeans might cringe at the thought of whaling, but what right have we to stop these old people from doing what they have done all their lives?

His gateway is made of jawbones and inside the little wooden building harpoons , painted whalebones and old newspaper clippings of famous people who have visited here, are all on show on his kitchen table and amidst the washing up.

Catch a bus back to Port Elizabeth, they cost an EC dollar a head and are minibuses carrying locals., crammed to the gills.

Big white letters across the top of the windscreen proclaim IVAN and there is a crucifix hanging over the centre mirror, and a marijuana leaf painted boldly on the rear window.

We squash in, the only white faces, each boy trying hard not to be the one alone on a seat, they do not want to be sitting next to strangers.

Loud religious songs preclude any form of conversation.

We really will leave tomorrow and so we go and stock up on drinks. Diet drinks of any form are hard to come by, the need for calories is still far stronger than the need for no calories.

"David, you carry these two cases, Brin that one and John can you take the bags?" The skipper picks up the heaviest. The boys don't move. "It's not FAIR!"

"Life's not fair."

"Mine's bigger."

"You're bigger."

But despite this dialogue they have each picked up a box and by now we are walking down the little street to where our dinghy is tied up to a jetty.

One of the Rastafarian market people is standing there and he hands me a breadfruit, large, light green and slightly spiky.

"Just cook it like potatoes," he says as I balance it on top of the cases of drinks that I am carrying. It rolls around and drops neatly into the dinghy as I hand the load to Martin who is already in the dinghy.

We finally make it out of Bequia and head for Mustique.

"I think there's a squall coming, lets get those reefs in!" shouts the skipper and we rush about, grinding winches until the sail is smaller and we have slowed down. We are just in time. A forty knot squall hits us as we are close hauled. (i.e. we are sailing almost into it.) The boat heels over as the wind hits, and we race along water rushing over the gunwale, but down below chaos is reigning, I have forgotten to shut the seacocks.

"Mum, the heads are full of water!"

Not only are the heads full of water but there is water coming through the galley plughole as well and pouring out of the sink. The books have come flying off the bookshelf and landed in the water, and the charts (pencil and all) have slid off the chart table, to join the books and the water on the floor.

"What's it like down there?" asks the skipper, with the wind and spray blowing in his face. He is in sailor's heaven.

"Wet."

He scowls.(yes of course I should have shut everything before we set sail) But not for long, he is enjoying the energetic sailing.

Water flows from the saucepan cupboard. It needed a good clean out anyway. I shut the seacocks, balancing myself against the angle of the boat, mop up the worst of the water and will do the rest when we are back on an even keel again.

Mustique is possibly one of the Caribbean islands that most British people have heard of, is privately owned and it is for the rich and famous, cruise liners don't come here, nor do many yachts as you have to pay for a mooring. Anchoring is not allowed.

Nobody comes rushing out trying to sell us things, there is only Antony in a beautiful white wooden boat.

"Good afternoon Madam" We are greeted by Antony (I think that was his name) as he takes a line from us to thread through the buoy. His wooden boat is immaculate, rubber rubbing straight so that he may not damage the pristine yachts and superyachts of the very rich.

"Wow look at that Mum"

"Don't we feel small here?"

There are two other yachts of our size and three huge motor yachts gleaming in the turquoise water, slightly obscene with their wealth, and perpetually running generators.

"Can we go swimming now?"

"No, come and help your mother get the sail cover on first."

"I'll do the binnacle cover."

And so on. And so on.

Ashore we are treated with extreme deference, just in case we are famous. Well for the time being we can pretend.

An antique shop, a designer swimwear shop and a shop selling vintage wines, caviar and cheeses are three of the four shops. The fourth is a grocer. Oh yes and there is a French bakery as well, it smells wonderful.

And a fish market. A small fish market where we watch them slicing up a barracuda.

There are mown lawns here, even a communal football pitch, and as I lie on the grass, with the boys playing football, I could almost be back in England. Except for the frigate birds flying far above, and the palm trees bordering the football pitch. At the end of the pitch is the little runway and every now and then there is a little buzz as another plane carrying another celebrity lands or takes off.

A wild tortoise (or possibly escaped?) ambles across a patch of grass and we make our way back along the spotless concrete roads, past a little yellow school to the boat to swim and snorkel and clean the impeller.

The impeller is a small rotating paddle beneath the boat that gives us our speed readings.

"Mum"

"What?" I am trying to read.

"There's whale baleen down here?"

"Is there?"

"Mu-um, sound a bit more enthusiastic, you sound as if you don't believe us."

"I do, I do," I say reluctantly putting down my book.

"And a bit of whale bone. Come and have a look."

I don my snorkel and mask and jump in to join them. The water is a pale turquoise above the sandy bottom. Sure enough beneath the boat there is what looks like pieces of whale baleen. I am not going to go down and get them. Despite my diving lessons I still don't like going underwater with my snorkel on.

David who is like a fish under water dives down and on about the third attempt comes up with the baleen in hand, neatly cut at the ends so it must come from a butchered whale.

It is quite deep but after two or three attempts he brings it up and once dry it sits on board on the bookshelf along with our ARC trophy.

The boys decide that the piece of whale vertebra is to old, heavy and disintegrating so they leave that to nature.

The fridge is still getting warmer, and the oven getting more temperamental, in fact sometimes it goes on strike and won't light at all.

Have expensive drinks at Basil's Bar, which is THE place to go to whilst on Mustique, or so we were told. Thatched and on stilts over the sea, we celebrity watch (of course we see nobody that we remotely recognise)and decide that we can't possibly afford to eat here. We go back and have pasta on board.

The next day we are drawn to a large group of locals (by locals I mean those that are employed by the rich and famous!) down on the beach. They are surrounding a turtle which must be at least five foot from head to tail. They are holding it up by the top corners of its shell and stripping its innards out. I feel sick, and try to shield the boys from the gruesome view but they are not to be shielded and watch in fascination.

"What are they doing ?"

"Why are doing that?"

"Is it alive?"

"Aren't they being cruel?"

For once I am at a loss for words and cannot give them answers.

Thinking turtles to be protected I ask the fishmonger if this is legal, and he says that at certain times of year turtles are allowed to be killed. I can only surmise that St Vincent and the Grenadines is not part of CITES.(convention of international trade in endangered species)

We leave this gory site, voicing our thoughts only amongst ourselves, and walk past huge mounds of empty conch shells, glowing pink inside, discarded after the 'lambi' or meat is taken out of them, and wander along to the 'other' beach.

This is the manicured one smooth and raked for the rich residents.

Here we can appreciate the benefits of a private island with very limited access, there is no litter, hardly any people, and we walk through woodland where paths have been raked clear of leaves in order that expensive leather clad feet may not be sullied.

On the beach we find dried out skeletal sea fans, and watch brown boobies dive bomb into the turquoise water for fish. These large brown birds fly over the water and then when they see a potential dinner they fold their wings so the they resemble a fat cigar and dive neatly into the water with hardly a splash. More often that not they come up empty beaked. Large brightly coloured lizards scuttle away as we approach and back on the road we step over a squashed snake. It has been a 'good diary ' day for the boys.

Back at the jetty there is a gentleman in an immaculately pressed white suit, white shoes on his feet and with a perfumed smell.

He is speaking into his VHF radio"......... I need the tender back here, you should be here waiting..........well what are you doing?…….. that'll do…." He is not happy, his tender has disappeared, along with its two crew (one to steer and one to take the painter and help the people ashore) He would like to go back to his yacht. We exchange pleasantries with him and decide against offering him a lift in our dinghy which is full of sand, discarded sandals, and no middle seat, I don't think his ironed white suit and leather shoes are compatible with the *Brandamajo* mode of transport! Also we had decided against putting the outboard motor on here as the distance to the shore was so small.

As we row away, the missing tender plus smartly uniformed crew appears, I wonder how much trouble they will be in, will they still have their jobs.

Barbecue ashore. None of this digging pits in sand that we were expecting to do out here. No sitting on wet sandy blankets like all our previous barbecues. No, here there is a ready-made barbecue, and benches and a table under a thatched roof. And not a soul on the beach except for ourselves. Watch a few more power burning superyachts come in, every light bulb burning, why if we had left a single light on(apart from that one necessary to act as an anchor light) we would be back out to the boat pretty fast to switch it off.

"Can I have the beer bottle lids?" asks John who wants to add them to his brewery smelling collection he is amalgamating in a box in his cabin. Probably a realistic memory, if not one that I wish our children to take back with them!

"Is there any more?" asks David looking at the now empty barbecue, sucking the last of the taste off his fingers before wiping them on his shorts.

The skipper silhouettes himself against the setting sun as he stands on the beach and ponders what it would be like, to have unlimited money and servants to do such things as fix broken generators. ….Nice

A pity Joe and Des have left us , they would have enjoyed Mustique.

We are ready to move on and leave the calm but unreality of Mustique. Haul up the anchor and head for Union Island, back to the real hustling bustling and relative poverty of the Caribbean.

Strong constant winds seem to be the norm here, so on reef down and have an exciting sail sailing fast to Union Is There is a twelve boat marina here and we decide to co we can charge up the batteries, and run the water maker.

"When I'm ready, you drop the anchor,"

We have not done a stern to mooring yet so this is a new procedure for us.

"Who is going to relay for me?" I yell sticking my head down below.

"Not me,"

Relaying's boring."

"Why can't I do the anchor?"

"You know why it's very temperamental going down,"

John comes up to relay, which means standing halfway along the deck and passing messages from the Skipper to the anchor woman......it is very difficult to hear one another, especially when there is a wind, which as usual there is.

Even so the communication is not great and I stop letting the anchor out too soon, we swing round, and end up coming in too fast and hitting a bit of protruding rusty metal that is coming off the pontoon. (these marinas are a far cry from British ones, or even the Spanish ones in the Canaries.)

The skipper's swears and blasphemes, there is a crack in the fibreglass at the stern of *Brandamajo*. John scurries down below and the anchor lady knows that she did wrong but defends herself anyway.

"It's just a graze," I say

"Yes and who's going to repair that graze?" asks the skipper.

But first we must get some power, so the boys leap ashore, happy not to have the chore of pumping up the dinghy, and go off exploring, whilst we try to connect the power cable to a dodgy looking power source.

The power we have come for is very inconsistent and seems to come in fits and bursts but there is enough to get the water maker running after the skipper hotwires it.

"Mum, come and have a look what I have found?" says David.

"What have you found?" says his mum, still recovering from her inefficient anchoring and the skipper's wrath.

"Sharks, Mum, real live sharks. They're Nurse sharks so they won't hurt you." David is doing his project on sharks and knows more about them than I do.

I follow him off the boat and sure enough in a large pool in front of the Anchorage Hotel, are lots of big brown sharks. Also some smaller tropical fish and a turtle. The pool is really a large bit of the sea walled off, but allowing the tides and seawater to come and go freely.

Martin gets out his sailboard, the boys and I explore, concrete streets, cows and goats and only a very few cars. There is a very pernicious smell of goat. There is a slight drizzle starting, we could almost be in Scotland, apart from the temperature and the lack of midges. Small planes come and land on a not quite grassy strip right next to the marina.

Round singing ladies try to sell us their fruit and vegetables from stalls along the edge of the road and I buy from the one that has some passion fruit, which the boys have developed a taste for. They are yellow or pink, and smooth skinned. "You know that you should eat them just when the skin starts to become wrinkled?" the white toothed smile asks me.

"Thank you," I say, wondering if they will last without being eaten until they get to that stage, and remembering the brown passion fruit in our supermarkets at home that bear no resemblance to these.

Batteries fully charged and water tanks full, and water maker run, we move off the pontoon to anchor, which costs us nothing. A reef to windward protects us against any waves but there is nothing to stem the twenty five knots of wind coming from across the Atlantic, except a tiny island where the reef breaks the surface.

Here a hermit has built a hut out of flotsam and jetsam. There is a pile of pink shiny conch shells by his door. We go and ask him if he minds us leaving the dinghy on the beach whilst we snorkel over the shallow reef, trying hard not to graze our knees on the delicate but vicious coral.

The wind generator spins as if it might take off, the skipper whizzes up and down on his sailboard and we try and do some schoolwork. The yacht periodically starts to shake as the mast and rigging reaches its resonant frequency, when it vibrates to a rhythmical hum in the wind.

"Please go and see if you can see Dad," I ask the boys periodically. They all volunteer readily as anything is better than Maths.

"Can't see him," says David.

"I can" says Brin.

"Where?"

"Over there?"

"That's not Dad, you daaw!"

"Who is it then if it's not Dad?"

We peer through the masts and the wind and a figure and a pink sail emerges from the water, teetering before setting off at high speed. "That's dad," I say, feeling safe to go back below before our next check.

He returns later, revitalised from his sailboarding fix.

"Did you have a nice time I ask?"

"It's fantastic out there, I don't know why more people don't windsurf. Nearly broke my arm though."

It transpires that he was sailing at full speed between the yachts and failed to see a submerged rope between two buoys. This acted as a tripwire and caught on the fin, (hanging down beneath the rear of the board), bringing the sailboard to a complete and sudden stop, catapulting him far and fast into the water. I laugh at the image but am thankful that he is unhurt.

We eat out at Jennifer's Café, really just the front room of (I suppose) Jennifer's house. She cooks us plantains, rice, dasheen (a root vegetable reminiscent of papier mache,) sweet potato, and then a choice of meat. Much to David's disgust I choose shark. "How could you mum!"

I feel so guilty under his accusing eyes that I am sure that I shall never eat shark again!

"Have you checked the shackle on the anchor?" the skipper asks as we open another bottle of beer, lovely and cold the antithesis of the boat beer at the moment.

"No" I say, "What will happen if it comes undone?"

"The anchor will come off and the boat will drift away."

I wonder how effective the chain minus anchor will be at holding the boat stationary. Not very I decide, especially in thirty knot winds.

Luckily we return to the boat and she is still where we left her. I shall check the shackle on the anchor when I bring it up.

Gravitas is back in VHF calling, her SSB (single side band, a radio communication which is effective over hundreds of miles), we are invited over for David's thirtieth birthday, so up anchor and sail under Genoa alone to Palm Island where they are anchored along with *Karma, Tristar* and *Tutela.*

First though, the skipper windsurfs over to them on this neighbouring island, probably going faster than we do in *Brandamajo*.

Now *Tristar* really does have a story to tell about their Atlantic crossing, at one point they were literally baling water out for their lives to prevent their boat from sinking, and that's not all........ but I should leave their story for them to tell. Our little adventures pale into nothing beside theirs.

We sit in the cockpit drinking and giggling well into the night, the boys have long since gone back to *Brandamajo*, not having any time for the grownups silly behaviour. She is anchored almost next to *Gravitas* and we have the hand held VHF with us for communication.

Have you ever played 'one spot'?

No?

Well imagine a group of perfectly ordinary sane adults sitting around chatting in the cockpit of a yacht named *Gravitas*. One says to the person sitting next to him/her "No spot,"

"Yes one spot."

"Tell two spot."

It passes round. "Two spot."

"Yes no spot."

"Tell no spot."

If you get the number of spots wrong, another spot is drawn on your face with the burnt end of a cork, which has to be reburnt about every two spots. So by the end of the evening the scintillating conversation is thus:- "Fourteen spot"

"Yes two spot."

"Tell seven spot."

"Seven spot."

"Yes fourteen spot."

"Tell.......ten spot."

"Aah.. who's got the cork.... Give it a blast..... here let me draw the spot...." the charcoal end is rotated neatly on the end of Emma's nose, it is her twelfth spot.

We are beginning to resemble coalminers in the dark.

And most of us are graduates! What has happened to all that university education?

We finally return to *Brandamajo* as it begins to pour with rain, the skipper singing full blast: "*I'm si-inging in the rain, just si-inging in the rain.*"

John is fast asleep when we return but Brinsley and David look at us with bemused faces., but I know that they would enjoy this game one day.

Tobago Cays.

This is the place that our friend back home, Matthew Baldwin, said we should be sure to visit, and I can see why. It is a haven. No shops no houses, just a few small uninhabited islands and vast areas of coral reefs, providing shelter from the waves but also death to the boat if you don' t anchor securely or navigate correctly.

We are of course not the only yacht, but it is not difficult to find a place to anchor where we can't see any of the other yachts so effectively are on our own. Although we are in the lee of a tiny islet it is almost as if we are alone in the middle of the ocean, it feels unnaturally exposed.

Our water pump seems to have broken. ....well the skipper needs to be kept busy! ....so although we have water in our tanks, the only way to get it out is to hand pump it (oh for the good old days when yachts had no need of all these power hungry gadgets!)

Instead of his head in the engine, this time the skipper's head is in the pump locker behind the shower.

"Pass us a tissue please."

Request is fulfilled, but what would we do without him?

Go snorkelling. Superlatives cannot describe the splendour of this undersea world. Martin tows the dinghy as he snorkels so that the children can hop in and out at will. Schools of little reef squid, glitter past, sparkling beneath us. Huge corals and a barracuda that elicits loud squeaks from the ends of the boys' snorkels. Big brightly coloured parrot fish with their sharp beaks that give them their name graze on the corals. It is eventually the cold that sends us back to the warmth of the dry air and the sun. Yes even here swimming slowly in the water for a long time can be quite cold.

The following day a wooden boat load of Seventh Day Adventists come on the scrounge for money. I ask them to sing, which they do in the beautiful deep voices of Africans. So I give them a few EC dollars. …. If you see what they actually do here in the islands, they do a lot more that any of the foreign aid or charities do for homeless, health education etc.

We have to head back to Bequia to collect the capacitor for the generator, which should have arrived by now.

A hard beat back and the first mate has once again omitted to close a couple of hatches, thus allowing invasion of the sea down below! The skipper eyebrows raise heavenwards.

The generator part is there. Hooray.

But the elation is short lived. It is the wrong part. Not good for the skipper's sense of humour.

Provision and walk around the island. Whilst the rest of us look at butterflies, flowers, hummingbirds and little brown snakes,

"Mum! Look what I've found" We all rush to see what little treasure John has found.

"What have you found?"

He picks up a dirty rusty looking beer bottle top, the smile of someone who has just found treasure on his face. "I haven't got this one!"

"And look, there's another and another." He is pointing and rushing along the muddy roadside. Even Brinsley is caught up in his enthusiasm.

"Why don't you just collect the ones you haven't got ?" I suggest.

"Well |I want to be in The Guinness Book of Records for someone having the most beer bottle tops," he says with the absolute logic of a seven-year-old. Nonetheless I see him discarding some rusty muddy tops further on. Luckily he accepts his mothers suggestions.

Now he has so many that periodically he tips the boxes of them onto the table in the boat and counts them.. I'm sure that I could use them in maths for statistics somehow.

At the end of a grey damp day we eat at Daphne's. Daphne has greying hair in tiny plaits sprouting all over her head, atop of which there always seems to be a hat. Not always the same hat, in fact she must have at least a different hat for each day of the week. Great pendulous breasts join her shoulders to her hips and she glows with pride when we tell her that the bread she bakes is the best we have found in the Caribbean. There is only us in the tiny cafe and she sits and tells us her life history as we eat her callilou soup, followed by barracuda steaks for us and chicken legs for the boys. They turn their noses up at the callilou soup. Callilou is a green leaf vegetable and the soup is vaguely reminiscent of nettle soup..

"You're not eating shark are you Mum?" asks David peering at our fish steaks.

"No" I reassure him.

"Yes." teases his dad, "I'm eating nurse shark."

"Da-ad!" says David.

"I'm never going to eat shark, Never!" David tucks into his chicken leg.

We must leave Bequia, but *Brandamajo* obviously thinks otherwise. First the water pump that has been sickly for some time, dies, then the GPS goes into a coma and refuses to work. However the skipper puts on his engineers guise and by noon we are several hundred EC dollars poorer but have a new water pump and a revived GPS. At last we can leave.

Saltwhistle Bay, Mayreau, is our next stop.

Mayreau is a one road island. We cannot be bothered to blow up the dinghy so we swim ashore. We walk across the island in our swimming things, much to the amusement (or disgust) of a group of elderly Americans who have just disgorged off a cruise liner for an hour, at the other side of the island. Here is the islands only car, used to taxi any overly large tourist who cannot manage to walk up the hill, up the short but only stretch of concrete road.

We only stop a night on Mayreau before heading back to Union island which is not far and due to the normal strength of wind and our increasing laziness, we sail there under jib alone, and still manage to make six knots.

'You must go to Lambis,' Dave and Emma from *Gravitas* had told us.

So we do. Safely anchored again off Union Island (and I have checked that the shackle on the anchor chain is secure this time.) the boys pump up the dinghy and it is launched into the water.

"Can I steer?"

"No, can I? David did the last time?"

"I'll steer. " says the skipper, much the best way to stop an argument., as we throw our shoes into the dinghy and follow them with ourselves.

The fruit sellers are still ashore. Still singing and still trying to persuade us that they each have better produce than the person next to them. But only one stall has passion fruit today and the lady remembers us. She grins. "You want some passion fruit for your boys?"

"Yes please."

"Here, I give you an extra one." She holds one of the smooth egg shaped fruit out to me.

"Thankyou." I say. I do not know if she really has given us an extra one but it is nice to think so, but taking it and adding it to the ones already in the bag.

Lambis that evening, is a restaurant cum entertainment hall run by Mr Lambi, who is a large man, an advertisement to his own good food.

"Eat as much as you want," he says , and rushes back into the kitchen dripping sweat, to make sure things are being cooked to his satisfaction there.

A steel band entertains us. Then an elderly bald Rasta man with two dreadlocks down to his knees and a slightly shorter dreadlock in his beard appears.

He sits on an old wooden chair and bends himself into al sorts of contortionist shapes, before jumping up and down on a bed of nails and then lying on it. The boys are intrigued.

The skipper is more intrigued when the limbo dancing girls come on and then invite everyone to have a go at limbo dancing under the pole.

The girls beckon the boys. They try to hide under their seats in embarrassment.

"Well if you're not going, I will" says the skipper and gets up to have a go at limboing.

Sandy Island

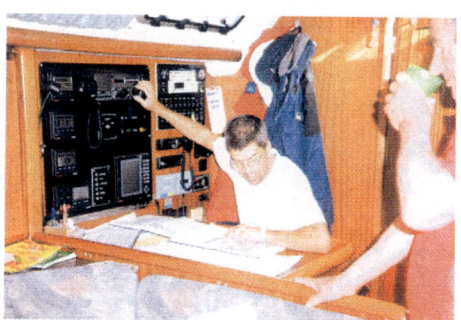

Skipper at the chart table

Festival feeling before the start
in Gran Canaria

Brinsley, Skipper David, 1st mate and
John, family afloat

Lookouts

Atlantic Skies

The skipper provisioning

Brandamajo at anchor in
Carolina, USA

"Oh Da-ad!" say the boys. But they are not to get out of it for long. With much embarrassment the boys soon follow their father, and giggle as the luscious beauties take their hands and start them off limboing under the pole.

John decides that much the best way to get under is by bending his knees! He is soon disqualified. However they all agree as we are walking back to the boat that they have enjoyed their evening. Just as well that none of their school mates from home were here to watch them!

Our next stop is Petit St Vincent.

It is so windy that we only put the staysail up this time. Apart from the storm sails we have in case of emergencies this is the smallest sail we have on the boat. And whizz across to this little island. Anchor in turquoise water with the reef to one side and the wooded island to the other. Petit St Vincent, more commonly known as PSV is another privately owned Caribbean island, reserved as a resort for the very wealthy. Although they like having yachts anchoring in the bay they are not that keen on having us ashore unless we are going to spend money in their hotel. We don't go ashore. But who needs to when you have the water, a tiny patch of sand by the reef and turtles swimming by?

We picnic on the patch of sand whilst pelicans dive and little sanderlings hop along the shore.

"They must be baby birds Mum, their wings are so tiny," says John.

The currents are so strong by this reef though that we decide not to let the boys swim. David doesn't want to after reports have filtered through to us that a diver was drowned here yesterday as a result of not being prepared for the strong currents. "No way am I swimming here," says David.

"Can we go in ." the other two ask in unison.

The skipper decides that he will test the currents when he goes and checks the anchor. The current is indeed too strong right here where we are anchored, it takes all the skipper's swimming abilities to swim back to the stern of the boat, so for the boys swimming is vetoed today.

David and Emma on *Gravitas* are also here and as they are dinghyless(their outboard motor having been left in Bequia for repair) but Martin goes off in our dinghy, hoping that the outboard will not break down, and after an afternoon with the boys jumping off a swing from the end of the spinnaker pole hung out on board *Gravitas* (the current is not so strong where they are anchored) we all congregate back on board *Brandamajo* for a curry.

"What are we doing tomorrow?" ask the children.

"Schoolwork?"

"No Mum, do we have to?"

"Lets go to Carriacou, then, but not until after we have dome some school."

So to Carriacou it is. What will I say to them when we are back at home and they ask, 'What are we doing tomorrow?'

Carriacou is another political country so this means that we have to check in and out of customs again. The town is called Hillsborough, and we anchor off, there being no marina. The wind whistles down the mountains and around the boat giving the skipper a sleepless night, and thus me his bedmate one as well.

Three a.m. I hear the outboard dinghy start. Martin is not in bed. I stick my head out through the companionway. "What are you doing." I shout into the gloom aft.

"I need some tissues please," comes back the reply. I should have known better and had some in my hand. Throwing some clothes on I go out into the dim light of half a moon, kitchen roll in hand and see what he is doing.

The wind had flipped the dinghy turtle, outboard and all. Convinced that our little outboard will not work after being totally submerged in the sea he is trying to start it. Miraculously it still works.

"Oh Mu-um" say the boys the following morning, "If it had broken we could have got a new bigger outboard?"

"Why, we don't need a bigger outboard?" answers their Dad.

"But think how fast we would be able to go" says David warming to the argument.

"Think how much more serious an accident would be if you had one," says their ever anxious mother.

"Ah but we wouldn't have an accident." Ripostes David.

They are willing us to get them an outboard bigger than our little 3.3hp one.

"Anyway it works, so we don't need to get another one," says their Dad.

At one stage during the year away, as parents we decide to change our names and I will only answer to 'Dad' and the skipper will only answer to 'Mum'. It is great for a day and then the boys quickly start calling me Dad!

Just off Carriacou is an island, known appropriately as Sandy Island, It is your archetypal Caribbean island of postcards, with only about six or seven palm trees, a big warm coral enclosed pool and long reefs extending off either end. The boys are in heaven and we all swim ashore, they build sandcastles and snorkel in the warm pool.

A big superyacht with a helicopter on board comes and anchors off and the launch comes ashore with several large elderly ladies who proceed to sit fully clothed in the warm pool, the skirts of their flowery summer dresses floating on the water, like lilies. It transpires that they have chartered the yacht off Elton John, and do this every year, get treated like royalty by the staff and flown in the helicopter to look for whales etc. I didn't ask how much the charter cost! They only stay for about an hour and then leave us to this idyllic island, where we can snorkel swim and just sit to our hearts content. But big grey storm clouds are gathering over the sea and we decide that it is not prudent to stay anchored here for too long as it is not the most sheltered of anchorages.

Tyrrel Bay round the corner on Carriacou is our next stop, and the damage wrought here by Hurricane Lenny is devastating. The shore road is no longer, it is now just broken up pieces of concrete, lying at broken twisted angles to each other as if hit by an earthquake, bits of metal sticking out. They litter the beach and are interspersed with uprooted poisonous machineel trees. There is or was of course only one street in the town, but we manage to find our way up a rutted track to where there is a workshop and we might be able to get the generator fixed.

We find the workshop, they don't have the right part for us, but by now that comes as no surprise so we chat and pass the time of day.

What would we do for a topic of conversation if our generator actually was fully functional?

This island has a hill, and one of our family's mini addictions is to climb a hill if there is one.

"Come on boys lets see if we can get to the top of this hill."

"Do we have to?"

"It'll be fun." We answer.

The boys have long since learnt that any further protest will be futile.

Walk through the forest on well used tracks looking for a way to the top, but each attempt seems to end up with the track heading back downwards, and to go straight through the forest looks well nigh impossible. So we eventually give up and the boys play with huge black millipedes that curl tightly around a stick when you pick them up. Each child runs ahead trying to find a bigger and more active millipede, which they then pick up with a stick and run back to us with. But they have to run carefully, rather like an egg and spoon race, otherwise the millipede will fall off.

"Are we going back to the boat now?"

"What's for tea?"

We opt for rotis and rum punches at the sailing club, run by Trevor. Trevor is an English West Indian, who has decided to return to his roots and try and run a sailing club, he lets us use his computer to send e mails.

It is dusk when he lets us into his little office to use his computer.

'Slap.......pause..... slap. Slap slap."

"Are you getting bitten?" asks Martin.

"I slap in time with his slapping, the big black mosquitoes are coming in and feasting on us. Sitting still at the computer is difficult, so we sit for a while, slapping each other waving our arms frantically and then send very short messages top those who need replying to. It is a relief to get out and go upstairs where we can eat our tea with the breeze blowing the beasts away.

Rotis are tortillas filled with spicy chicken and vegetables and are usually very cheap. The rum punches are as usual served without optics so we roll back to the boat and make sure we tie the dinghy up.

There has been a spate of lost dinghies lately, but how many are due to the strength of the rum punches and how many are due to theft?

"*Alice Ambler, Alice Ambler, Alice Ambler*, this is *Brandamajo, Brandamajo*, Over.", John is sitting, the mouthpiece of the SSB held closely to his mouth, hoping for an answer from his friend Toby. We know that they are in the vicinity. Silence.

"*Alice Ambler, Alice Ambler, Alice Ambler*, this is *Brandamajo, Brandamajo*, Over."

No response.

"Can I try *Duchess*, Mum?" This from Brinsley.

"OK"

"*Duchess, Duchess, Duchess*, this is *Brandamajo, Brandamajo*, Over"

No response.

David is still in his bunk, reading , he is definitely showing signs of turning into a teenager.

"Pass it to me Brin, I'll try *Alice Ambler* again." Brinsley passes his brother the microphone.

"*Alice Ambler, Alice Ambler, Alice Ambler* this is *Brandamajo, Brandamajo*, over."

"*Brandamajo, Brandamajo*, this is *Alice Ambler*."

"Hallo Toby."

"Hallo John, what are you doing today?"

There is silence from John as he is overcome by a fit of not knowing what to say.

"Hurry up and speak John", says Brinsley.

"I don't know……what are we doing Dad?.. " he looks at his father.

"Sailing to Grenada." Replies his father.

"We're sailing to Grenada."

"We are in Prickly Bay, it's lovely here, are you coming here?"

John looks towards us for confirmation and we nod.

"Yes, I think so, so maybe we will see you."

The conversation ends there, but they have made their communication, which always seems so important even if they are lost for words when they speak.

CHAPTER SIX

THE COUSINS ARRIVE

Early in the morning we up anchor and leave. As usual the wind is blowing but as we have a relatively long sail to Grenada this is no bad thing. I remember to shut the hatches and seacocks before we leave, endless mopping up of water is beginning to reap its rewards in my memory bank.

Crash, bang! "Wow what IS happening!" the boys appear on deck clutching at everything as they try to steady themselves against the rocking and rolling of the boat as she is tossed this way and that. There are large confused waves, throwing us every which way.

"This must be Kick 'em Jenny," says the skipper taking the helm over from George. Our trusty autohelm cannot cope in these sort of seas.

"No wonder it is called Kick 'em Jenny, I say, holding onto the railings so that I don't get pitched across the cockpit.

The boys clip on their harnesses and crawl into the cockpit. "What is Kick 'em Jenny?"

"That," says the skipper pointing to a steep rocky island sticking out of the water. The Atlantic waves are getting churned up as they come in passed it.

"And…" he continues, "we are going over an active underwater volcano, which is pointed and high and helping to cause all this turbulence.

"It's not erupting though is it?" asks David.

"I hope not," we both reply in unison, "..if it was I don't think that we would be here." In fact when the volcano is erupting, all boats keep well clear of the area.

Not long past this and we are in the lee of the island of Granada, then all of a sudden we are becalmed, the first time since we were half way across the Atlantic. It is strange to have to switch on the engine, and to have our full sail complement up.

As soon as we arrive, almost before the anchor is dropped, the children all jump in and swim over to *Alice Ambler* where John and Toby catch up on seven year old gossip.

Grenada is another island and we must check into customs and immigration here. Despite its turbulent recent history it is now a full democracy, and have probably forgiven the British for giving them independence when they didn't really want it, or in 1974 weren't ready for it.

Grenada has tarmac roads, traffic, a yacht club, steel band and yet more rum punches. And the first place I have found since St Lucia that will develop my photographs for me.

Can't remember what day it is, but does it really matter?. However we soon find out what day it is. Sunday, as our walk into the town of St Georges tells us. Things are shut on Sundays, in fact they shut on Saturday afternoons, and reopen again on Monday, so it is usually at the weekends that we catch up with what day of the week it is, especially if we are planning to reprovision, which is usually the case.

But there is a man here called Basil who will repair the fridge, despite the fact that it is Sunday, and so he does, he also knows a David who will be able to take our cooker away and repair that as well. Hooray. No, unfortunately his friendship circle doesn't extend to someone who can repair the generator.

"Hey, this'll give you a chance to clean behind the cooker," says the skipper, as we struggle to disconnect the gas pipes from behind it. It must be taken ashore in the dinghy to be repaired.

"You could do it if you like?" I offer.

"No thank you, that's your job." He replies, as he carefully carries the now disconnected cooker out into the cockpit and into the dinghy.

Now in the empty space where the cooker was I find all sorts of things, some shrivelled peas, wrinkled beyond recognition, a curled up piece of onion, that must be quite recent, it is not completely dried up, a used match. And a nest of long black hair. How on earth did that get behind the cooker? Oh and there's that teaspoon I remember dropping down there not so long ago.

Having seen the cooker, Basil and the skipper into the dinghy with David to act as chauffeur and take them ashore, I have a wonderful time cleaning up this mess, much better sense of satisfaction when you clean something really dirty!

Nikki from *Alice Ambler* has told us about this idyllic peaceful island called Calvigny island, and we arrange to meet up for a barbecue, but first we must get our cooker back, it returns and is once more fully functional. We arrive last at Calvigny Island.

Before we have even rounded the point that will take us into the sheltered harbour we hear a loud thump thump of disco music.

"Do you hear that?!" I ask the skipper, not quite believing what I am hearing .

"Disco music?" he asks.

"Yes." All around us we can see nothing but islands with not much more than the occasional house.

"Where on earth can it be coming from?"

"Maybe a fishing boat." But the sound is totally incongruous with the surroundings. We round the point and there are *Alice Ambler*, *Shilling* and *Viva* (other ARC boats) all anchored side by side, but also there is large disco boat that has moored alongside the old ruined jetty and is blaring loud music whilst a mass of bodies black and white are gyrating in the heat on board. Some go ashore to leave their litter under the palm trees.

As we edge through the clear water to anchor, I am in my usual position standing on the bow looking into the water for telltale shallow patches and waiting for the signal from the skipper to drop anchor.

"I thought this was meant to be a secluded anchorage that nobody knew about! I shout across to Nikki as we prepare to drop anchor.

"It was!" she shouts back above the noise of the music. "I'm sorry!"

But I must concentrate on my job as anchorwoman.

"Whoa!" I shout. The depth very suddenly goes from fairly deep to very shallow, as the almost vertical wall of a coral reef rears up before us. Simultaneously to my shout there is a frothing of water all around and I know that the depth sounder has set off an alarm ant the skipper has thrust her in reverse very quickly. We are lucky this time, and manage not to put ourselves aground on a coral reef.

We have just settled down to anchor when the noisy disco boat decides that it is time to leave. Not a moment too soon. They start pulling their anchor up, under brightly coloured disco lights the bodies are still gyrating and moving, the beauty of this deserted palm clad island is obviously lost on them, inebriated with alcohol they can think only of the beat of the music and maybe of the sexuality of the person next to them. As they pull themselves away from the shore on their anchor, the large boat turns, ominously close to us anchored yachts, the stern swinging out. *Viva* is closest to them, thankfully we are furthest away.

They also start pulling *Viva*'s anchor up with theirs. We look on. Both *Viva* and *Alice Ambler* have started their engines, trying to keep out of the way of this ungainly boat, disco still blaring and one poor unfortunate throwing up like a sad figurehead over the bow. A few of the dancers stop their movement and watch what is going on, our lifestyle as alien to them as theirs is to us. Simon the skipper of *Alice Ambler*, (a surgeon working in the middle east doing lots of kidney transplants) swears and gesticulates. The disco skipper shouts at his minions , gesticulates and if it is at all possible for a black man to blush (it is) he is by now bright red under his dark skin. The boat gets more and more tangled up and it seems that he will not be able to leave without hitting someone. We can only watch.

Finally he leaves, fitting between the two yachts, the vomiting figurehead still in action but thankfully nobody injured and no boat damaged. But it was a close call.

The peace is blissful, though it takes a while for the ringing in our ears to die away. At last we have the deserted island to ourselves and our friends. Nikki is smilingly shamefaced at having suggested we come to this hideaway!

Night falls quickly here in the Caribbean, and so we start our barbecues early, but first we must clear up all the litter so that we can pretend that the monstrosity was not here earlier. The children dig sandcastles whilst we adults build the barbecue, using grates from our grill pans to cook on. Rum punches and beer help us, and the skipper throws some beer on the flames so that we don't have everything burnt on the outside and raw on the inside.

"Come and get it!" The men stand brandishing cooking implements and the children leave their football and sand castles and come , the smell of food drawing them like a magnet.

"Hot dog anyone?"

"Can I have a spare rib?"

The night darkens we sing songs under the palm trees to Dennis' (from Shilling) guitar. The night sounds of frogs and owls begin, there are no mosquitoes and the children disappear with seventeen year old Paul to the videos aboard *Brandamajo*. The jokes get sillier, the stars get brighter and it is hard to imagine life back in Cheshire.

It is one of those perfect evenings that will be framed in our memories for a long time to come.

But even paradise has a price. "This bed STILL has sand in it!"

Time to explore our little paradise the following morning. We climb up old concrete roads, cracked and with plants growing in them. At the top of the little hill is a deserted house, the roof has come off, and the encroaching plants are well ensconced. The ghosts of a once vibrant place are with us at every step, this must have been the house of the Calvigny family, but it is difficult to tell when it was last occupied.

Remnants of a planted garden with strangely British flowers, has been almost suffocated by the jungle, and a radiator lies on its side in what must have been a garage of some sort. Pieces of broken china are embedded in the rotten window frames that have long since left their original homes. Another ghost feels its way amongst us and I tell the boys that here is a great idea for their English, they can write a story about this deserted house when we next do schoolwork.

We scramble amongst the ruins for once not talking very much each of us has our own imaginations to provide us with entertainment.

Leaving the house, we wander back onto the broken concrete road and the bright sunshine, with great ideas about buying the island as a retreat. "How much would it cost?"

"We could have our own anchorage, and rebuild the house?"

We meet the *Alice Amblers*. "We've decided that this island would be a great place to buy" says the skipper.

"Sorry, we've planned to do that?" answers Simon. The two men start discussing sharing it. All great dreams of course knowing full well that in real life and once money and school once again become all important, it is totally impractical. But how nice to dream.

"What do you think, could I climb that and pick us some fresh coconuts?" asks the skipper, looking up at a coconut palm later on. The green heavy coconuts are nestled among the fronds like testicles.

"Not a chance," I say, hoping that he won't, I don't really want a skipper with a broken leg. It is the wrong thing to say, the challenge has been thrown.

"Go on Dad, Go on Dad!" say Brinsley and John.

"No Dad don't," says David wearing his worried frown. I agree with David. But the skipper has taken off his belt and has started his way up the tree. He has definitely left his corporate persona behind.

Using his belt like Mulan (another of our video tapes we have on board) he works his way up and plucks three fresh coconuts from the tree,. Holding onto the tree with one hand he pulls the coconut off with the other. "Watch out! Here it comes. We stand well away as the first nut comes hurtling down.

The boys rush to pick it up.

"And again!" comes the warning from the top of the tree." We dive out of the way. I am thankful when he is on solid ground again. Maybe I won't have to manage the boat on my own after all.

We have jobs to do and believe it or not a certain time schedule to keep to, so we must leave our little paradise and head back into the mainland Grenada.

We come into a marina full of charter boats in Secret Harbour, Grenada.

"OK boys, no school today, we are going to hire a car and explore the island."

"Hooray!"

The car arrives two hours late, has no rear seat belts, no fan, makes a worrying clonking noise as it goes round corners, but it goes.

The walk to do here is apparently one up to an impressive waterfall which goes by the name of the 'Seven sisters' or so someone tells us in the little forestry hut where we stop to find a map.

However it is mid afternoon by the time we are there and when we suggest that we are planning to walk today the official steeples his hands on the desk and looks at us as if weighing us up.

"Ooh you won't have time to go there now," he says looking at his watch. "And I don't think the children will manage it......If you do go make sure that you don't swim under the waterfall, someone was drowned there last year."

"How long does the walk take?" asks Martin, trying to get his facts sorted.

"Ooh about three hours, and that is only if you walk fast, Ooh you won't have time to go there now." He shakes his head at us mad white people.

"Ooh it's a very difficult walk, I wouldn't advise it."

"OK" we say leaving the hut, maps in hand, and climbing back into the hot white car.

We go anyway. When we get almost as far as we can with the car, there is a hut, we have been told that we must stop here and ask permission to climb up to the waterfall. Here there is little wrinkled lady sitting on the step of the hut, flowers that we have as house plants at home are growing in a straggled flowerbed beside the hut.

"I'm thirsty", say the boys who have clambered out of the car to join us.

"There's some water in the car," I say, smiling a greeting at the little old lady at the same time.

"Mu-um, we can't drink that, it's ROASTING!"

On the step next to the lady is a huge bag of red mace clad nutmegs. As she talks to us she doesn't stop what she is doing, which is shelling the bright red mace from the nutmegs, so to the other side of her is small basket of mace like vermilion lace, and another bag of plain brown nutmegs looking more like the nutmegs we buy in the shops at home.

"We thought we would like to walk to the Seven sisters waterfall," we say.

She smiles, she doesn't have many teeth left, and her black hair has strands of white in it. "No problem"

"Will we have time to do it before it gets dark?" we query, the forestry official's warnings ringing in our ears.

"Of course, I was down there myself this morning collecting all these nutmegs, just pick up a stick, you will find in a pile at the bottom of the path, and be careful, its a little muddy at the moment.........you can drive and park over there." She stands up, putting down the nutmeg in her hands and wiping the sweat off her hands on her skirt, and points vaguely behind the hut over the banana trees, where we can see the track winding through banana plantations.

We give her some money as we had been advised to do, as we are on private land, and she sells us some cans of coke.

There is another car parked at the bottom of a small path and as we are getting out a couple emerge from the trees. They look as if they have had a mud bath. He grins, she doesn't look so happy. "It's VERY muddy," he says looking at his wife or girlfriend, "we didn't get to the waterfall, it gets very steep."

"Where are the sticks?" we ask him.

He points to a pile of roughly chopped pieces of wood not far from where we are standing. "You will definitely need one of those," he says .. His wife/girlfriend is trying ineffectually to wipe some mud off herself with a tissue.

We choose our sticks and set off. Through rainforest and nutmeg trees. The nutmeg trees are laden with golden fruit which open up and drop letting the bright red mace clad nutmegs drop out and litter the forest floor. It is indeed muddy, and the steep slippery walk both up and down would be difficult without sticks.

You dig the stick into the mud at the edge and use it as a support as you haul yourself up through the slippery mud.

"Mum I can't walk, it's too slippy," says John. He is unsuccessfully trying to get up a steep muddy slope, but every step forward results in at least the same backwards again. And this is despite some 'stick use' instruction from his parents.

"I'll help you, grab hold of my hand," I say holding out my hand to him. He grabs hold of it and we both slide down the slope backwards.

"Whoops!"

Mud is accumulating everywhere and it is like glue on the bottom of our sandals (John and I are the only ones stupid enough to be doing this walk in sandals.)

"OK. Let's try taking our sandals off." I say. We do and thereafter things are much easier, barefoot it is possible to dig your toes into the mud and give yourself a grip. I briefly wonder what bugs and parasites there may be in this tropical mud, but it doesn't stop me doing it.

The water fall when we reach it is lovely, it falls clear and high from the jungly trees around it, falling into a deep pool which shallows, and tumbles over big boulders to find its way to the sea. We strip off and swim naked, washing mud and salt off us.

137

"You're not going to swim NAKED?" ask the boys.

"Why not, there's nobody else here?" we answer. And the boys rather sheepishly follow suit. (yes I know someone drowned here not long ago, but we don't stop driving in cars every time someone gets killed in one) The current beneath the fall is so strong that you can swim your hardest and remain stationary, a bit like a swimming treadmill, it is very invigorating. We all get tremendous pleasure from swimming in fresh water after the sea.

We get back to the car as the forest is beginning to get dark, having collected a few windfall nutmegs for their beauty, and maybe their use. Perfect timing. I would like to go back to the forestry hut and tell the officer there that we have just walked up to the waterfall. We don't of course.

We walk the following day round a caldera (a long-extinct volcanic crater) lake called Grand Etang. It is pouring with rain, Ballachulish (West coast of Scotland where Granny lives) style, the path is as muddy as the last one.

"Ssh if you walk quietly we might see some monkeys" says the skipper.

The boys momentarily stop the loud talk, and we all look in the branches around us, but there is not a sign of the animals, and conversation resumes once more.

Soon the skipper and Brinsley are far ahead and David and I are behind. Only John is walking alone for a while and he is the only one of us lucky enough to get a glimpse of these shy Mona monkeys as two monkeys cross the path in front of him, The rest of us were making too much noise., and thereafter however silent we try to be they do not show their faces or tails again.

In the capital of Grenada, St Georges we manage to buy a capacitor for the generator, maybe we will be able to get enough power out of it to run the water maker.

Something else that has not been working lately on this boat, and that is the holding tank. Now the holding tank is what we use to collect sewage when we are in harbour, and then we pump it out when we go out to sea. Unfortunately the pump that pumps it out has given up, so we have this full holding tank and no easy way to dispose of the contents. It has been full for a while now and we have been wondering how to solve the problem. Now we really must do something about it so decide to start pumping the sewage out of it with a hand pump.

It is situated in the saloon under one of the seats so we have to remove the seat cushions to get to the stainless steel holding tank, which until we start pumping is odourless.

Set the boys some school work, they are not very keen to participate in this particular job. But it is not long before the job in hand seems to overpower everything else.

"It honks in here, we can't possibly work in that smell," says David.

"Put a peg on your nose," I say, only half joking, but Brinsley has beaten me to it and is already handing out clothes pegs from the clothes peg box, and all thought of Maths goes out of the window as they try to fix the pegs on their noses, trying different positions for the greatest degree of comfort.

"You know, this wouldn't be allowed back home, making us work in a sewer," says David, the peg now firmly in place on his nose.

I must admit the boat has smelt more pleasant, wafts of sewage smell almost have me asking for a clothes peg......maybe if I just breathe shallowly.

"Don't tell me you lot don't like this smell?" says the skipper with a grin on his face, though he is not enjoying the job any more than the rest of us.

We finally decide that the easiest way round the problem is to unbolt the tank from the floor, pump and all, and carry it to the toilets ashore. We have to take the pump off and put a bung in, what can honestly be described as a shitty job. We do this over the stern of the boat. It is unfortunately impossible to remove the pump without emptying the tank first.

"Pass us a tissue will you boys, please?"

"Do you want a whole roll Dad?"

"Good idea."

Finally hands covered in excrement, a vision of the corporate persona flashes through my mind, but the holding tank has successfully had the pump removed and a bung put in, and we have not polluted the surrounding sea too much.

We then carry this tank, and it is heavy, ashore. "Can I give you a hand with that?" asks a clean looking gentleman watching us struggle up the pontoon.

"No thank you," we reply despite its weight. I'm sure that he has no idea what we are carrying, luckily we no longer smell.

I'm not sure if we really want to tell him. We pass newly arrived charterers on board their yachts reading books and sipping gin and tonics and decide that maybe we'll charter next time. They certainly won't have to do what we are doing right now!

We stop for a rest outside the toilet and showers and the skipper does a reconnoitre "Well?" I ask.

"No we can't do it in there, there are people having showers. I would probably get lynched!" he says emerging from the gents. However the ladies are empty, so with the boys on guard outside we go and flush the contents down the loo, it takes a lot of flushes! Thank goodness this is one of the better toilet facilities we have been in.

There are down sides to this boat gypsy way of life, I suspect this job is one of them.

By early February it is time to start heading North, Granny, Jess(my sister), Gordon and their two boys James and Calum are coming for two weeks, we are supposed to be picking them up on St Lucia. We are nowhere near St Lucia at the moment.

So we start sailing rapidly North stopping briefly at Carriacou, Union Island, Bequia, we have spent two months in these islands and have some great memories stored.

Then to Young Island Cut on St Vincent. We are mostly sailing against the prevailing wind now so have to beat, it is not at all like the reaches and runs we have had sailing south.

Arrive in Young Island Cut after a dawn start from Bequia, we want to climb the volcano here, called Soufriere. Actually all the volcanoes here seem to be called Soufriere, it means sulphur springs.

Sam who meets us in St Vincent rents us his car for the day. Another car which bangs and clatters it's way along.

"This seat belt doesn't work," comes a voice from the back.

"Well you're lucky, I haven't even got one!" says another.

"Hold on tight then," I say. Where is my motherly concern?

We drive round the twisty roads of St Vincent, which is one of the poorer islands of the Caribbean. Over a rocky river bed of lava which has washed away the road, then through a large banana plantation before finding a place to park the car surrounded by bamboo. We set off up this 4000ft mountain, first through cool jungle then gradually the trees get smaller until they are just knee high shrubs. The air is colder but we have a clear sky and the sun as usual is burning down. By the time we get to the top we are walking through rock and grass.

Soufriere is next to Mt St Helens, the most monitored volcano in the world, being of the same type and therefore there is the eventual possibility of a violent explosive eruption.

"I would love to see real lava flows," says David, whose other ambition is to see a tornado. Us adults are not quite so keen, especially on this trip, whilst the boat is our home. Two local walkers pass us barefoot, and my feet cringe as they walk unflinchingly over the very spiky old lava gravel, and we stop to take a drink of water.

The lava does not flow, the sun shines, and at the top we eat our sandwiches looking down the sheer thousand foot vertical wall drop into the crater below, where a sulphur smelling steaming mound is slowly building. Eventually it will not be able to contain the pressure held within it.

"Do you think that could explode now?" asks David., peering into the crater at the mound of steaming rock. I pull him back from the sheer cliff face, he is getting a little too close to for comfort.

"Possible, but don't worry you'd be dead so quickly that you wouldn't have time to feel anything " we answer.

"It does stink a bit up here," says Brinsley. "What else is there to eat?" I rummage around and find them another sandwich, before we pack up and head downwards.

"Let's make things easier and check out of customs and immigration tonight" says the skipper, as we begin our descent, feeling the air get warmer with every step we take down.

"OK." I say, rubbing some more sun cream onto my arms.

What is not far by boat is a very long way by car, and some three hours later, ("Was this really a good idea?") we have finally managed to check out, customs at a police station and immigration at the airport. We now understand why Sam offers a service of checking out or in for visiting yachtsmen. We just thought that we would save a bit of money.

Close hauled, windy and bumpy we sail up the outside of St Vincent (thereby getting the full force of the Atlantic swell) as it is a much more direct route to Vieux Fort on St Lucia. Generally speaking yachtsmen tend to sail up in the lee of the islands as it makes for a much more comfortable and safer sail, but we are now short of time.

Leaping around on the waves trying not to get too close to the formidable looking shore of St Vincent, big black cliffs with the Atlantic waves smashing against them bordering them with white. The fishing line suddenly whizzes out, rattling against the ratchet as it goes. "A fish, a fish!"

The boys throw on their life jackets and come out.

"Don't forget to clip on!" we say .

'Snap, snap, snap' the harnesses are clipped on to the metal D rings in the cockpit.

"What is it, what is it?"

"Can I reel it in?"

"No can I? Brin did it last time." John trips over the tangled web of harness lines as he comes out through the cockpit.

"Shall I get my camera?" says Brinsley, climbing back over the harness lines to go down below and get his camera, balancing with both hands against the motion of the boat.

The skipper does not want to leave the helm, but as he is our fish dispatcher he trusts the bucking helm to the first mate for a short time. It is a wahoo, long, pointed nose and beautiful, about 15lbs, and what we had been trying to catch unsuccessfully all the way across the Atlantic. Safely despatched with Dave P's rock hammer, and put in the red shoe box(the shoes having been tipped on the floor down below,) until the boat is still enough to deal any further with it we progress to Vieux Fort.

Vieux Fort is the non touristy end of St Lucia, but it is close to the airport. The anchorage we are heading for no longer exists, in its place a new dock or something seems to be being built.

"We could go over there, where there are some other boats?" says David pointing. There are a few fishing boats anchored, no other yachts at all, but it seems the only place to go. We drop anchor and the wind comes down the hillside causing us to turn almost 360 degrees on our anchor chain, not the sort of anchorage you want to leave the boat unattended.

"Guess what we're going to do now boys?" asks the skipper, relaxing for a while a packet of Pringles in front of him, but being eaten by his sons.

"What?" they ask......then without waiting for an answer "can we have a drink please?"

"In the fridge " I say. They disappear without finding out what it is their father has in store for them.

"Clean the boat!" he shouts after their disappearing forms.

"We can't," says John.

"Why not?

"We have to do school work!"

"This is a practical lesson in polishing and cleaning." I say

"Oh Mu-um.".

On the dock side we watch large container ships come and load up with crate loads of bananas, probably destined for the U.K. or Europe.

As the wind drops the mosquitoes home in on the human feast we provide. This little sheltered bay seems to be a haven for the little monsters. They attack from all sides whining and buzzing as they land, feast and escape,(or quite often they get murdered by our hands before they manage to engineer their escape.)

"We should have got some Mosquito netting," says the skipper.

I silently agree, somehow it wasn't at the top of our priority list when we were preparing to set of and sail across the Atlantic.

"Are you sure that you don't get malaria here?" asks David, frowning, all sorts of horrible pictures going through his head., and slapping a black mossie as he asks. Too late the mosquito has already sucked his blood and he smears a red streak across his arm.

"We're sure."

"What about Dengue fever?"

"Yes you can get that."

"Oh no..... I'm worried," says David. "Does it kill? Do you think that that mosquito has just given it to me?"

Dengue fever is in reality not very common here although it certainly does exist. We spray ourselves with citronella leaving us sweet smelling though slightly sticky, and light mosquito coils, which keep the mozzies away but probably poison us in the process.

The next day Brinsley and I go ashore to meet our next guests, leaving the skipper and the other two boys polishing the chrome work on the stanchions. We have already spent the morning polishing and cleaning inside.

We walk to the airport, about two miles, only to discover that their flight actually is coming in at the other airport, right at the other end of the island. We leave messages for them to make their way to this airport so we can show them where the boat is. However after at least an hour, Brin is back on the radio.

"*Brandamajo*, *Brandamajo*, *Brandamajo*, this is *Brandamajo* Mobile, over."

"*Brandamajo* mobile this is *Brandamajo* over."

"Hello Dad, have you heard from Granny, Jess and Gordon yet, over?"

"Ye-es, they are here right now. Over"

"Did you hear that Mum?" he turns to ask me.

"Tell them we'll be right back." I say.

"Dad, we're coming back, this is *Brandamajo* mobile standing by."

"See you soon, *Brandamajo* standing by."

Martin has had to paddle ashore on the sailboard to collect them (is he practising to be a boat boy?), as we had the dinghy padlocked ashore with the keys in my pocket.

There are ten of us on board now. The boys are wild with excitement at seeing their cousins James and Calum and immediately jump in the water, three brown bodies and two white bodies, leaping on and off the dinghy and sailboard, like puppies. Granny is neatly nervous at the prospect of two weeks afloat, her stomach is very apprehensive, but the first anchorage is a least calm, though the mozzies are back and give a full blast mossie attack. Gordon wakes with forty seven bites distributed over his body.

"It's not normally as bad as this." We say. "Honestly!"

He was last with us for the trip from Portugal to the Canaries, which was wet and windy, and life aboard is very different now.

"We've got wahoo for tea," I say proudly. "Fresh, we only caught it yesterday."

"Brin, pass us a bag of rice please from behind that cushion?"

He holds it up to look at it. "It's full of weevils," he says . But without shock, we have discovered that much of the rice and pasta we buy here has incipient weevils and keep it too long and it soon becomes crawling.

The Russells are intrigued though and we show them the bag with little black insects crawling amongst the rice.

"It's all right," I say. "I won't use this pack......but you should enjoy it, all part of the experience of boat living, you can imagine that it is a hundred years ago!". The next one proves to be weevil free.

"No thanks!"

Sail a short sail up to Soufriere. Gordon tries fishing. Doesn't catch anything. We plan to moor between the pitons, the two pointed mountains sticking out on the edge of St Lucia. Long before we are there, a boy in his wooden boat comes out to meet us. We warily watch as he comes a little too close to the skipper's other woman, he does not want the shiny white sides to be scratched. The wooden boat is tatty and sharp at the edges.

"You want a mooring?" he shouts, having realised that we do not want him coming alongside.

"Yes please " we yell back above the sound of the engine and the wind. There do not seem to be any spare white and blue mooring buoys left.

"I take you to a buoy." He points to a large white one and we follow him. It is metal but we tie up nonetheless, we are not allowed to anchor here on account of it being a marine national park and anchoring kills the coral. The wind is strong and seems to be in the right direction.

"I am from that hotel, I must take fees from you," he says , white smiling at us. We are not surprised and duly pay up , but not without getting a receipt of some sort.

'Crash.'.........'Bang'........We are asleep. Something metal is clanging against the side of the boat. We lie half awake now wondering if the noise will be repeated.

'Crash'.......'Scrape'..........'Bang, bang, bang.'..... *Brandamajo* is being beaten up.

Time to go and investigate.

145

Luckily the moon is out, but the wind has dropped (a rare occurrence here at this time of the year) .We are swinging and banging against the big metal buoy.

In the moonlight, and dressed in our yukatas the skipper climbs atop the buoy and I pass him down fenders which he ties around the buoy like a necklace, thereby protecting the boat against any more scrapes.

Back to bed and the banging is muted now, and hopefully not damaging the boat. We can sleep.

There is a knocking on the window, but at least we are up and dressed.

I stick my head out of the companionway "Hallo"

A lad in a not so scruffy wooden boat is there with an older gentleman. "we have come to collect your fees for the Soufriere National park."

"We have already paid," I say and show him the receipt.

He tut tuts "They're not allowed to collect money, and you'd be better off on one of those small buoys over there." He points to a recently vacated buoy. We move, sweet talk him and give him a donation for the upkeep of the park, and at least we are now attached to a plastic buoy, but there are scratches along the blue waterline of *Brandamajo* to remind us of the damage that big metal buoys can do.

Another wooden boat arrives, looking even more unstable than the previous two, but this one is our pre arranged transport to the island, they have arranged a tour for us. We all pile in, all ten of us.

"Come on, in you get........careful......DON'T ROCK IT!........Are we all here?.....Have we got everything?" The skipper and I shepherd them in , and the younger of our two boat boys (along with Granny, who is clutching tightly at her bag and camera) looks alarmed the boat teeters precariously on the limits of its stability. I should have put my camera in a plastic bag.

"Sit still Calum," says Jess as he leans over putting his hand in the water. All the boys are giggling and full of high spirits. I'm sure that they would find the whole expedition highly exciting if we capsized.

We have to negotiate around Petit Piton, thus leaving the shelter of the bay, Of course nobody is wearing lifejackets, I wonder what the

British law would make of this kind of paid transport! Thank goodness there isn't a swell.

Around the Piton without mishap and he pulls up neatly beside a wooden jetty, we all pile ashore still dry. There is a minibus driven by a cousin of the boat boys which is going to take us to see the sights that we should see in St Lucia. Faded fake leopard skin seats and bits of plastic hanging off, so it doesn't matter when the children eat sticky buns on the back seat, as they wait in the heat for Granny and myself to try and get some money from the bank.,

We are good St Lucia Tourists and I can look upon this as part of school work. Sulphur springs, Cocoa and coconut plantations, banana plantations, and then the waterfall where Superman picked an orchid for Lois Lane....in the film *Superman 2*, I think...

The different things they do with all the different parts of the coconut is a revelation to all of us, and with a glimpse of the old colonial way of life, I can convince myself that we are doing history and geography today.

It is windier on the way back to the boat, and this time we do not return totally dry, but at least the wooden boat doesn't capsize....despite it being pretty close to at times. Of course it is loaded well beyond capacity ("No ma'am, it can easily carry this number of people.").

Back at the boat we introduce the visitors to the delights of snorkelling, and getting worried how easy it is to get carried away with the currents as we float face down watching the fish below.

Decide to take our visitors to do some shopping in Castries market. Castries is the capital of St Lucia, and somewhere there, there is a parcel that Granny sent me for Christmas, but it took a long time to arrive, and has to wait in customs for me to retrieve it. I still haven't.

"We'll just stop in the boat on the way to Rodney Bay" says the skipper.

Gordon and Calum are at the back of the boat, trying to catch fish.

"Are we having fish for supper then?" I ask.

"Of course, just we haven't caught it yet," answers Gordon.

"Time to reel in the line," says the skipper, "we are almost there......Engine on!......sails down.....come on, boys, and give a hand up here, please."

"Are you ready to do the anchor, Bub?" he asks me.

I scramble up and head to the foredeck, before giving him the thumbs up.

We anchor fairly close to the shore so that we don't have to row too far, after all we are only going to be here for a couple of hours.

Ashore, the skipper goes off on a hunt for parts for the generator. The rest of us split up and grockle shop, to buy souvenirs and presents from the market here. Brightly coloured dresses, scarves, tee shirts and African wooden carvings. Periodically we glance over at where our home is lying peacefully at anchor. We all meet back on the quay.

"I hope you haven't bought anything Bub?!" says the skipper suspiciously looking at the bag that I have in my hands.

"No," I say hiding it behind my back.

"Come on, let me see." I show him the carved flying fish, carved by a local lad, crudely carved but we have seen so many flying fish that it will be a nice souvenir.

"It won't take up too much space." I say.

"It's nice," he says.

We sit dangling our legs over the quayside waiting for everybody to gather. We will have to do the trip in two dinghy loads, so chatting and relaxed we load children into the dinghy and the skipper and I take them, leaving Jess, Gordon and Granny ashore for the next load.

"I think *Brandamajo*'s moving?"

"No she's not."

"She is Dad, she is?"

"I don't think so……..or is she?…."

"She is."

"Come on Brinsley, let me take over the rowing," says the skipper, knowing that he will be able to row much faster than his son.

Brinsley hands over without a murmur.

By now *Brandamajo*'s speed is obvious to us all as she makes her inexorable way towards the open ocean, and Mexico. It is hard to believe that she has an anchor attached.

We of course had decided that it wasn't worth putting the outboard motor on the dinghy for this short trip, so now with the wind against us the skipper is rowing like mad to try and catch up with *Brandamajo*, whose escaping speed is rapidly increasing.

"You're not getting any closer Dad."

"Thanks Brin." He starts to put even more effort into his rowing.

Thankfully there is a charter yacht anchored between *Brandamajo* and the open sea, and if it wasn't for her *Brandamajo* may have continued the remainder of the year on her own!

Her anchor snags and she slows her escaping pace and she comes to rest against the charter yacht, its occupants catching hold of her gently. We can now catch up with her.

Shame faced and apologetic we thank her captors and set about hauling up the anchor, the remainder of the crew can only watch from the shore as we try and get the anchor up. It won't come.

"I can't get it up!" I shout back.

"I'll try driving forwards!" he shouts back. "I can't leave the helm, though!" The children have disappeared down below to the computer.

I fear the anchor winch is going to break, but the skipper drives her forward and finally covered in stinking mud and a lot of effort later it comes up attached to another chain, obviously the reason for her slowing down her escape. The anchor is almost impossible to remove, from the chain to which it is attached, the skipper must remain at the helm, all the other helpful adults are sitting ashore so the first mate must cope alone. With the help of a boathook , lots of swearing, cursing and tears, I finally free it, but as the chain drops back into the water, so does our boathook which is still attached to the chain.

"It's free!" I yell, and walk back aft to the cockpit. "but I've lost the boathook."

"You've what!?"

"You heard me. The boathook has disappeared."

I absorb the skipper's wrath in silence, but at least we are free and can collect Granny, Jess and Gordon from the quayside for the rest of our trip to Rodney Bay.

Rodney Bay is empty of post ARC boats and people and is being dredged. What a different place, quiet and almost eerie, but is an opportunity to fill up with water, fuel and catch up on a bit of paperwork. And we can collect post here.

"OK folks, this is going to be you first taste of real sailing. We are going Inter Island," says the skipper a couple of days later. "Come on lets get that sail cover off, boys you can help."

Granny goes ashore to post some cards and we get ready for sea.

"Has everybody got a scopaderm patch?" I ask.

"Do they really work?" says Jess.

"Yes."

Granny looks doubtful. Gordon has declined to wear one; after his sailing to the Canary Islands with us, he is a seasoned old hand.

We are barely out of the shelter of Pigeon Island., a peninsula that protects this large bay against the full force of the Atlantic waves, and we are crashing down on waves, head to the wind and the boat is slamming and banging. She rides up one wave and then crashes into the trough of the next, the whole boat shuddering as she hits the water. Sometimes it feels as if she might fall apart, but logically we know that this is nothing compared to what she might meet should we be sailing in the southern oceans,(God forbid!). It is because at the moment we are motor sailing so are going more directly into the wind and waves than we would be if we were just sailing.

This is definitely the least comfortable point of sailing. A particularly loud bang shudders through the boat. Granny is sitting in the corner of the cockpit looking green, with a look of 'I knew it would be like this' on her face, maybe scopaderm isn't working for her.

Gordon is sitting astern trying to get his fishing line sorted out.

"Oh s-----" The skipper utters an expletive.

"What?"

"We've lost all of our instrumentation."

"Oh." We all wait for what the skipper is going to do. We can see Martinique from here and it is not all that long ago that sailors didn't have such things as GPS.

"What are you going to do?" asks Gordon.

"We could turn around and go back to St Lucia,.......... but we are much more likely to get this fixed in Martinique."

"Let's go on then. " I say. We decide to go on and when we switch off the engine things are slightly smoother, but being inter island and having the full Atlantic swell coming in, not very much smoother we still have a functioning compass, and an emergency hand held GPS, .. Jess is thoroughly enjoying sailing without the dreaded seasickness, the wind in her face and a smile as the spray hits.. Gordon, without a scopy patch has succumbed and is hanging off the stern of the boat, all interest in fishing temporarily forgotten. "It's all that rum punch I drank last night," he says trying to be cheerful. Jess just grins at her husband in glee.

James appears from down below where all the children are playing on the computer, despite the motion. "I don't feel very well Mum." He also looks worried and pale, but disappears back down below into hibernation in the cabin.

No fish are caught but there are surely some sighs of relief when we reach the shelter of Marin Cul de Sac on Martinique.

The skipper manages to fix the instrument panel, it is just a loose connection.

As soon as we anchor in the flat water, James reappears from the cabin where he had gone into hibernation and Granny's colour and Gordon's humour return to normal. The transformation is rapid.

Martinique is very French, and if we hadn't just sailed from St Lucia, it would be hard to believe that we were not back in Europe. A truly well stocked supermarket, a truly well stocked chandlery, French prices, French food, and even French traffic. Speaking French is definitely an advantage. The advantages of not becoming a small independent island are very apparent , the French government can feed a lot of money into the island, and not only benefiting the islanders but also the French tourist industry. When Christopher Columbus first saw Martinique the Carib Indians who lived there called it Madinina which means island of flowers, but now it has a lot of agriculture, fast roads and on the mountains, forestry.

"Mum, I'm hungry."

"There's something in the cupboard."

"Anybody down there going to give me a hand with the dinghy." The dinghy is partially deflated and lashed onto the deck. Pumping it up to get it as firm as it needs to go is a tedious job, but then having guests does have its advantages....you can get them to pump up the dinghy!

We move up the coast of Martinique, pausing only briefly at anchorages where there are loud discos and horrible, noisy, polluting, jetskis. They scream around, water shooting up, and I hope that I will watch them fall or break down.

"Should be banned." I mutter as I follow one with my eyes, before going down below to start preparing something to eat. Most of the islands so far have not had jet skis, either because they are banned, or because most of the inhabitants are far to poor to be able to afford them.

As the gentle swell rocks us to sleep, Granny and Jess feel queasy and the boys have made a cigarette manufacturing plant. They make cigarettes by rolling slithers of paper, colouring one end brown and the other has orange and grey ashes on. They are then wrapped in Sellotape and put in packets they have also made from paper and Sellotape. All five boys now play Martinique monopoly with the remarkably lifelike fags hanging out of their mouths. Granny looks on disapprovingly.

"You do know that I wouldn't really smoke cigarettes?" says David looking for reassurance that his parents don't think that he is already is on the slippery slope to addiction.

We just smile an acknowledgement.

A little bay called Anse Noir, barely big enough to fit us in, but we do get in and drop anchor, we are still looking for a 'Jessica beach' that is a beach long, golden and empty and bordered with palm trees. The kind that Jess had envisaged before they came out to the Caribbean. We may have had plenty of them further south, but we have not come across a good one since the cousins arrived. I'm not sure that we will on Martinique.

"I don't believe that there are deserted islands and beaches out here!" says Jess, who is wearing a skimpy black dress.

"There are, only you just missed them." I say. But here in Anse Noir there are palm trees, there are not loads of people and there is a little beach made from black volcanic sand. Steep cliffs with kingfishers flitting about and nesting in the rock faces surround the rest of the bay. The wind circulates off the cliffs coming from all directions, meaning that we swing every which way on the anchor.

But there is also a confused swell coming in, not good for some stomachs.

"I think I'll stay on board," says the skipper, "in case we drag." We have lost some confidence in our anchor holding after the little episode in Castries.

"I think I would like to go ashore," says Granny as a large swell causes a jar of Marmite to roll off the table and Granny to not want to venture down below.

The boys jump in. The saucepan cupboard spits out saucepans angrily as I try to extract one in which to cook the tea, and Granny and Jess go ashore.

I join them ashore and in the dwindling light walk with Granny through the jungle up a dry river bed. The tourism, roads and supermarkets of Martinique can be forgotten for a while. We scramble over large boulders and I top up Granny's anxiety by telling her about the poisonous snake called the 'fer de lance', but she is much happier ashore and only reluctantly agrees to come back on board so that we can move to a place with a little less swell.

An exhilarating sail up to St Pierre, which everybody enjoys, though Gordon still manages to catch no fish.

"I suppose we'll have to eat out tonight then," says the skipper as Gordon hauls in the empty fishing line again.

Here off St Pierre there is much less swell. "Is that better Mum?" I ask Granny.

"Mmmm," she says, not entirely convinced, but definitely looking happier as she sits in her corner of the cockpit.

The town of St Pierre was destroyed by a volcano some one hundred years ago, killing all 30,000 inhabitants but a prisoner, Cyparis who was ensconced in a thick walled cell, thereby avoiding the noxious ash and heat. Walking around the town it could almost have been ten years ago, not one hundred, so many buildings have been left as they were, gaunt burnt out skeletons.

We walk up to where there was once an aristocrats garden, it has been raining so everything is lush, green and steaming. We have to leave the road and head towards where the garden is, on a track.

Jess points out mimosa to the boys. "Touch the leaves and they all close up." We all peer down at the ground and spend some time touching the leaves, watching the tiny leaves slowly recoil at our touch, folding themselves flat along the stem. I have been looking for this for some time and it has taken my non biologically minded sister to find them. "I think they die if you do it too often," I say spoiling the fun, and not even sure of the facts. They're bored of this game by now so luckily it doesn't matter.

Gordon picks up fallen coconuts. "This is how we used to break them open in South America," he says demonstrating with a stone. The boys squat in a circle around him, each wanting to have a go at breaking the coconut. The coconut remains obstinately green and round, their efforts merely making scratches and dents on its hard surface.

"Let me have a go," says David.

"No me." Brinsley has found a larger stone.

"I will try."

The children all try. The coconut wins, but it comes with us and periodically a new suitable stone is thrust at the coconut.

"Hey look at this." We look. We have now arrived at the ex garden. It is weird and eerie, tall has been trees now covered in creepers as are the steep sides of the valley. The vines weigh down the bamboo clumps and small brightly coloured banaquits(bright yellow and brown sparrow sized birds) and humming birds flit in and out of the shadows, but as at the deserted house in Calvigny you can feel the ghosts of a once elegant maintained garden, and where the French aristocracy might have walked twirling their parasols.

There is a waterfall cascading over a tall cliff which must have been the reason they chose to build the garden here, but now it is draped in overhanging creeper clad branches. Stands of bamboo, provide a lighter green and some sort of uniformity in their tall straight stems, but even these clumps have the creeper crawling up them.

Now there is just us and the banaquits and their avian mates.

"I've done it!" a triumphant voice comes from behind us. The coconut has been opened and thirst is quenched with the milk inside. Now mission accomplished they can come and Ooh and aah at natures architecture. The garden ghosts have obviously not reached Gordon and the boys yet!

Back in St Pierre we find a café where we eat and drink, and the boys spill their coke. Just before tucking into a huge pile of chips, David has his usual daily worry "I won't die of a heart attack if I eat these? He asks. Then "Am I too fat?" Of course he is not, he is beautiful (I AM his mother!)

"You're fine I say."

We wander back to the boat to relax and doss.

Gordon fishes off the back of the boat. He has even tried fishing during the night to no avail.

"I can see all these fish swimming around and rising, why do they not come and take my bait?" he says . He has done more fishing during their time with us than we have done almost on the entire trip and not caught a single fish, I can only think that it is something to do with us being off this highly populated island of Martinique.

It comes the time when our family must leave us and head back to Scotland, and we must go and get the boat lifted out of the water for some essential maintenance. We set sail in pouring rain back down the coast of Martinique heading for a little bay called Trois Islets from where they will catch the ferry and then a taxi to the airport.

"I hadn't really thought about the rain here," says Jessica putting on one of the boat oilskins.

The rain is a constant heavy drizzle and the visibility gets less and less good. There is for once no wind and so we must motor.

"Can we run the inverter?" come the voices from down below as soon as the engine is switched on. Engine noise equates to power which means that the boys can play on the computer and we can have the fridge going full blast so have cold beers!

The visibility does not really slow us down as we have both the radar and we have put waypoints in so good old George should take us to the right place. We approach Trois Islets. I stand in my oilskins trying to work out where we are on the chart. "Its OK," I say to the skipper, I can see exactly where we are, I point to where I think on the chart, as some land emerges from the drizzle.

"We can't possibly be there, says the skipper, look how far we have got to go to the waypoint."

"Oh," I say, and look at the land again, No maybe I WAS wrong, maybe we are in the next bay, after all. I try to make the land look like it should from the chart. The rain is coming down in sheets and it is difficult to see. But I manage to match land to chart, or so I think.

I go up forward, it has temporarily stopped raining. The sea in front of us suddenly is getting ominously pale (you can tell how deep it is here by the colour of the water). "STOP!" I yell, "It's getting very shallow over here."

The engine is already in reverse, the bleeping of the shallow alarm having warned the skipper, but we are still too late. We are stopped by physical and not mechanical means as we come aground with a gentle bump.

"We're aground." Both the skipper and I say simultaneously to our family, though this statement is rather superfluous even to them. Luckily it is sand and not a coral reef, and thank goodness we had slowed down.

"We can't possibly be aground, there's nothing to aground on here." Despite the evidence the skipper has the chart in front of him and does not want to believe our situation. But we are irrefutably aground. "We should be able to come in on a straight line" says the skipper. Our guests are wisely keeping out of this skipper/first mate discussion.

"Well there's definitely a problem here," I say, going down below to plot exactly where we actually are, (using the GPS) not where we think that we are. Meanwhile we manage to get off the sand and have time to ponder our error.

We are of course in the first bay that the land had identified, and were heading towards the right bay, but would have to cross dry land to get there. This is what is known as a GPS induced collision(as a result of approaching from a different angle than originally planned.)

So we retreat and come into the right bay feeling slightly sheepish at our mistake, how much better it would have been to make the mistake without visitors, but that chap Sod has been at it again with his rotten law.

Here the bottom is thick and muddy and we can't even begin to judge the depth. We do our best to rely on the echo sounder. It is still pouring with rain.

"What can I have to eat?" comes a small voice from down below.

"Can you wait until we have anchored?"

"I'm starving."

"Well you'll just have to wait."

"What happens if we can't wait?"

"Bri-in!"

Brinsley knows when he has said enough, and his parents have other things to think about.

The water in here may be muddy, but it is flat and calm. .

We find what appears to be a clear spot. It is the route for the local ferry.

"Pas ici, pas ici!....You can't anchor here!" a little man comes out on a boat and tells us. We haul up the muddy anchor, spattering mud all over the boat and myself, stinking and gluey.

A new space is found between two rather decrepit looking boats. The skipper and I drop the anchor.

"No good," says the skipper a few minutes later after seeing that our swinging circle would take us into another boat. "Get that anchor up again." It is very heavy, but I am sure that here we are nowhere near any coral. It should just be soft mud.

Gordon comes up. "You OK?"

"It's very heavy," I say. "I hope we're not attached to another anchor again!" This time it comes up with a sack on the end of it. The sack is covered in mud and well hooked into the anchor. What looks like claws are sticking out of the bottom of the sack I don't want to investigate any further, and push it off the anchor with the boathook, letting it splash into the water. It drops heavily and sinks to the bottom. I am sure that it was a dead dog or some such, and once the image of a dead dog in a sack has got into my mind it is impossible to erase.

We finally anchor successfully, and as it is so calm everybody manages to eat a great meal. It is the skipper's birthday tomorrow, and the cousins and Granny are leaving.

CHAPTER SEVEN

AND SO TO THE LEEWARD ISLANDS

Who is Pengy?

Pengy is a small knitted penguin that ended up on the boat by default, i.e. he is one of those small things that the removers left behind and got shoved in a pocket, as a stowaway not to emerge until we were safely under way.

Anyway Pengy has provided hours of fun, and is now one of the best kitted out penguins around, he has a full superman kit, a rucksack into which is folded a tent and a sleeping bag. All made out of paper , and you have to bear in mind that Pengy is about the size of my hand. Who needs expensive toys?

Anyway the family left us and the boat suddenly seems quiet. We have almost had enough of Martinique, but we must remain here for a little while longer, work to do on the boat, new anode, etc, but still no generator parts.

"Our two hours must be up," says David, looking hopefully at me. I am trying to explain fractions and decimals to Brinsley.

I look at my watch, it's warm down here in the cabin. "Go on then, pack up your things, that's enough for today."

"Hello-o I'm ba-ack!" the footsteps on the deck herald the skipper's return.

"Guess what I've found?" he asks.

"Generator parts?" I hazard a guess.

"No, not a chance, but what I have found is a sailing competition here on Martinique, next week."

"Dinghy sailing?" I hand him a more or less cold beer.

"Yup, I can hire a laser and we can hire oppies for the boys." (Oppies being Optimists, a small sailing dinghy that the boys sail back home).

"Where?" I am not all that enthusiastic as I was hoping that we would be able to leave Martinique soon.

"A place called Schoelcher, just north of Fort de France (the capital of Martinique).

"Great," I say trying to sound enthusiastic.

"Yes, Mum, please can we?"

"Go on then I don't mind." Believe it or not the skipper is actually having sailing withdrawal, he doesn't count sailing a 47ft yacht across the Atlantic as real sailing! (Well I suppose it's not the same as dinghy sailing.)

But before we come to that, John and Michelle, electrical engineer and vet, and friends from way back arrive with two year old Claire for a flying three day visit, they are on their way from America to New Zealand.

The skipper goes to pick them up from the shore.

"Can I come with you Dad?" asks Brinsley. He is John's godson.

"Can I drive?"

"Yes, get a move on though, they are waiting for us on the quayside."

They soon arrive back at the boat, dinghy laden with the paraphernalia of a toddler, Claire is already in her lifejacket.

"Hello John." I greet them, taking their luggage.

"Hello Anna, I've got your flour......but never again."

"Thank you," I say, dropping the bags through the companionway into the saloon and following them.

"I hope you appreciate that it nearly got us arrested. I thought we were never going to get here!"

I pass cold beers up to them.

I apologise profusely and decide that I won't tell them that finally here on Martinique I have been able to find bread flour! Clare is now heading full of confidence into the cabin and nearly falls headlong down the companionway, but is quickly advised by her father that a better way would be to go down the steps backwards.

"Come on Clare, I'll show you around," says David, shepherding her down the steps, and the little girl is quickly taken under the bigger boys wings.

"I'm sorry that the bag of flour has been torn open, but the customs could NOT believe that we were bringing only flour in, they were convinced it was cocaine or something."

"I'll make you the best bread ever," I promise.

"They need a sample to test it for drugs."

"If that was a bag of neat cocaine, I think you'd carry it in a safe!"

I am truly grateful. As for the breadmaker, bread flour is by far the best thing and until here in Martinique we have been quite unable to get any, so when we have been asked 'what can we bring?' I have always been unhesitating in saying 'bread flour.'

John and Michelle are definitely a little stressed after their near arrest, so we fill them full of beer and bonhomie and the following day sail round to Baie des Anglais, full of uncharted reefs, no other boats and quite idyllic, even if it does hold the risk of us getting stuck in there should the seas get up, as it is on the windward side of the island.

"I wonder if Clare gets seasick?" asks Michelle, cuddling her daughter, who up until now has been helping her father unsuccessfully to fish.

'Whoops' The answer is not long in coming as Clare throws up her lunch over her mothers shoulder, and into the cockpit. Luckily nothing that a bucket of seawater can't clean, if only our living rooms back home were so easy to clean of children's vomit!

"She does," says her dad John B.

However she is quickly recovered but we are more circumspect what we give her to eat whilst we are sailing.

Sailing back round to Anse L'Ane where John, Michelle and Clare are going to leave us, we sail past Diamond Rock. This is a steep barren pinnacle of rock pointing out of the water, which in 1804 was commissioned as a ship. Martinique has always been largely French but the British tended to rule the seas. However as they were always short of ships, someone decided to use this pinnacle of rock as a ship, thus giving many nasty surprises to the French.

We are sailing past it on a broad reach. "Let's retake it!" says John B. It is still an empty barren pinnacle of rock. They sit and discuss the best method of approach.

"What do you think would happen if we went up and left a Union Jack?"

But we are soon past the island, leaving it to the nesting birds, the French and the annals of history.

We spend a week in Schoelcher, where Martin hires himself a laser radial (sailing dinghy) and David and Brinsley, Oppies.(or as they call them here in Martinique, Optis.) John and I will have a restful week sorting out cupboards and relaxing. The competition here is an open one and dinghies from all over the Caribbean are attending, as well as some of the Olympic laser team from France

"I feel ill Mum," says David on the first day of the competition. He is curled up like an armadillo in his bunk.

"You poor thing," I say. "Just try the first race and then see how you feel?"

"No I'm really ill this time, I think I'm going to be sick."

"Well make sure you're not sick on the bunk then," I say. David is always ill before any sort of competition; if he is winning he gets better, if he is losing he doesn't.

We persuade him to sail and, with his Dad and Brinsley, we take them ashore in the rubber dinghy, and watch them disappear.

John and I return to *Brandamajo* to charge up the batteries and do some tidying.

The batteries on the boat are giving up, and not holding their charge, and we had bought new ones in the Canaries before we left.

John and I are sitting on deck watching the remainder of the family through binoculars. "Mum, I think that is Brinsley coming back," says John.

I take the 'bins' from John and peer through them. Sure enough Brinsley is returning and he has only just set off.

He sails past our boat, in his little Oppie, with FRA (for France) 8 on the sail, and I know that I am going to have to go ashore to help him haul the dinghy up the beach. And just when I had settled for a nice long relaxing morning dossing and sorting cupboards.

"What are you doing coming back in?" I ask as he sails past.

"It's too windy," he replies.

Back ashore when we have to fill in a form giving reasons for retirement from the race, the organiser looks at the form in astonishment. "Trop de vent?...Vraiment?.....non, pas de vent" He cannot believe that we are finding it too windy. Little does he know what it is like sailing on Budworth Mere in the heart if Cheshire!, a lake surrounded by trees where the wind is patchy and anything approaching twenty knots of wind and the lake becomes bare of boats.

The skipper and David return.

"That was hard. I hurt everywhere!" says the skipper, creaking and groaning as he gingerly moves down the steps into the cabin.

He creaks across and looks at what the battery charge is reading. It is not good "They should still be under guarantee." And indeed they should, but trying to get that sorted when the batteries were bought in Spain and the French people don't want to have anything to do with them. What is all this about Europe? Try explaining that to a French battery dealer in the heart of the Caribbean islands! I think we will end up having to buy some more new ones.

By Shrove Tuesday, the four day sailing competition has come to an end and Martin has come second, so is in very high spirits especially as the competition was so much younger. He is still creaking and groaning around as all those muscles that haven't been used for a while are brought into action again. The boys have not done so well, I think finding them selves in a large competitive fleet was quite a shock, but they have enjoyed themselves.

The atmosphere has been great and the sailing club most welcoming to this British boat that has moored outside it, and crew entered into their competition. Out of anywhere I have ever been, I can honestly say that Martinique is the most racially integrated, with absolutely no discrimination between black and white.

It seems that in a few generations they will all be the same colour, a sort of golden brown!

We toss pancakes on the boat and then decide to go ashore to experience the Mardi Gras Carnival. It is a carnival that goes on all week , and I had been told that today's theme was black and white. What I didn't realise was that everybody is meant to wear something black and white so we go into Fort de France all in our matching bright red *Brandamajo* tee shirts. Everybody else is wearing black and white.

Shouts of "Noir et blanc pas rouge!" greet us as we step off the bus and it dawns on us that the theme of black and white is adhered to by almost everybody, spectators and participants alike. Well at least we won't lose the children!

We sit on the pavement getting dirty and drinking cold drinks from a booth behind us and an assortment of bangers and bikes pass in front of us.

"Look at those bikes!" shriek the children as motorbikes do wheelies in front of us. A few lorries dressed up parade past, and at least two bands of 'nuns' (or is it the same one passing by twice?) we buy hot chestnuts from street vendors and not candy floss.

"Quick boys, duck sideways!" I shout as a shower of flour comes pouring out of an upstairs window. We have already had water squirted on us and several people with a combination of flour and water glue plastered on their bodies pass us by.

"Mum, Dad, look there's a Macdonalds. Can we eat there? I'm hungry."

As parents we throw questioning glances at each other.

"Go on then." Can we really be in the Caribbean, we wonder as we sit at this universal fast food place and watch the boys enjoy themselves.

After seeing the same black and white band pass for the third time, decide that we have seen enough and head back for the bus to take us back to Schoelcher where the boat is anchored.

Find a Varta dealer (the make of our batteries) in Fort de France.

"Let's take the batteries then and see if we can get our money back?"

They are exceedingly heavy, too heavy to try transporting by dinghy and bus so we up anchor and return to a marina at Marin, towards the south of the island, and from there we sweat and strain ourselves and lug them into the back of a hired car.

We park the car French style, half on the pavement and half on the road almost outside the battery shop and leave the boys to guard it whilst we lug a battery into the shop. They are tested and all the readings come up OK.

"They are the wrong batteries for your boat." It is explained to us in a mixture of French and sign language.

"Pas possible!" we exclaim catching onto their Gallic gestures.

"Oui, c'est possible, these are not deep cycle batteries."

We wave, we gesture and we give in, it seems that they are right, but we can't possibly go back to the canaries and change them now.

Use the hire car to buy vast amounts of food, these French supermarkets are far removed from the little shops we have been buying our provisions from up until now. and look for a beach(unsuccessfully) with waves on for the boys.

It is time to leave Martinique. I for one am ready to go back to the less crowded and less developed Caribbean that we have come to know and love.

So it is with no regrets that we head north towards Dominica, but we needed to come here to get jobs done, and the supermarkets were great.

Leaving Martinique, we also leave the Windward Islands and progress into the Leeward Islands. Dominica is green and mountainous and probably the poorest island we have been to so far. The Caribs called the island Waitkubuli, which means tall is her body, and Christopher Columbus on trying to describe it to King Ferdinand and Queen Isabella of Spain scrumpled up a piece of paper to demonstrate the mountains. He discovered it on a Sunday and so named it Dominica, and the name has more or less stuck.

At Roseau, where we drop anchor of an hotel, a bright green wooden boat with a dark black Rastafarian with shoulder length dreadlocks in a bright yellow tee-shirt comes out to meet us.

"You don't want to anchor outside the town" he says , smiling and motoring along beside us. "Many drug problems."

We weren't going to but thank him anyway.

"You want anything, anything at all, don't forget me, just call me. My name is Geo," he says whilst trying to help us attach a mooring line to a rather dicey looking buoy.

"We would like to walk up to the boiling lake," we say.

"No problem." He heads back into the shore in his green wooden boat with large new looking Yamaha outboard.

"Mum, why has he got a finger missing?" asks John as soon as Geo has left us,

"I have no idea," I answer, having not even noticed the missing digit. "You'll have to ask him. Come on, let's get that sail cover on."

"He says he's Rastafarian, but doesn't like the long dreadlocks, that's why he has cut his off to shoulder length," says Brin, opening the locker and getting the tatty grey covers out.

Next to the hotel there is a diving operation and so the next day we go diving. We opt for one of the easier dives still being relatively novice, and go on what is nicknamed the 'champagne dive'. The boys stay in the dive boat chatting up the Canadian lady steering it whilst the skipper and I explore the corals and seahorses amongst bubbles rising in thin lines from the cracks in the Earth's surface. We pass vents in the rocks where hot water comes out and mingles with the cold. I am getting better at diving now and more able to concentrate on the sea life rather than my inability to stay down. Unfortunately this time there is a slight leak in my oxygen tank so by the time we have finished the gauge reads zero.(luckily we were never very deep)

"That was fun, can we come out in the dive boat next time?" ask the boys. "You didn't go very far though, we could follow your bubbles."

It rains all night, but we are up at 6.30 am and look out. We can see Geo sitting in a big inner tube and paddling with his hands to his green boat with is moored a little off the shore. We get our bags and picnic and row ashore to meet Geo who is going to take us up the mountain to see the boiling lake, it is apparently a long walk, and yesterday people had looked askance at us when we said that all five of us were going to go up there.

"You can't take your children up there, it is too far," said a fat American. "We tried to go up yesterday and had to come back down."

"Don't worry our children are used to being dragged up mountains and on long walks," we reply, "Why we took our youngest John up a fourteen thousand foot mountain in the canaries." The fat Americans who are staying in the hotel next to which the dive boat operates, just shake their heads in wonder, or is it disbelief, that we can be such hard parents?

"You enjoyed it didn't you boys?" nudge nudge.

"Yes, yes," they all dutifully reply.

The boiling lake is the second largest in the world, the largest being in New Zealand, and the one attempt that was made to build cable cars to it by some foreign consortium was soon laid to rest by the total non co-operation of the local people.

Ashore we stand outside Geo's hut, waiting for a cousin of his to arrive to drive us up to the mountain, but he seems not to be here. Geo gets more and more concerned. He looks at his watch. It is gone seven thirty. "I told him we must leave at seven, but he is not here!" he states the obvious.

"Don't worry," we say, "we are used to Caribbean time".

Geo relaxes slightly and the cousin arrives.

"I'm hungry," says Brin as we all clamber into the ubiquitous minibus, with peeling plastic seats and turned up lino on the floor.

The cousin leaves us at the foot of a large wooden hydro electric pipe, efficiently built by a German company, along which we start to walk, balancing carefully along the top, it is quite a long way to fall either side. "We could go up the path," says Geo, long after we have started on the pipe, "but this is a much better way and goes directly to meet the path."

"No, that's fine."

We cannot disagree as he is our guide, and the boys think it is a wonderful way to walk, balanced on top of a large circular pipe. Geo has never been abroad except once to Holland.

We join the path where the dam is that collects the electricity generating water into the superbly built pipes.

It starts to rain, but no matter: we have our cagoules and at the moment it is still warm and humid.

We join the jungle and whistling birds whistle to one another in the canopy over our heads, and Martin and I try to enthuse some tropical biology into our sons (going back a bit....and I won't say how long we are going back!... Martin and I met whilst on a tropical Biology course at Aberdeen University.) but they are not very enthused.

"We KNOW that Dad, you've already told us!"

"Ah but look at this," we point out another strangling fig, its golden brown stem flowing in intricate patterns up the trunk of the host tree, that it will eventually kill, or a beautifully shaped leaf so cleverly designed to drip the water off.

They dutifully look, having learnt that sometimes it is easier to show an interest.

We descend through the jungle into a valley where there is a rushing adolescent river strewn with large boulders, around which it pours and gurgles. It is time for breakfast, so I unpack egg sandwiches and for a while it has stopped raining, so we can take our hoods down and lets our bodies steam in the humidity. Geo rolls a joint, and the big black mosquitoes appear from the rotting leaves and damp nooks and crannies to feast on the bare flesh that has so conveniently stopped in their midst.

'Slap.......slap........slap,slap,slap,...' "Ah got one." The skipper holds up a squashed mosquito on the palm of his hand and I spray citronella on the bare arms and legs of our children.

"Don't copy me at home," says Geo to the boys, drawing on his joint. The mozzies don't seem to be bothering him, and the boys have no idea that he is not smoking an ordinary cigarette. (or so I think) The sweet smell of marijuana means nothing to them yet,(thank goodness).

We climb through the jungle along an ever-narrowing path and reach another ridge. The temperature is getting cooler all the time, and the rain becoming heavier.

"That there is the Valley of Desolation," Geo points below us, but all we can see is clouds and mist below us.

"Mmm," Martin and I say.

"Where?" say the boys.

We could well be in Scotland. "We have to walk through it anyway, you'll get a better view then," he says , bounding on his long athletic legs ahead of us. Brinsley and David keep up with him, but John needs encouragement from us, it is wet and as we get higher it is also getting colder and colder, and more and more like home.

"Is he all right?" Geo reappears from in front , looking queryingly at John.

"He's fine," we say, firmly pulling our youngest son up the steep hill.

Soon we are scrambling down a path that is boggy and mossy, by now being above the height of the jungle, the terrain like the weather is very Scottish, and we descend into the valley of Desolation. Here boiling water bubbles up and hot sulphurous steam belches from the ground, from white and yellow heaps upon which nothing can grow. "Make sure you don't fall in the stream," says Geo Looking as the boys jump over these streams of boiling water. "Hey this is COOL" says David standing in the steam, which is lovely and warming.

"No it's not David. It's actually very hot," says John who has perked up now we are not climbing.

We peer at each other through the sticky damp sulphurous steam which condenses on our cold wet hair in fine droplets.

We could have stayed warming ourselves in the steam for much longer, but we must go on. Nobody even suggests turning back. The wind gets stronger the rain gets harder, sometimes almost turning to sleet and we battle against it up our third hillside., it is almost too windy to talk so we plod on, faces turned inwards away from the wet wind. Even John has stopped complaining. We finally get to the top and stand on a plateau of clay all vegetation worn from it, where people have stood to view this natural wonder.

"That" says Geo, pointing down below, "That is the boiling lake."

All we can see is cloud, but beneath the cloud you can hear the bubbling of a vast cauldron and every now and then the cloud and steam parts to give a brief glimpse of the cauldron some six or seven hundred feet below us. Big brown bubbles growing and bursting then the cloud and steam covers them again.

And by vast, I mean vast. It is apparently some 207 foot wide, and the sound of its belching bubbles gives us some idea of its size, even if we cannot see it.

"You mean we came all the way up here just to look at a cloud?" says Brin.

"We could wait for a while and see if the cloud clears?" suggests Geo. "Someone fell off this cliff last year into the boiling water," he continues as we carry on peering hard into the cloud and steam below us almost willing it to part so that we can get a good view of what we actually came up here to see.

I instinctively draw the children away from the cliff edge.

"Did he die?" asks David.

Geo smiles. "He was skinned."

We finally give up waiting for the weather to clear, it shows no sign of going to and we are getting very cold, it is time to descend

Stop to heat ourselves up again in the steam coming from the vents in the Valley of Desolation, it is difficult coming away from the steam vents a bit like getting out of a very hot bath into freezing cold air, but we do it, our next warming station being the river. We race to get to it before another group of descending people do. The river is milky white and warm

"Not as warm as usual," says Geo, dropping his haversack under a dripping tree and wading into the river, "because of all this rain." Nonetheless we sit in it beneath a waterfall. Our clothes couldn't possibly get any wetter. We eat our picnic lunch., by now soggy biscuits and soggy sulphurous sandwiches, but we are hungry and no one complains. Geo takes the boys to the top of the milky white warm waterfall and they play in the warm water for a while before we know that the time has come that we must get out of this tepid bath and descend.

"I have never known the weather to be so bad," apologises Geo pulling his tee-shirt over his head.

"Don't worry," we say, "It's like this in England, but we are trying to forget about it!"

The path is now a raging torrent but at least as we get lower the air becomes warmer. David and Brin run on ahead with Geo, leaping in great strides ahead of us and out of sight, he tells them about marijuana and his teenage years of running up to the boiling lake by moonlight and they tell him about snow, and how the trees are bare in winter. They are learning how what is normality to one culture is strange and intriguing to another.

Back at the bottom of the wooden hydro pipe, the cousin is waiting to take us back and Geo peels off his boots, his feet rotten and wrinkled. He is obviously more used to being barefoot than shod.

"Why did we walk all that way in the rain to see a boiling lake we couldn't see?" asks John as we strip off our wet muddy clothes back at the boat and throw them in a tub of water used for cleaning wet suits of the divers.("We'll rinse it out I promise!" the skipper says as the proprietor of the diving centre looks on). The sun is now shining and it is hard to believe that we were actually cold not so long ago, the difference between here and in the mountains is so extreme.

The skipper tries to start the generator. It won't start, he shrugs his shoulders, as the year goes by we are learning not to let such things worry us too much, which to a perfectionist (no, not me) is quite an achievement.

Following our trip up the mountain we decide to go whale watching. We have heard that there are whales that live in the deep waters off Dominica.. It is a flat calm day and we set off from Rousseau, scanning the horizon as we motor slowly out from the island. Not a whale in sight. Plenty of dolphins. But not a single whale. We are thinking of a sperm whale a la Moby Dick of course; a blue whale would do, or a grey or humpback. But whales are not playing today.

"I'm bored Mum," say the children and disappear down below to play on the computer. The inevitable 'pubbajackas' from down below soon follows.

"Well, what do you think, should we give up?" asks the skipper, looking at me. I am reluctant but we can't spend all day scanning a mirror surface of water for a spout, even if you couldn't have better whale spotting weather.

"I suppose so," I say. The boys return on deck

"Have you seen one yet?"

"No." We slowly turn and head towards Portsmouth a town further up Dominica.

"Whale! Whale!" John has spotted one right on our stern, and we have time to watch a huge spout of water before it dives, its great big flukes lifting high in the air, right behind us. It was indeed that of the Moby Dick variety, a fifty foot sperm whale, and we nearly missed it, and I take a perfect shot of the ripple of water it leaves behind, with my camera. We stay out and wait for forty five minutes for it to surface for it's next breather and sure enough it does but this time not quite so close to us. How lucky we are to have seen it. Another school of dolphins comes and plays around our bow as we head into the anchorage

The sun is going down and we have eaten and washed up. We have been swarmed by small flying ants and the boys are having a funeral parlour for them, catching them and extinguishing them on the mosquito coil.

"Another stiffy," says Brin, adding a dead ant to their growing pile.

"If you catch one you can hold it over the hot end of the mosquito coil 'til it dies," says David, doing just that.

"Here's some more David," says John opening his hand and tipping several live ants onto the plate holding the coil. The children soon have a death production line going, and I hope that their enthusiasm doesn't progress beyond ants!

In the background Caribbean music is blaring. The locals are gathering for a jump up on the beach (that means it must be Friday or Saturday)

"Before I go to bed, I want to count the ants." John is looking at the growing heap in the ant morgue in the corner of the chart table.

"You'll need to move the morgue before tomorrow." The skipper momentarily lifts his head from his book. He is reading through the whole Patrick O'Brian series of nautical books.

"I think we should do some school work today," I say putting on my metaphorical teachers hat the following morning.

"Oh no, do we HAVE to?" say the boys almost in unison. It is now an automatic response that expects no spoken reply.

"Think of Mrs Barrington," I say. She is their teacher from home to whom Brinsley and John will go back.

I get the school books out. I think that we will do English today.

The skipper emerges from the shower.

"Mum! The headmaster's naked again!"

It is not long though before the headmaster has turned engineer and is back asking for tissues to be passed to him.

But the man who left Plymouth six months ago is now an engineer, a functioning dad, a part time headmaster, a plumber, not to mention of course a skipper.

Have a brisk sail up to Les Saintes, a group of French Islands off the coast of Guadeloupe. The skipper is in his element as he stands at the helm, the yacht racing along, wind on the beam, and no appreciable seas to speak of.

"Lazy Duck, Lazy duck, Lazy Duck, this is *Brandamajo*, *Brandamajo*, over." It is not too difficult to sit at the chart table whilst at an angle because the seat is curved.

Silence, we haven't been in contact with them for a while, so much for our ideas of being able to use the SSB all the way around the world.

"Mum, can I try *Alice Ambler*?" says John.

"Of course."

"*Alice Ambler*, *Alice Ambler*, *Alice Ambler*, this is *Brandamajo*, *Brandamajo*, over."

171

Alice Ambler is not responding. The airwaves are quiet this morning,.

As we drop anchor, the engine seems to be coughing, but never mind, let's worry about that tomorrow. I suppose that we're due for another problem.

Terre de Haute is a lovely island but completely spoiled by hordes of fat red French tourists, we hire bikes and cycle around until we find an almost totally empty windward beach at the end of the little runway. We push our bikes past a sign that says 'Danger, swimming forbidden' Probably why it is empty. There is only us and a south African family and we are all swimming, and enjoying the waves, and they're yachties too.

Walking back along the shore. "Mum, that's *Gravitas* there."

"It can't possibly be, they're in Trinidad."

"No it is, I'm sure, look where the ensign is, and I KNOW where they put their fenders," says Brin.

We peer at the boat and sure enough if it is not *Gravitas* then it is their twin. It will be nice to see them again.

It is indeed Dave and Emma, and they try to pay us a surprise visit, not realising that we are already aware of their presence.

Back at the boat the skipper does his now standard turning of the generator to see if it will kick into life, it hasn't for some days now. A soft purring indicates that it has decided to start. Why? We have no idea, for the moment, Sod at least is sleeping.

We are heading north now towards Antigua. The engines mild cough has developed into something much more serious and it is very reluctant to get started, so we cannot risk going up the central canal of Guadeloupe,(which would require a reliable motor) we will sail up the outside. Of course when you really want to sail, the wind is inconsistent and variable.

"He's going about now," says the skipper. looking at a catamaran who we have been sailing more or less with for the past half an hour. "We'll just get that patch of wind over there, and then we'll gub him!"

"You're not racing him?" I say.

"Of course not, but just get that Genoa in a little. Come on grind that winch and we will be able to catch him yet."

"Come on Dad, get more sails up, let's gub him!" David has appeared on deck at the merest hint of a race.

"Sorry Dave, we've got all the sails we can up.

And so we race the catamaran. Each time we cross tack we are a little bit closer. Once we have overtaken him, the skipper relaxes. And so does the first mate!

We anchor in a little bay called Deshaies at the north of Guadeloupe. It is almost dark when we get there. It has been a long sail in very light winds but we will just spend the night here before departing for Antigua at first light in the morning.

The skipper goes ashore to try and check in, but it is too late and everywhere is closed so I suspect that we will spend the night here without the knowledge of the customs people.

We sleep, as always, under sheets alone, it is too hot to have anything heavier, and most of the time too hot to cuddle, I wonder if couples from tropical climes cuddle as much as couples from the cooler Northern climes? Crash!! Crash, bang, bang. We are being pounded by waves coming in and slapping against our stern. The wind is from forward but the waves are coming from aft giving the boat a jerky uncomfortable motion, each wave pushing her forwards into the anchor chain and then she falls back with the wave only to be brought up short with a loud yank on the anchor chain.

"I suppose I'd better go and try and do something about that." The skipper rolls over in the bunk , thinking for a bit before hauling himself out of our bear pit and going out into the dark to rig a warp from our stern to the anchor to try and bring us facing the waves more. However finally at five a.m. we decide that there is no point lying here wide awake waiting until morning, we might as well leave. So we do, the first pale glimmerings of dawn are showing in the eastern sky.

The boys sleep on through the clanking of anchor chain, the flapping and hoisting of sails and the starting of the engine.

The day progresses the children get up , the wind drops and we are left with calm glassy seas, but thankfully the engine is working after a fashion, so we use it when the sails flap uselessly, we have quite a long way to go to Antigua.

"Look at that squall coming behind us Dad!" David is poking his head through the companionway and looking over the skipper's shoulder.

"Is that a line squall?"

"I can see the rain falling from the cloud!"

"Let's put a reef in, no lets put two reefs in," says the skipper. We are only just in time, the squall hits, violent, wet and windy, pouring rain and 20 to 25 knot gusts of wind, then it is gone as quickly as it arrived, we are back to glassy seas and feel as if we have just been put through a washing machine.

Montserrat is smoking quietly to our port side and Antigua is getting bigger as Guadeloupe gets smaller. There are no whales, no dolphins and even no fish to break the glassy calm. We have got the lines out as we usually do when sailing inter island in the hope of catching us a free fresh meal.

We arrive in Antigua, with no fresh fish for tea. Never mind, it looks as if will have to be pasta again.(If I can find a weevil-free pack!)

Christopher Columbus named Antigua after a church in Seville in Spain. Under British rule for a long time, it only became independent in 1981, and during British rule became highly fortified, making it one of their main strongholds in the Caribbean.

It is much flatter than the other Caribbean islands we have visited so far and almost completely surrounded by beaches, they say that there is a different beach for each day of the year. Our first view is from the marina and a part of the Caribbean we have only glimpsed so far, that of the super rich yachts. We go alongside the marina in Falmouth harbour, but at $36 a night plus water and $20 for electricity I don't think that we will be spending longer than one night here.

But our sad batteries need charging up and our sad generator needs mending.

"Mum! Mum! *Gravitas* are here!"

"So they are, right opposite us on the marina, the two of us look like little paupers compared with the other yachts. Our white hulls now look slightly off white and our worn ensign looks quite rag like, befitting the nickname for the British ensign of 'red duster.' (actually in all honesty ours is quite rag like, tattered at the edges from the non stop battering by the wind and sun it has had!) All day the big yachts are being washed, or varnished or polished, so that the owners may not sully their clean ironed clothes, and so that their guests may comment on the beauty of their yacht (or do they take it all for granted?)

As the owners walk down the pontoons to their yachts they do not even notice that we are there, but I bet they don't have as much fun as we do!

After one night alongside we untie and go out to anchor, having got the engine fixed and the generator almost fixed. We can now swim of the boat, and the boys can take the dinghy to the beach.

Now next to Falmouth Harbour, is English harbour, a short walk across the isthmus and above English Harbour is Shirley Heights where we had been told to go for a good Caribbean jump up.

I am pegging out the towels on the railings, salty and sandy they are now faded and ragged after their almost continuous life on the railings in the hot sun. "We'll take the dinghy round shall we?" asks the skipper who has appeared from down below.

"You can't possibly!," I say aghast, standing up and dropping yet another clothes peg into the water. It sinks.

"Why not?"

"It's the open ocean."

"So. It's flat calm and we can take the VHF with us."

I crawl under the sun awning back into the cockpit. "Our dinghy is far too small to take round there!"

"We'll never be far from shore, and if we don't, we will have to get a taxi!"

"Come on Mum, pleease let us go in the dinghy?"

It seems that I am outnumbered, and maybe it will be fun anyway. So we go.

Who said you couldn't take a small craft into the Atlantic? Luckily the seas are flat calm. The little outboard goes at full pelt and we pass a deserted beach before making it round the peninsula and tying up at a little jetty on Freeman's Beach.

The walk up to Shirley heights is through thick scrub and large cacti known as Turks Heads. Half way up the steel band strikes up and we finish sweating our way to the top to the sound of the steel band playing classical music, getting louder as we draw closer.

Phew.

"Mum we're up here!" The boys are standing looking down as I step out of the scrub onto the cobbled hill top, Stalls are set up selling rotis, (chicken and potato in a tortilla wrap)hot dogs and beer.

People are gathering , but few have come up the same way as us , most of them have come by car or taxi via the road.

"I'm hungry!"

"OK here's ten E.C.'s. Go and get yourself something."

They are slightly gobsmacked that I have given in so easily. But they are not the only ones who are hungry. First a cold drink. Our tee-shirts are sticking to us.

As the hilltop gets crowded we watch the sun set over the two harbours, both crowded with yachts all lying neatly into wind. We can pick out *Brandamajo*, by her two red jibs, which few other boats have. She is still there.

People appear in all sorts of get ups from the skimpy hardly dresses to elegant long skirts and of course those like us in shorts. I wonder how many new couples will partner up tonight. We can almost feel the heat emanating from the sunburn and sweat as everybody starts to sway in time to the steel band music.

But the sun has set, the boys are not yet interested in the opposite sex and so we leave the crowds to their beers, rum punches and sweaty dancing and wend our way back down through the scrub.

It is now pitch dark, but we think that there will be enough light left to see our way down.

"Ow!"

"What?"

"I've walked into a cactus." This is from David.

"Well that wasn't very sensible was it?"

"Is it sensible to walk in pitch black through a cactus forest?"

Point taken, let's not lose the path.

"Can you see me Dad?"

"No can you see me?" We shout through the black prickly scrub.

"Here grab hold of my tee shirt and see if we can feel out way down this path."

Brinsley has a torch and every now and then we can see a bit of its dim light, but the battery is now so low that it does not light up much of the path.

"I'M HERE!" the shout comes back to David and myself and we know that the advance party has found the road. We are not far behind, but David at least and I suspect some of the rest of us, have some cactus thorns deeply embedded. I think it will be a long session with a pair of tweezers. These fine cactus hairs do not relinquish their flesh targets that easily.

A couple of days later we move round the peninsula and anchor of Freeman's beach near the entrance to English Harbour.

Morning. "Duchess, Duchess, Duchess, this is *Brandamajo, Brandamajo*, over."

"Hallo Martin this is Chris here."

"I heard that you were in Antigua, how's the generator?"

Needless to say generator malady is common amongst small generator bearing yachts.

"Fixed. Yours?

"Almost fixed."

"A beer to celebrate tonight then?"

Our generator is now at the most functional it has been since the fateful day three across the Atlantic.

The boat is measured for race week, we tie up alongside a rusty old wreck and the official race measurer comes aboard and spends ages measuring this and that and this and that, but finally he is done and we can go back out and re anchor.

"Come on boys, give your mum a hand with these fenders please!" shouts the skipper.

"Coming!" says John in one of his willing to please co-operative moods today.

The fenders are untied and lugged up forward where they need to be placed in the generator locker.

"Aaagh Muuum. Daaad. Help me! Help me!"

We are all gathered round John immediately , he has let the lid of the locker drop on his toe. There is blood everywhere.

His screams reverberate around. "Sshh. Let's have a look" say his worried parents.

"Oh yuck I can't look!" Brinsley quickly turns his head away after peering at the pulpy mess that is John's toe."

David asks "Are you all right John?" trying hard not to look at his toe.

"Don't worry I'll clean your decks Dad." Brinsley rushes aft to get a bucket , as we get a bowl of disinfectant and wads of cotton wool to see if we can ascertain the damage.

"Mum it hurts, it really hurts," he says between sobs.

There is so much bloody mess that it is difficult to see how bad it is so we decide that we must take him to a doctor, but the local doctor is not very interested in seeing him and suggests that we take him to hospital. This entails getting a taxi(well a minibus with 'stingray' emblazoned across its windscreen) to a hospital in St John's, fifteen miles away. He sits quietly on my knee, worn out from crying and the initial shock has gone ,the toe well wrapped up in layers of bandages, all gore hidden from sight..

Ray from the Stingray taxi offers to wait for us as we seem to be well out of the way from anywhere and we go inside the hospital. A receptionist greets us and we follow her, dripping blood along the corridor as we go.

"Here you can wait here, while I go and try and find a doctor." She says drawing aside a curtain and leaving us in a cubicle.

Apart from us, a couple of nurses doing nothing, and the receptionist, the hospital seems totally empty, certainly no other patients. It is clean, but the beds are rusty and the curtain on the window is a bit of flowery material tacked onto the frame. The whole wooden building is painted grey. We sit in the silent building waiting for a doctor to appear.

A buxom nurse pops her head round the door. "Are you all right?"

"Yes thank you," I say. "Is there a doctor coming to see us?"

"We have phoned for one. I am not sure where he is, but he should be here soon."

Meanwhile Stingray waits patiently outside. I go out to tell him that we may be some time. But he is happy to wait and only charge us for the two journeys, not the waiting. He is obviously not too busy at the moment.

"How is the boy?"

About an hour later a doctor finally arrives. We see the car pull up through the window and an Indian doctor get out.

"Hello there, what can we do for you?" The doctor looks at John's tear-streaked face, so we recite the story again. "Have you filled in the forms and discussed the method of payment yet?" he asks.

I shake my head.

"Maybe you'd better go and do that now. He nods his head towards the door. Obviously he is not planning to do anything until I have sorted this out, so I go, whilst John has to wait some more. He turns his head towards the wall.

Once I am back, having given the necessary reassurance that I will not leave without paying, the doctor slowly peels off the bandages, John renews his lamentations and the doctor pulls off the toenail.

"I don't think we can stitch that," he says , having cleaned it up. "It is too ragged, but I will put a splint on it and bandage it up. Would you like it x-rayed?"

"What will you do if it is broken?" I ask.

"Oh I won't do anything other than I am already doing , but I am quite happy to give you an x-ray if you would like?"

"And how much will that cost?" I ask

" About $200 American dollars."

"No thank you," I say.

We leave, John now proud of his newly bandaged and enormous toe, splinted with one of those little wooden tongue spatulas.

Stingray is pleased to see that 'little John' is OK and he asks after him every time we pass whilst we are in Antigua.

"Mum, why can't I go swimming?"

"Your toe mustn't get wet."

"We could put it in a plastic bag" Brinsley is already rummaging through the cupboard for a suitable one."

"Give it here Brin. Let's see what we can do." David has his little brother's foot on his knee and is taping a plastic bag round the whole foot.

"I'm not going around with a plastic bag on my foot!" John is indignant.

"Well you'll just have to stay on the boat then." I am trying to put a saucepan in the cupboard. I kick it hard with my foot to shut it.

"I'll wear a plastic bag." The capitulation is almost instant.

"I don't think that you can swim yet," I tell him, "but that at least should help keep some sand out of it." He may now go to the beach with them and in theory not get his bandaged toe wet. The skipper varnishes the woodwork in the cockpit, and Alex (same age as Brinsley) from *Duchess* goes to the beach with the boys. Alex subsequently comes and has a sleepover on our boat, but the poor boy is so overcome with excitement,(being an only child) that he is sick in the night. He still tells his parents that he had a fantastic time!

There are rumours that *Alice Ambler* is in Jolly Harbour, also on Antigua, we try calling them "*Alice Ambler, Alice Ambler, Alice Ambler*, this is *Brandamajo, Brandamajo*, over."

No response. Maybe their SSB is not working. Nikki will be at a loss without the morning gossip channel!

We are going up there anyway. A brisk sail, and we arrive just in time to join in the start of a yacht race, so of course we do, especially as since we are now officially measured to conform with the Caribbean racing rules, we are eligible to race in any yacht race here.

"Look they're just about to start!" says the skipper before we have even got close to mooring, "let's join them!"

"Oh do we have to?" The crew is not exactly as enthusiastic as the skipper, but we start rushing around hauling ropes hither and thither, putting reefs in and taking reefs out as squalls play with us.

The skipper has managed to produce a map of the course, obviously picked up and then secreted whilst in English harbour! So I do my best to navigate between hauling on ropes.

"We'd better go about here, it's getting very shallow" The water is a vivid turquoise and getting brighter and paler by the minute, quite a stunning colour, but no time to look and appreciate the colours, we are in a race!

"Ready about!.........Lee Oh" the sheets go flying, the sails go flying, there is a splash. The sheets are pulled in the sails are trimmed and we are one winch handle less.

"Well that's thirty quid down the drain," remarks the skipper.

"No, in the sea," answers John.

Finish the race, well reefed down in a prolonged squall, and head for the marina.

Alice Ambler are here as are *Pimpernel*. John is delighted to see *Alice Ambler* and his friend Toby, and runs along the pontoon to play with him.

The mosquitoes here are large and vicious, no wonder it used to be called mosquito cove.

"Does THIS island have dengue fever?" asks David, examining a bite. "What about malaria?"

"Don't worry David," we say handing him the citronella and lighting yet another mossie coil with which to pollute our lungs.

John can now manage to swim but one of us adults has to walk with him and hold the injured foot out of the water. It creates a lot of amusement especially for Toby, who wants us to do the same for him, so on the each we walk through the shallows with these two small children holding one of their legs out of the water while they swim with their other three limbs. Not as easy as it sounds.

The marina at Jolly Harbour is relatively cheap, you can walk to a good beach, and the supermarket and it is nice to have unlimited power and water for a bit. We can even let water run down the drain! Well not too much.

Sail a rough bumpy sail up to the North of Antigua, a place called Green island. We are all undrugged so the boys lay strewn around the cockpit, and I refuse to do very much down below. John collects the seeds from sesame baps (that we had for lunch) into neat little piles and plays with them on the cockpit floor, that sort of game doesn't require much movement!

We anchor in calm and the crews vitality is immediately restored.

The skipper takes a break from engines and generators and whizzes around on his windsurfer whilst we catch up on some school work.

We snorkel over eel grass and not much else. John can snorkel by lying in the dinghy which Martin tows while snorkelling, and sticking his face in the water, keeping his body and the injured toe in the dinghy and relatively dry..

" I can't get my mask on," says David.

"I'm sure you can, if you try harder," I say not looking at him and concentrating on getting my own mask on.

"Mum, listen will you? There's BLOOD!"

The magic word is uttered, sure to get their mother's attention and I stop doing what I am doing and look at my son.

There is indeed. His tooth is about to come out, it is extremely wobbly and I cringe as he wobbles it with his fingers, but it is exactly where his mask fits close against his face so it is no wonder that it is hurting. He gives up and sits, being towed in the dinghy .

Later that night. "Mum, I can't eat anything, my tooth hurts." I hate wobbly teeth. "Look at it Mum."

"Ugh no."

"I can't go to sleep."

"Come here David," says Dad who is sitting at the chart table planning tomorrows route to Barbuda. "I'll pull it out.

"No, Dad, No."

"Yes, Dave, Yes"

"No you can't do that."

"Well stop making so much fuss about it then."

"OK.....no.....yes......no.......yes.......yes.....no...."

"David!"

David finally walks gingerly towards his father who pulls the offending tooth out. But now there is peace, and David can get to sleep.

CHAPTER EIGHT

HAVE YOU EVER RACED YOUR HOME?

Barbuda is a long flat island surrounded by reefs and at least 200 wrecks so far. The sailing books say it is inadvisable to go to unless your insurance is up to date and you are happy to do 'eyeball' navigation, i.e. look out for reefs and when you see one swerve or stop.

The charts just have the big reefs marked and 'numerous small reefs' on the other bits, or even 'uncharted'.

However our insurance is up to date and (as if we haven't had enough adrenaline buzz) there is nothing like a challenge. So whilst the boys are still sleeping we set off from Green Island.

"What does David Jones say?" asks the skipper from the cockpit as we slowly motor out from the sheltered bay of Green island.

I have been listening to the local weather forecast on the SSB.

"The usual, occasional squalls, wind out of the North, 18 to 20 knots," I reply making my way up to help the skipper get the rest of the sails up.

The wind is against us, so we sail close hauled, but we are racing along, I just hope that the boys have got their lee berths up to stop them from falling out of bed.

"I think that is a squall coming." The skipper is looking in front of us and sure enough there is the dark line of cloud scurrying across the sky to meet us.

"Get that reefing handle out!"

We grind the reefs in making the sail smaller, the squall hits and batters us with wind and rain, but we come out the other side unscathed.

"Let's get those reefs out!" the skipper is smiling at the moment, and the reefs are shaken out and the sail hoisted again.

"Any chance of a drink ?" he says hopefully as the dark sky recedes, heading towards Antigua.

I start to go down below looking ahead as I do so. I pause. "Do you think that that is another squall coming?" I ask pointing northwards.

"You'll have time to put the kettle on."

I do and am soon back on deck winding in reefs again.. Too much sail area in the strong winds that accompany the squalls and Martin (or George) would not be able to control *Brandamajo*.

"We could always turn back?" say I, stretching my aching arms, rain dripping off my hood and pictures of unseen reefs we will have to navigate when we reach the island, in my head. I glance at the skipper as I ask the question, half hoping that he will suggest that we turn back, he is biting his fingernails, a sure sign of non relaxation!

"We could," he says , but lets get a bit closer first, the weather might clear up yet. The spells between the squalls are getting shorter, so we don't bother shaking out the reefs, and the weather at the moment shows no sign of clearing.

"Are we there yet?" A voice pipes up from down below, the children have awoken and are getting up, I think that they will be on deck soon, it is far too bumpy for them to stay down below for very long. I am at least drugged up, the buff coloured scopaderm patch securely behind my ear, dispensing its life saving anti nausea drug through my skin.

"No, not yet……….and DON'T forget to clip on," Brinsley is climbing out into the cockpit, the end of his safety harness in hand.

"Sorry Mum, I forgot."

"Well don't forget." Adds the skipper.

The sun temporarily comes out, giving us a respite from the wind and rain. We still cannot see Barbuda though we are only a few miles away, but the clouds above it have a turquoise colour, so we know that we must be near, as the turquoise of the clouds will be the reflection from the shallow waters. I read this in a book and am fascinated by the phenomenon.

"Boys look at these clouds!"

"Mu-um, clouds are clouds!"

"Yes but these are green clouds."

The boys look up, "Where?"

"Over there!" I point ahead of us where the clouds have a definite turquoise colour on their undersides.

"Oh yes." They return to their books and their toys. I suppose it is no different from the clouds back home reflecting the orange of the sodium street lamps, but somehow I feel it is.

Then another squall hides it all again. We slow down waiting for another gap in the weather, according to the GPS we are getting close to Barbuda and are now sailing under jib alone.

"Listen to that," says the skipper. Ahead of us there is a thundering and crashing of waves breaking. We cannot see them, the rain is coming down too hard, but they sound ominously near. They must be on one of the reefs surrounding the island. Thank goodness for GPS, if it wasn't for that I think that we would be on our way back by now.

"Are we going to get wrecked?" asks David, peering through the rain to where the sound of breaking waves is getting louder.

"I hope not."

We slow down and look at the sky we cannot attempt to get into the shelter past the reefs whilst the weather is still like this.

"There is some blue sky over there." David points.

"And it's coming this way."

Then as quickly as it started, the squall passes and we have blue sky and sunshine.

"Let's go then," says the skipper. "Let's get that engine started, just in case."

"Land, I can see land." Without the rain we can see very clearly now a long strip of flat land, and all along the edge there are breakers roaring at the reefs. It is time to make a dash for it. We ride the waves in, almost surfing, they are fairly big now that the water has shallowed out. We follow a gap through the reef and as soon as we are behind the shelter of the reef the water flattens out. What a difference to the maelstrom outside, all of a sudden the sun is shining and this eyeball navigation lark seems feasible.

I am standing on the bow, looking for the tell tale dark patches that are little reefs.

If we keep over the pale turquoise water we know that we are over sand and even if we do touch the bottom, it will not do any harm. The lighter and less blue the water, the shallower it is.

"Couple of degrees to port!" I shout, reinforcing my verbal with a hand signal.

"Port again!......... starboard!.........OK now a straight line ahead."

185

It is not long before we are at anchor off Spanish point, in turquoise waters and a peace, broken only by the big wave thundering on the reefs. The eyeball navigation was surprisingly easy, but not something that you would want to attempt if the sun was too low on the horizon, or the sky was too overcast.

Not a soul here except for us, no other yachts, no other people, and not even any houses in sight.

Blissful. The oilskins are hanging up, the sound of the waves thundering on the reefs is no longer threatening and even the rush of squalls seems to have receded.

(Although there are apparently two very exclusive resorts here, one of which Princess Diana used to come to get away from it all, I don't however think that we will be patronising them)

Barbuda is politically part of Antigua but has virtually no tourists and due to the difficulty in navigation is also off the beaten track for most yachties, there are fantastic beaches and unfortunately some of the sand is shipped off these beaches to boost the touristy beaches in Antigua. But to us this isolated island is a kind of heaven.

"Can we swim?" the anchor is hardly down, and the boys are already in trunks waiting for one of us to say yes.

"Go on in you go then."

"Mum, when can I get my toe wet?" this from John.

"As soon as it has completely healed up." I say, hauling the dinghy over the side, making sure that I don't drop the painter as I do so, it is still windy and the rubber dinghy would be off like a rocket if I let go.

Ashore, the place is deserted, only occasionally a feral donkey, peers at us through the scrub, before galloping off when we get too close. We wander through the scrub and sit on the windward shore watching the waves break before heading back to the dinghy to go and do some snorkelling.

In the dinghy, heading towards one of the reefs to do some snorkelling. "Oh ----"

"Da-ad, you shouldn't swear."

"I've just dropped my mask in the water."

So the skipper (with my mask and snorkel) and Brinsley jump in and start swimming looking for the fallen mask, whilst we try and retrace our steps in the dinghy . Not an easy thing to do as it is difficult to remember exactly which patch of water we came over.

"Anybody found it yet?"

We lean over the side of the dinghy trying to search the bottom through the ripples on the surface.

"What are you doing over there?"

Brinsley is heading back fast towards us in the dinghy.

"Mum, I need to get back into the dinghy."

"Why?"

"There's a big fish out there" says Brinsley

"Don't be a wimp," says David, who is sitting with me and John in the dinghy trying to keep stationary whilst they search, "Fish don't hurt you."

We have given up trying to search from the dinghy and are trying to keep it still so that Martin and Brinsley have a point from which to search.

"Well I'm coming anyway." He hauls himself over the edge and flops seal like into the bottom of the boat.

He keeps quiet about the fish, it is soon forgotten in the search for the missing mask.

"I've found it!" comes Martin's triumphant shout, holding the lost mask in his hand. What a relief, we can carry on snorkelling.

The underground world is almost as good here as it was on Tobago Cays. Huge brain corals and some bright yellow fire corals, and then as we are drifting silently along an evil looking barracuda appears.

'They can't really hurt you' we had been told.

But when one of these fish swim towards you, sharp teeth and an evil glint in their eye, and under water things look at least a third bigger than they are in real life, then you don't feel like staying to test the theory of whether they will bite.

They have black spots down their sides and are streamlined for a very fast attack on their prey.

Swim towards them and they carry on coming. Stop swimming and they carry on coming. Start swimming away from them and they carry on coming. I don't test the first two options for very long, I am too busy swimming hell for leather towards the rubber dinghy. The feel of the rubber dinghy is a very welcome comforting feel. The boys have already hauled themselves out of the water.

"Is it still there Mum?" the boys ask full of shrieks and giggles.

"Is what still there?" I ask nonchalantly, I can afford to be nonchalant now that I am holding onto the dinghy.

"That big barracuda."

"What big barracuda, I didn't see anything, only a few innocent looking fish." I don't let go of the dinghy and put my face under the water, and there sure enough there are two of them slowly but surely coming towards us, getting closer and closer.

"Out the way boys, I'm coming out!" I shout, hauling myself into the dinghy.

"Ha, ha, ha, ha,....where's the little fish now then?" ask the boys.

"It's grown and there are two of them." I answer.

The skipper meanwhile has slowly but unobtrusively also got back into the rubber dinghy"

"Wimps!" he says watching the fuss we are all making. . Not until we are out of the water does the big fish turn and swim away. Maybe I won't swim back to the boat after all.

"Mum, that was what I saw when we were searching for Dad's mask!" says Brinsley.

I grin, "Well no wonder you were so keen to get back on board then."

Then we see a large stingray lazing around at the bottom of the anchor chain. I decide against going down to investigate it.

The following day, once the sun is high enough, we 'eyeball' our way out. Weaving our way between the dark coloured bits of coral actually seems quite easy now. We sail under Genoa alone along the island, and anchor off an eleven mile Jessica beach. (sandy, palm trees, no buildings, no people) There is nobody here except one other yacht, along the whole of this eleven miles of beach. This long stretch of sand glows dark pink at the waters edge, where fragments of bright red shells have gathered. There is a group of palm trees half way along the beach and a deserted ruined building. We drop anchor, and rock gently to sleep on a gentle swell.

It is the tenth of April and Brinsley's birthday. Five a.m.

"Squeak, look at all these balloons, " rustle, rustle, I will myself to stay asleep and hope that Brin will sit quietly. Vain hope.

"Can I open my presents now?"

I open one eye, Martin moans and rolls over. "Can we wait just a little longer, it's only five o'clock."

"OK then." He disappears back to his cabin.

Seven a.m. "Mum, can Brin open his presents now?" John and Brin are both up. David is heading towards teenagehood and is not rushing out of bed.

"Yes, go on then. Happy Birthday, Brin." We duck our heads back under the sheet, pretending that we don't have to wake up yet.

"Happy Birthday to me, Happy birthday to me." He is squeaking and excited (Brin often squeaks when he is particularly excited about something)

"We don't have to do school work today do we?"

"No, not at all, you don't even have to think about it." Even for me it is nice not to even have to try and fit school work in.

"Oh wow!" Brinsley has opened a very sharp multitool knife, and is immediately pulling each tool out and examining it.

By now we are up. "Careful, Brin. Remember that you are not to use the knife blades unless we are supervising you," says his dad. I nod vigorously behind him.

We take the dinghy ashore and carry it up the beach. The other side o f beach is an enormous emerald green lagoon, the other side of which is the islands only town, Codrington.

"I've got my knife with me, just in case we need it," says Brinsley holding up his tee-shirt so that we can see where it is on his belt.

"Are you ready to jump in boys?" asks the skipper holding the dinghy steady against the small wave, which are lapping against the boat.

We all jump in and get very wet as we set off in search of the Frigate bird colony,(or is it called a rookery?) that we know is here.

It is quite windy and the waves lap and spray us as our little dinghy with its 3.3hp outboard pushes us along.

"I think it's over there," I say pointing to where I can see some frigate birds wheeling.

"No I thought it was meant to be over there?" says the skipper pointing in a totally different direction. "I don't suppose you brought that book with you?"

"No. Did you?"

"No"

After a detour round the lake we find the colony. There are hundreds of the large pterodactyl like birds flying around, long bent thin wings and long beaks slightly hooked at the ends. When they are not flying they are perching on the dead branches and the mangrove trees, or feeding by now very large chicks, some of them still in their white fluffy down. It is an impressive sight. They seem to take no notice of us as we motor under the mangrove bushes to see them.

White egrets roost with them looking elegant in comparison.

"Can we go and get something to eat now?" asks Brinsley.

We are all ready to move on, our little outboard has already used three tanks of fuel to get to this far end of the lagoon and we will now head towards Codrington. It is one of the few times that a larger dinghy might be beneficial.

In Codrington, a small town geared only towards the locals who live there, we have virgin pina coladas for the boys and not so virgin one for us. Little boats come in and unload box after box of lobsters onto a lorry, until the lorry is full. They are apparently all going to be flown to Guadeloupe. Lobsters with eggs on are replaced in cages to be taken back out to the reefs, as they are not allowed to sell them.

"Shall we buy a lobster for your birthday tea Brin?"

"Oh yes please"

We manage to buy a fairly big one for six dollars, its feelers are broken so it is not perfect enough for the French market, and we put it in a piece of sacking which the boys trail over the edge of the dinghy keeping it cool.

Back in the boat 'Lobby' is kept in a bucket, of seawater. "We've got a pet now" says Brin, who is forever persuading us to have a pet. The three boys are squatting around the bucket looking at Lobby, who in turn is waving his broken feelers at the boys. The lobsters here are not like the lobsters at home, they are spiny lobsters and don't have the huge vicious claws that our temperate lobsters have.

"Do you mind eating your pet?" we ask.

"I suppose I'd better not get to know him too well," comes the reply.

We barbecue Lobby and some sausages on the beach that night.

"Brin, can I borrow your new knife?" The skipper is thinking of a way to cut up Lobby.

"Here you are, Dad." Brin eagerly unattaches it from his belt and hands it to his father.

"Ouch!"

"What have you done Dad?" The boys cluster around their father who is clutching a bleeding finger."

"I've cut my finger!"

"Da-ad, and what were you telling me to be?"

""I don't know Brinsley what was I telling you to be?"

Very careful Dad, the blades are very sharp!"

We eat as the sun sets and the most voracious mosquitoes we have met so far come and attach them selves to our ankles, legs, arms and any bit of flesh they can find. They are not very quick though so it is not too difficult to squash them as they land, or more realistically after they have had a good sup of blood. It is the mosquitoes that finally chase us back to the boat where we eat chocolate bread that we had made for Brinsley's Birthday, It is not very nice, I think that the fish will get quite a lot of it.

Brinsley's diary for his birthday reads *Today was the 10th of April MY BIRTHDAY, so I woke up and opened all my present and I got a kite a sticker making book some shorts a T-shirt and a leatherman knife which is a pen-knife with five screw-drivers a saw some scissors a serrated blade a file a nail file a can opener a knife and some pliers then we went to the frigate bird colony and we saw frigate birds 6 feet away we then went to town and had a pina colada. Then went back to have a BBQ on the beach with a lobster we had bought.*

(And I thought we were beginning to master this punctuation!)

Well we have had a fantastic time here on Barbuda but must return to Antigua as our next visitors, Judith and her nine year old son Sammy are joining us for a week.

Judith is a clinical psychologist, full of enthusiasm and joie de vivre. When I meet her, she has had her dark glossy her hair cut Cleopatra style. Sammy, with the big brown eyes and luscious hair of his mother is always full of high spirits and I have had to read the riot act to our children to ensure that they make him duly welcome aboard. They are quite capable of being a bit of a gang. The skipper reads the riot act to Sammy and assures him that any misbehaviour will result in him getting thrown off the good ship *Brandamajo*.

"I'll be good, I promise," says Sammy, "I won't touch anything. He regards the instrument panel from a distance.

I'm not sure if our guests really know what they are letting themselves in for, they are the only non boaty people we have had to visit, but I have done my best to warn them what life aboard a yacht will be like and they still decided to brave a visit.

"It's quite cramped on board." I had said, "And you may well get seasick. Are you still sure that you want to come?"

"Our flights are booked. We're game."

The weather is not conducive to a gentle breaking in to yacht life and Judith's vision of sipping gin on a yacht is rudely smashed as we introduce them to sailing at the deep end. The trade winds are very strong and the seas are building but we set sail for Nevis anyway, we are going to spend enough time in Antigua with Race Week coming up as it is and would like to explore some of the other islands nearby.

As soon as we are out of the shelter of Antigua, Judith begins to lose some of her ebullience, slowly turns a pale shade of green and lies motionless in the cockpit, despite the scopaderm patches. It is raining so that she has a slightly bedraggled look about her. Sammy fishes with the boys for a while before deciding that he is also not feeling too well, his mother cannot do more than give him a sickly grin of sympathy.

I lay an oilskin over Judith (we are in a squall) offer her a cup of tea, which makes her even greener and unsympathetically tell her that there is an airport on Nevis! Perhaps I am feeling too cocky that it is not me in this predicament as it usually is.

We anchor off a perfect Jessica beach with the mountain rising in the background and swim ashore to play, luckily our visitors have regained their sense of wellbeing. We spend a day here on Nevis, there are pelicans drying their wings, balanced on the edges of wooden boats at anchor. Apart from the beach there is not a lot ashore, then sail to St Kitts, the neighbouring island.

St Kitts and Nevis are one political internally governed federation and the smallest nation in the Western hemisphere. It was also the home of the first British colony in the West Indies.

For the short trip between the two islands there is a strong thirty knot wind blowing, and after broaching (when the boat is over powered and control is momentarily lost so she slews round into the wind) under our Genoa alone we decide that we had better reef the Genoa down a little! Or even change down to the smaller sail.

There is a marina here in St Kitts but it has been badly damaged by the hurricane and has few facilities. The wind is blowing so strongly that the skipper is very apprehensive about manoeuvring *Brandamajo* in the small spaces. I would like a bow thruster, it would make life so much easier. (a bow thruster is a small propeller set sideways in the bow of the boat thus increasing the manoeuvrability of the boat. Without one the wind catches on the sides of her and at slow speeds can push her round.)

Charlestown Harbour, Charlestown harbour, Charlestown Harbour, this is sailing vessel *Brandamajo, Brandamajo* over."

We are doing our usual call up of any harbour where we are planning to come into a marina. There is not an immediate response so we try again. We can see the harbour wall and the forest of thin sticks that are yacht masts projecting over the top of it.

"Charlestown harbour, Charlestown Harbour, Charlestown Harbour, this is sailing vessel *Brandamajo, Brandamajo*, over."

"Station calling Charlestown, this is Charlestown Harbour, how can I help you?"

"We would like a berth in the marina if at all possible, and due to the strong winds we will have difficulty with our steerage so we would appreciate one facing into the wind if that is possible, please."

"No Problem." He proceeds to give us some directions to where we should berth.

I go up on deck and relay my conversation to the skipper. He is dubious. "That is going to be very tricky, in this wind. The wind is still blowing between 25 and 30 knots.

"*Brandamajo, Brandamajo*, this is *Pelagic, Pelagic* over." Another yacht is calling us, we are now in sight of the harbour wall.

"*Pelagic, Brandamajo*." I answer his call.

"*Brandamajo*, I was listening to your conversation with the harbour master, I think that you will find it difficult to get in where he is telling you, it is still very windy in here but there is a space next to us I suggest that you come in there, we will give you a hand."

"Thankyou very much *Pelagic*, *Brandamajo* standing by."

We drop the sail and motor carefully round the harbour wall. Much of the marina has been ripped apart by the last hurricane and there are empty posts and torn planks in places where it has not yet been repaired.

The skipper looks briefly at the space we were initially asked to go "I can't possibly get in there, don't these people know anything about wind?!" he says so we go next to the yacht called Pelagic and manage to tie up with remarkably little banging. Once tied up, with all our warps secure we can sit and silently laugh over our beers and gin and tonics at a charter boat banging from post to post as the wind blows him to and from over on the other side., and that is where we were going to go... but there is plenty of room both sides of this tiny little man made harbour.(No us yachties are not always nice people!)

"Mu-um I've dropped my shoe in!" This is from Sammy.

"I'll get the boat hook," says Brin unclipping the boat hook from its place on deck and leaning over to try and scoop up Sammy's sandal with it..

"How do you possibly expect me to get down from there!" says Judith in horror, looking at the steep step she has to get down from the bow to the jetty. Getting off the boat in many of these marinas entails squeezing the gap in the pulpit (railings around the bow) or climbing over them and often dropping some way onto the pontoon. Judith has a bad back, from an old injury

St Eustatious or more commonly known as Statia is our next visit, it is a Dutch island, and used to be an important Caribbean trading post, due to lack of duty. As with many of the other islands it has a volcano, and as we are making it a family hobby to climb volcanoes up we go. It is a hot dry day and the shade of the trees is very welcome.

"Go on, you go on, I'll meet you on the way down," says Judith who has yet to get used to the heat.

"Are you sure?" I say not wanting to abandon her.

"Of course, I might even enjoy the solitude." she answers. We carry on walking and finally reach the crater rim. It is an old volcano and looking down into the crater we are looking down on top of lush forest.. We haven't got time to explore down in the crater. "let's go up here?" says the skipper pointing up a steep path. So we scramble up, holding onto trees in some places to pull us up a particularly steep part.

"Careful here" calls the skipper looking back. I am bringing up the rear with the four boys(we have Sammy with us). But we make it to the top of this part of the crater and manage to scramble back down.

"Stop mucking around, I don't want any broken limbs!" I shout watching the boys try to swing down the slope on the tree branches, sliding on the shale between them. This is more or less what we have to do, only I was hoping that they would treat the descent with a bit more circumspection.

"Hello Judith!" she has made it to the first bit of crater rim and is very pleased with herself.

Beautiful black and yellow butterflies drink from a stream and a long snake crosses our path as we wend our way back down the slope, just in time to get thoroughly drenched by one of those sudden heavy rainstorms with which we are becoming so familiar.

Due to its duty free status we are going to stock up on beer here in readiness for the sailing club crowd who are coming out for Race Week, so we load our dinghy full of cases of bottles of Dutch beer, and return back to the yacht.

The anchorage is very rolly; we watch her mast sway from side to side as we come alongside, and then have the task of unloading all these bottles of beer and stowing them.

We get the children into a working chain, one person in the dinghy unloading the bottles from their cardboard cases (Don't want any cockroaches aboard), then they are passed along until they reach the cabin where I am stowing them. Unfortunately I cannot stow them at the same rate as they are arriving.

Crash! "Quick catch that bottle, Oh no there goes another one."
As the boat rolls bottles of beer start rolling across the table, across the floor and Judith and I catch one, only for another one to appear from

where it has been put waiting for me to find a suitable stowage place for it.

"Where shall I put them?"

"I don't know, wedge them behind the cushions, anywhere where they won't roll."

The bottles are wedged everywhere and anywhere and then stowed wherever we can find places for them. We have bottles of beer in food lockers, with the towels, with the saucepans, in fact anywhere that one might fit and not roll around, it is put.

We do a night sail back to Antigua, it is just a little too far to sail during the day, calm sailing, in fact so calm that for much of the night we have to motor.

It is about midnight, the moon had not risen yet so it is extremely dark. The children and the skipper are asleep, Judith is just deciding if she can sleep and I am on watch.

All of a sudden a bright light passes across the cockpit, like the headlights of a passing car, except that we are at sea and there are no cars, or even boats in sight. Am I hallucinating?

The next thing I know is that a large silent fishing type boat is almost alongside us and the bright light is shining at me almost blinding me, then she pulls away as silently as she came and disappears. She has no navigation lights and as soon as the spot light is switched off I can't see her.

My adrenaline is pumping but we are obviously not what they were looking for.....Drugs, maybe?

"Are you all right up there?" Judith asks sleepily.

"I am now," I reply . She comes up to join me for a while as we sail past Nevis which seems to be in the grip of a large forest fire, and then watch the full moon rise, red and glowing, to give us light for the rest of the night. It is beautiful and a gentle breeze blows us back to Antigua.

Back in Antigua Judith and Sammy leave us, I think they have enjoyed themselves? They will certainly have a few stories to take back home.

It is Easter day and Classic Race week. Antigua is filled with old and beautiful elegant yachts, what is it that often makes old things look beautiful?

196

"Shall we go out and sail with them?" asks the skipper.

"I suppose so," I say not too enthusiastically as it is somewhat windy and I am not drugged up with Scopaderm.

It is windy, but the yachts are quite beautiful and apart from the RIBs (rigid inflatable boats) and helicopters flying overhead it could be a scene from a hundred years ago.

"There's *Endeavour*, Mum. Don't you think that she is the most beautiful yacht afloat?" says David.

Come on let's go about so that we can catch her as she comes by on the next leg," says Martin.

She is indeed graceful and racing along at such a speed that we can't even think to keep up with her.

The boys and skipper ooh and aah at Endeavour and the other yachts, and finally wet, windblown and beginning to feel distinctly queasy, we head back into English Harbour and drop our anchor.

Antigua is beginning to fill up for race week and finding a spot to anchor without swinging and crashing into another boat is not easy.

It is mine and David's birthdays. David has also been given a knife and seventeen year old Paul from *shilling* has made a cake for him which is delivered in all its glory. Martin has arranged for me to go for a ride. The lady who owns the place comes and picks me up in a rusty white pickup truck.

She is very English and very horsey, but has been on the island for some years now. Her face is weather-beaten and aged by the Caribbean sun and wind.

"I'm afraid there was a disaster last night." She says

"Oh no what happened?" I say hoping that I am not putting her out too much.

"A stallion belonging to a local Rastafarian escaped and got into our land . He killed one of my prize mares. I was hoping to sell her soon."

"I'm so sorry" I say. Not knowing what else I can say.

"Also, I don't know if your husband told you but the farrier has decided to leave the island and we haven't got another one, so none of the horses are shod." Antigua and being horsey does have its limitations! Riding as a leisure pursuit here has not really taken off yet. I am given a little bay pony which I ride bareback down to the beach, where we swim., The beach is small and today the sky is overcast and the waves choppy, but the gallant little pony several times gallops and jumps over the surf into the sea, until finally we are bored of that game and take him back to the stable, anywhere else to ride is too stony for his unshod feet, but for me it is nice to be back on horseback after so long away.(bearing in mind that I was riding almost every day before we left)

Back on the boat the boys hand me their presents.

"Go on Mum, open them, open them now!" they are excited and full of pride at what they have managed to do with no prompting from their parents "We bought them ourselves. I hope you like them, but there are not many shops here."

In fact the only shop within easy distance for the boys is a drinks shop, so they have bought a bottle of wine, a mini bottle of champagne and a bar of chocolate.

"How on earth did you manage to buy the alcohol?" I ask. By no stretch of the imagination could any of the three pass for over eighteen. (unless you add their ages together)

"We just told them it was for your birthday," says Brin.

I am truly emotional, maybe our children are growing up.

"Ahoy there!" I look up at the voice, I am just finishing of cleaning the boat and we are moored to the stone harbour wall in English Harbour in Antigua.

"Matt! Kate! glad you managed to find us, Luckily your cabin is ready." John has moved out as he has the other big double cabin, so he is always the first to move out.

"Hiya Mate," the skipper appears from up forward, we can stop doing chores now our next lot of visitors have arrived. Matt and Kate are with us now, for Antigua sailing week and then a holiday beyond. A lot of the excess living baggage from our home, such as the canoe, windsurfer, bimini etc, etc., are put into storage above the customs shed in Antigua for the week we are racing.. "Got to make her a bit lighter" says the skipper.

The first day of racing and the others have not yet arrived so we will do this race by ourselves.

"We must get out there early to get some tacking practice in," says the skipper.

We cower (well I do anyway, Matt gives as good as he gets having crewed for Martin in the laser two dinghy and being just as competent a sailor)

We start and if you have time to look at the sight it is lovely, perhaps not quite so dramatic as 250 yachts starting the ARC, but not far off it.

"That was a s---- start!" says the skipper,(well that's not EXACTLY what he said) and it wasn't a very good start, but we don't do that badly.

"I think I understand why you don't like racing with him!" says Kate

And so the week goes on, Josh, John, and Matt B. join us for the rest of the week, and set about racing our home, lads from the sailing club, to do some 'home' racing, and get a small sample of our year. Kate and I can be boat bimbos for the week, Kate looking like a model in her leopard skin bikini, bought especially for her Caribbean holiday and me some fifteen years older keeping to a more demure swimming costume.

"Ready about!.....Lee oh!" and the angle of the boat goes through at least forty five degrees as the men rush around hauling ropes and Kate and I slither in an ungainly fashion across to the other side of the yacht, carefully avoiding swinging booms, rushing ropes and lethal sails. The boys if they are on deck are helping to haul ropes as well.

Peace reigns for a while do we can sit on the rail with our legs hanging over, watching as other yachts loom frighteningly close to us, particularly at the starts. And of course keeping everybody supplied with drinks and snacks.

"It's very hot..........I could do with a drink....... Watch your legs, aren't they going pink?!" and so on.

"Where's my pencil?!" The skipper and Josh are planning today's tactics to see if we can't do a little better.

"Here use mine Dad."

Thankyou, but where IS the chart table pencil?"

"Probably on the floor."

Matt B. is recovering from his hangover, having met an old skipper friend of his(Matt B used to crew aboard a yacht over here so he is enjoying bringing back old memories) and had a good few rum punches. "Mum is Matthew not feeling very well" the boys only half tiptoe around his pale looking morning face.

"I think we should go about now, there is a rock dead ahead of us."

"Ready about......Lee oh!" Kate and I hardly have time to slither across. We have to slide across the cabin top, avoiding the boom coming across, that would knock us out and also into the sea, and avoid any ropes that might be flying. We crouch half way waiting for the sail to be set so that we can resume our positions on the 'up' side again until the next time we have to go about.

"Come on Matt run that jib round." Matt B. shows us how the professional crew do it and gets hold of the bottom of the Genoa and runs around the foredeck to get us about as quickly as possible, without losing any speed.

"GRIND that winch!"

"PULL that sheet !"

"Do we need some kicker?"

The dinghy sailors have been trying to get every inch of speed out of *Brandamajo*, they are probably among the best group of sailors here, just that the other boats won't be laden down with the paraphernalia for a family of five liveaboards.

"Yacht on your port side!"

"Yes I see it thankyou."

"There's the finish boat, get the numbers of the boats in front of us and behind us!"

And so the week goes by. We are in a different harbour each of the first three nights, where parties go on until the small hours and the locals set up stalls and sell every kind of food. Antigua race week is probably the biggest festival and biggest money spinner during the Island year.

Last day, we are not winning, but everybody is enjoying themselves, the skipper has relaxed enough to launch into some Gilbert and Sullivan and the wind has decided to disappear.

"I am the captain of the *Brandamajo*-o"

"And a fine good captain too-o"

John Chapman and Josh are flying back tonight so sods law decrees that we be becalmed for the latter part of today's racing. We drink beer and bite fingernails and wonder if we'll have to retire and motor in order that they may catch their flight. We don't, though Sod throws in another aid in that the outboard dinghy decides not to function properly.

So for six days, with one day off in the middle we race our home and eat drink and be merry in the evenings and then it is over.

Antigua is rapidly clearing as yachts make their way north or south to be out of the way of any potential hurricanes during the hurricane season.

"Well boys shall we take Matt and Kate up to Barbuda?"

"Yes please, do you think that we will see any more barracudas?"

So we take Matt and Kate up to see one of our favourite islands, second time around it is much easier, helped by the weather being much more clement, and we catch a small tuna fish on the way up.

This time nobody can be bothered to blow up the dinghy so having anchored we put our clothes an black bin bags and tow them behind us, hopefully keeping them dry.

Carl in the ubiquitous wooden boat meets us in the lagoon (we have pre-arranged this) and takes us to see the Frigate birds. We get there twice,...no four times as quickly as our little rubber dinghy had, it does help that he knows where he is going. And he has a 70 horsepower outboard on the back.

"Mum why can't we have at least a ten horse power outboard on our dinghy? Ours is FAR too small."

"Would you like a lobster?" asks Carl.

""That would be lovely," we say.

"I'll take a look at one of my pots."

We motor over closer to the shore, and all of a sudden, Carl stops the boat, sticks a boat hook in the water and comes up with a lobster pot. No buoy or any marker to tell us where it is, and the lagoon is not small.

The lobster pot is crawling with lobsters, about thirty at a rough guess.

He looks at them, "Some of these are too small, but how many would you like?"

We don't quite know what to say, not expecting there to be more than one or two lobsters.

He ends up giving us about ten, and throwing the small ones back in. "

"I'll cook them for you if you like?" he says , "while you go for a walk."

We watch two small boys trying to make reluctant donkeys swim, and then return to the boat for lobster. But even all seven of us cannot eat all the lobster that has been provided. Never mind we can always have lobster for lunch tomorrow.

Matt and Kate return to the grey skies of Manchester, we will miss them, but they have to return to work and we must move on. And after all the visitors we have been having lately it is nice to have the boat back to ourselves for a while. The generator is broken again. We must waste precious time waiting here for a new cylinder head gasket for it, when we should be heading north before the hurricanes. Antigua is now almost totally empty, and we feel like migrating birds who have somehow missed the flock.

"Mum, ple-ease can we go to Montserrat?" David has been pestering us to go ever since we first saw the plume of smoke rising from its volcano.

I look at the skipper. "What do you think, we have got to wait a few days for the generator part?"

He ponders for a while, considering the wind direction. He is not very keen on getting the boat covered in ash.

"Go on then, let's go."

Some days volcano warnings are given out depending on how much ash is being spewed forth and how volatile the volcano may be on that day.

Montserrat is still a British dependency and until the Soufriere volcano erupted in 1995 was unspoiled, lush and green, and little known about. In 1997 the volcano erupted even more violently and since then the island has been divided into various exclusion zones thus keeping people out, depending of course on the mood of the volcano.

David has been pestering us to go to ever since we first saw the plume of smoke rising from its volcano. Two of David's wishes are to see a tornado, and to see lava flowing.

"Cool Mum,!" says David as we get closer and the volcano belches letting forth a huge cloud of black steam and smoke. Luckily the wind is blowing the ash away from us so that hopefully the boat will not get covered in ash.

The brown rivers of ash are very clear against the green of the hillsides. I hope it doesn't explode whilst we are anchored beneath it.

It is flat calm so we are motor sailing. "Good day for school work today boys?" I say, donning my teacher's guise.

"But MU-um." Their automatic response comes at the same time as they sit down around the table to accept the inevitable.

"Will my writing be good enough for Mrs Barrington?" asks John, concentrating on his handwriting at the moment, and sticking his diary under my nose. I hold it away a bit so that I can see it.

"Well you know John, when you are in Mrs Barrington's class, you will have to do real work," says David full of the superiority of one who has been there.

Mrs Barrington is the class one teacher in Great Budworth School, and little does she know how much her influence has been with us this year.

"But Mu-um, Mrs Barrington SAYS ...." an all too common refrain when my method of teaching is not approved of by the pupils!

Drop anchor beneath the cliffs at the opposite end of the island to the volcano. It is hot and the water is very inviting. By the time we have finished anchoring we are dripping in sweat.

Brinsley is in first. He is out pretty quickly. "Ow!"

John is in next and swims a bit further, "Ow something is stinging me."

David, Martin and I follow. "Ow, ow, ow," we are all pretty quick in getting out of the water. The water is stinging.

"What is it?"

"Look ! I can see all those little black and white jellyfish. Lots of them!"

We peer into the water and sure enough the culprits of the stings are drifting innocently around. We decide against swimming any further.

Ashore, there are no tourists, but we find a Montserratian who is willing to take us into Plymouth, the capital that a few years ago was completely destroyed by the volcano.

"Do you really want to go there?" he asks. "Yes please" answers David, "Will we see lava flows?"

"No, we just have ash flows here, there is nothing in Plymouth, and we may not be allowed there."

We drive slowly through the island its lush greenness belying the devastation at the other end. "The English government keep sending us money, and what is it used for? ......building new government buildings, with flat roofs so that the rain collects and they have to rebuild them, with more of the aid that comes here," says our guide as we drive past the government buildings.

"Would you like to be an independent island?" we ask.

He ponders for a moment before answering, pointing out houses where British people we should know about have lived.

"We would nave no money if that was the case, at the moment the only money that we have comes from your government. And then that Robin Cook came here did a lot of talking but nothing seems to have happened, we are still all living in temporary houses that were put up after the eruption."

We arrive at Plymouth, luckily today the volcano is not on red alert, so we should be OK. We pass through various barriers on the way, but they are all open.

Our guide is not going to come out of the car and walk with us, his house was buried here, and he cannot understand why we want to go and explore, the place holds too much fear and bad memories for him.

The place is quite eerie, the trees are all dead, the buildings are covered and filled with ash, some of them up to their roofs and there is no sign of life at all, no footprints, no birdsong, not even any cats or dogs.

Towards the edge of the ash flow though grass is beginning to recolonise, spreading its way over the grey ash.

Behind the ghost town, the volcano is emitting a steady stream of smoke. The whole thing is quite moving.

"Mum, look at my feet!"

I look, and not only at John's feet but all of us are now covered in a fine film of grey ash, which we have kicked up as we walk along.

"At least I can write about a real volcano I have seen," says David, who is doing a project on volcanoes. He seems to have accepted that he is not going to see flowing lava.

"I'm hungry ," says Brin, as we head through the ashen ruins back to the faithful minibus waiting for us. His scrawny body obviously doesn't have much storage space for spare food. "What's for lunch?"

"I don't know Brin," I say, not even thinking about lunch yet.

We drive back passed more deserted houses from which people were evacuated, but which have just escaped the bulk of the pyroclastic flows of hot ash that still regularly disrupt this little remnant of the British empire.

Back at the boat the jellyfish have gone. "Da-ad, will you tow us on the surfboard?"

The sailboards that we brought with us for the children to use has been used as a swimming platform, it being almost continually too windy for beginners to even think about windsurfing.

"OK"

"Me first...."

"No, me."

"Can I go first Dad, ple-ease!"

And so the skipper does some dad duties and the children, either singly or individually sit on the surf board whilst he tows them in the rubber dinghy, round the boat. One of them invariably falls off as he turns too sharp a corner, but that is half the fun of it.

Back at Antigua, the cylinder head gasket has still not arrived(apparently it has not even left the U.K.) and after a couple of days we can wait no longer, our insurance company decrees that we be further North than 35 degrees by the first of July, and at this rate it will be a lot of hard sailing.

We will sail overnight to St Maarten.

It is a full moon, there are gentle following winds and so we run goose-winged, (jib out one side and mainsail out the other side, like a goose) there are no big waves, no water over the deck and no throwing up....actually enjoyable even glorious sailing!

St Martin is split into two halves, the French side, St. Martin and the Dutch side Saint Maarten, we drop anchor in the Dutch side, at the town of Philipsburg. We are here purely to stock up with provisions to keep us going until we reach the States.

This island is Duty free, and we do some serious shopping, shoes, shorts and swimming costume.

"Mum, guess what?"

"No what?" I say, trying to choose between a blue swimming costume with flowers on it and a bright gold and yellow one.

"Listen, I know you're not listening, you've got that 'I'm not listening face' on."

I put down the swimming costumes. "We've found Pokemon cards, REAL Pokemon cards, can we have some please?"

Sure enough in the shoe shop (I'm sure they don't sell Pokemon cards in shoe shops back home) there are Pokemon cards for sale. I think of all those lovely drawings the boys have been doing and can see that the end of their home made Pokemon cards is looming as we get closer to America.

"All right, I'll buy you one pack each, after that you each have to buy your own.

"Thanks Mum!" they go shrieking up the street ahead of me.

The following day, Brinsley goes with his Dad to look for engine parts, and the other two and I do a mammoth shop at a supermarket that promises to deliver.

"You do deliver, don't you?" I check with my two trolley loads at the check out.

"Of course, no problem, just wait outside and we will load your things into a van.

So surrounded by shopping we wait. And wait. And wait a bit longer. The heat is almost oppressive, as we are sheltered from whatever breeze there may be.

"Don't you think that you had better go and see if they have remembered?" asks David.

So I do. "He is just coming." They say. I must try to remember that this is still the Caribbean. However a van duly arrives, but one of the front tyres is flapping and clinking with flatness as it pulls up.

"You have a flat tyre." I point out to the young driver, surprised that he hadn't noticed it.

"Oh" he says grinning "Would you like to load your shopping into the van and I will go and find someone to change the wheel. " So we set about loading the stuff into the van, it is hot and sweaty but the boys have found Mars Bars ice creams. And then we wait, and wait and wait. We sit leaning against the open door of the transit, all our perishable goods must be perishing inside the metal van by now, or we sit on the concrete pavement. I am beginning to wonder if it would have been easier to get a taxi, but by now we seem to have different people popping out every now and then to look at the flat tyre and then disappear again. I wonder if I should volunteer to change it for them.

It is very hot.

"Shall I just get a taxi?" I ask.

"No, no, you can't possibly do that, we said that we will deliver and we will."

"I decide against asking them 'when?'

It finally transpires that the root of the problem is that it is a Saturday and the person who mends tyres is not here. Of course all the spare wheels and tyre changing equipment is locked away in some shed somewhere. I suspect that delivering shopping to yachts is not all that common, or perhaps we are getting too close to the end of the season.

A salesman is trying to sell windows outside the supermarket and watches all that is going on.

Eventually he says "Come on I'll take you." so the problem is resolved and we pile all our shopping into his tiny jeep and then John climbs and lies on top of the shopping in the back and David and I squash into the front seat. It is quite a relief to get back down to the marina. Where we begin the mammoth task of transferring it all onto the boat.

Provisioned, we are ready for the next sail to Virgin Gorda.

Another overnight sail, but again with a nearly full moon, and we arrive early in the morning to what are known as the 'Baths'. Here huge boulders , and by huge I mean twenty or thirty foot in diameter, lay strewn across the beach. This is charter boat territory and by the time we have been for an explore, the yachts are beginning to arrive in bulk, it is time to go and spend a night on the marina before heading off for the Turks and Caicos.

Here in the British Virgin Islands the American influence is obvious, and even this late in the season there are lots of charter yachts. We are glad that we had not planned to spend any longer here.

We move to the marina to fill up with water and spend a few hours before moving on. "Come on boys let's go and have a shower!" I say. The next leg is going to be about five days.

I walk into the shower room and am hit by a welcoming blast of cold air. Air conditioning! Definitely American holiday country. But it is lovely.

They are the most fantastic showers.(We have seen all sorts in the different islands we have been on.) We all have at least two in the short time we are there, luxuriating in their luxury. We had almost forgotten what air conditioning was like.

"Mum I'm just going to go and stand in the toilets to cool off."

We have a five day sail (or four if we are lucky) to the Turks and Caicos and it will be the longest sail we have done with just us.

Decide on watches of two hours on and two hours off. If you are on watch for four hours at night it seems such a long time. After the first couple of nights I have discovered that the best way to stop yourself falling asleep is to stand up and so then if you fall asleep you will fall over, which of course wakes you up again!

"Quick boys come on up and look at these dolphins!" The skipper is on watch and there are dolphins just to the side of us. All of a sudden one of them will leap up and spin very fast on its vertical axis, (head up) and then flop back into the water. It is as if they are showing off.

"Wow, look at that one!" shouts David as one makes a particularly spectacular spin.

"Pass us the Dolphin book up, please John!" I say. John hasn't yet made it up on deck.

It turns out that there is a species of Dolphin called Spinner Dolphins and after some studying of these lovely animals we decide that they are probably Short Nosed Spinner Dolphins.

"How about the spinnaker?" asks Martin. I had always said that if it was just the two of us sailing, I did not want to use the spinnaker, but we are going slowly and the winds are light. I can feel my resolve wavering.

"Go on then." I give in, we put the spinnaker up, (not that easily, it is a big sail) and the boat speed almost doubles. I take the helm whilst the skipper gets the big yellow and red sail up.

"Mum." This from John.

"Yes."

"What's that thing called when you blink lots of times and then go to sleep?"

"Do you mean forty winks?"

"Yes, that's it. Winking is blinking with one eye, isn't it?"

"Yes."

A few minutes later. "Mum."

"Yes."

"I've just done forty winks and I'm not asleep."

Brinsley and David are playing Pokemon with their newly bought Pokemon cards.

"Charizard is the most valuable you know," says David. "James and Calum haven't even got it and Calum has got two hundred and fifty cards!........Brin you can't do that!"

"Why not?"

"Because it's the rules."

"Who said?"

"James told me." Retorts David.

"Well he didn't. I don't want to play any more."

We listen to many conversations such as this through the day, that is when we are not doing schoolwork.

"Your watch David," The skipper calls down to the boys. Each boy has a watch of one hour during the day, and can come on watch with one of us during the night.

They can helm if they want to, or let George helm. It is during these three hours that we get a lot of schoolwork done as I only have two boys to teach at a time instead of three.

Thunderstorms flicker through the night, and we have to decrease sail as we do not want to arrive at Provodencialis during the night.

We notice a commotion of birds ahead, and as we pass through them.

"Fish! Fish! We've caught a fish!" the sound of the line reeling off the ratchet alerts us to the fact. Martin feels the other line (we have two out).

"We've caught two fish!" he says . Indeed we have. We reel the lines in , both of them jerking and bouncing and discover we have two tuna fish. We let one go, we cannot possibly eat them both especially as the fridge is not working at the moment. Correction the fridge is working but the generator is not, so we cannot afford the power to run the fridge.

"Wow it's huge!" The big fish gives quite a fight as we reel it in, splashing and flashing through he water.

Martin has the tuna on the end of a gaff.

" Will you look at that. Isn't that a lovely fish?"

The fish is quite beautiful. It is a yellowfin tuna, and the fins are a bright luminescent yellow. It must be at least fifty pounds and is about the same size as John.

"Get some Vodka please Brinsley, and can someone pass me the rock hammer?"

So with vodka, to make the fish sleepy and the rock hammer, the tuna is dispatched and admired. It is so big that we will not be able to eat all of it, so we cut two large filets of its back and consign the rest back into the sea, where I am sure that it won't last very long before being eaten by some hungry mouth.

"Guess what we are having for lunch then boys?"

"Tuna."

So we have fresh tuna for lunch, tuna for tea and tomorrow we will have tuna salad for lunch and tuna curry for tea.

By then we are tuna'd out.

Flat seas and warm breezes and the days turn out to be some of the best sailing we have had of the whole trip.

Turks and Caicos.

Eight a.m. We are outside a huge reef that separates us from the harbour.

"Provodencialis, Provodencialis, Provodencialis, this is Yacht *Brandamajo*, Yacht *Brandamajo*, over"

"Yacht calling Provodencialis, this is the harbour master at Provodencialis, over."

"Hello there, this is Yacht *Brandamajo*, we are presently outside the reef and would like an escort in."

"That's no problem, how much do you draw?"

"Six and a half feet?"

"OK, that will be all right, a boat will be out shortly.

We wait. Soon zig zagging through the reef we can see a small motor launch coming out to meet us. He seems to brush over places where it appears that the reef is touching the surface of the water.

He beckons us to follow him.

We do. "You can't possibly follow him there," I say as he goes through the brown seaweed on the surface, it looks convincingly like a shallow reef. But he is still beckoning us.

We progress slowly avoiding the brown reef, and follow his zig zag course through the reef, which n a couple of places has been cut to allow boats to pass through.

I peer closer at the brown reef as we pass over it.

"We're fine" I shout back to the skipper. I am standing on the bow watching the depth as we motor in. "That reef is lots of jelly fish"

There are so many tiny brown jellyfish that the mass is almost solid, they appear to be in huge rafts but even in the water between the are several million.

We are now at the entrance to the harbour.

"Follow us very closely," say our escorts over the radio.

We do. But it is not good enough.

"We're aground," says the skipper as the boat thumps to a halt

We are. We manage to back off and follow the advice of the guide boat and try another route. Thump. We are aground again. This time we cannot get off,. Luckily it is sand here. We try going full in reverse, and then full throttle forward. No we are firmly stuck.

"OK everybody," says Martin. "I want you all up on deck and we will try to rock her off. First stand on side of the boat leaning over and then when I give the word, run very fast over to the other side and we will see if we can't get her off that way."

But trying to rock a forty six foot yacht with only two adults and three children is not very effective. She rocks ever so slightly but remains firmly stuck.

The tide is rising, all two foot of it and finally with the launch towing us around sideways, we manage to get off. We are not going to attempt again yet, so anchor off and wait for the tide. So much for getting someone to guide us through and prevent us going aground!

Too many little brown jellyfish to make swimming an unattractive prospect, so fall asleep to the sound of bubbajackas until the tide is higher enough for us to go into the harbour.

"Mum, can we have pizza ashore?"

After five days at sea, I have no intention of cooking so we eat pizza and drink rum punches.

The following day the customs man comes to clear us in and out, we are only staying here for one night, enough to catch up on some sleep and have a quick run ashore.

"Any firearms?" he asks, now sitting his slightly oversized bulk by our table down below. It is hot and he mops sweat off his brow.

"No. " Martin and I answer in unison.

"What are firearms?" asks Brinsley.

"Guns and things." I answer.

"We've got a gun." Pipes up John. The customs man looks at us without a smile.

"No, no," we say "We only have paper and cardboard guns." At which point Brin disappears into his cabin to show his gun he has made.

"Can we go ashore and have a pina colada?" asks David.

I am getting more and more embarrassed by the minute. "Virgin ones, maybe." I say, hoping that we won't be held for feeding children alcohol as well as maybe hiding firearms!

Luckily the fat customs man sees the funny side of things and disappears all the necessary paperwork in order.

An osprey watches us as we walk along the beach, and try to get photographs of it. Little do we know that soon we are to see ospreys every day in the states, but thinking of their scarcity back home it seems very exciting to see our first one.

"Who's going to go for a snorkel?" Everybody looks at the water, still more brown than blue with the jelly fish, but the snorkelling is supposed to be very good here so we decide to try anyway.

The boys soon give up. "I'm not swimming with all, those jellyfish." They say and proceed to build sandcastles instead.

"This is boring " says David.

But the skipper and I persevere. It is a strange sensation swimming with the myriad of these little jellyfish brushing against your face, but to begin with we can manage, it is only when the cloud becomes so thick that you cant see. Then I discover that not only do they sting, my face is tingling, but they are getting caught down my swimming costume and as they get squashed on my front, they definitely sting. I give up the uneven battle and return to the shore with the boys. Martin is fairly hot on my heels.

CHAPTER NINE

WE ARRIVE IN THE STATES

We would love to stay here and maybe do some diving, but we are already behind schedule and must head north.

We leave the Turks and Caicos islands and this time we know the route through the reef so do not rely on an escort, and as soon as the tide is almost at its highest we head out. The solid mats of jelly fish are still there but we can plough through them and just hope that they are not hiding a reef underneath them!

Both fishing lines out in the hope of catching another fish.

"I hope we don't catch another tuna, I've had enough tuna fish for a while," say the boys, giving an unenthusiastic feel on the lines before going back down below to their endless games of drawing ships on pieces of paper, which they then use to play with.

No fish, but there is lots of Sargasso seaweed, little yellow ochre coloured clumps of the curly stuff which keeps getting caught in the fishing lines. In places there are huge mats of the stuff, and we can imagine what the Sargasso sea must look like at times.

There is less and less wind as we head north, the bright red and yellow spinnaker is hanging like an empty paper bag and as darkness falls we have to resort to the motor disturbing the peace of the day.. As soon as it is switched on. "Can we use the inverter now please?" from the boys who have long since run the computer battery dead, and are dying for a chance to charge it up. So away go the paper boats and out comes the computer. I really should be teaching but at the moment it is very hot and for once we let the boys play uninterrupted in the calm weather.

The saucepan cupboard wins the long battle it has been waging with me and refuses to open. I hit it hard. It still doesn't open. I try swearing at it along with the hit, it refuses to budge. Pleading doesn't help either.

"Mum, you know that the cupboard can't really hear you?" comes a boys voice from behind me. I smile to reassure them that I am not totally off my rocker.

"I know." I say.

"I am the Captain of the *Brandamajo*...o," comes the skipper's voice from the cockpit

"And a fine good Captain too" the boys response from down below is almost reflex, after nearly a year of Gilbert and Sullivan indoctrination (with a few word alterations) it is second language to them.

"And very good, let's be it understood, I command a right good crew." He is now letting George helm and sitting on the edge of the cockpit looking out for anything that might hit us.

"He's very good let's be it understood, he commands a right good crew." The boys carry on with their game as they respond.

"I can't get this cupboard open!" I mutter, trying to kick it again. It crashes open to the floor. I won't shut it again.

"I'll put a different latch on it," says the skipper between verses.

"Mum, I've got really bad toothache," says John.

"How bad?"

"It really hurts, he comes closer to me and opens his mouth.

I look at his tooth and can see nothing but it reminds me of the nagging hole I have had in my tooth for some time now, ever since a bit of filling broke off somewhere in the Caribbean..

"Give them a good scrub," I say and offer him half a Paracetamol.

We motor through the night, with thunderstorms flickering in the background and the Paracetamol seems to have worked, the next morning his toothache seems to be better.

As we approach the Bahamas, the thunderstorms that have been flickering in the distance for some time now, become all the more real.

"Attention all shipping, attention all shipping this is a weather warning.' The announcement comes over channel 16, the VHF channel that is for emergencies and all listening.

We change channels to get the full warning. 'All shipping are advised not to leave port as there are severe thunderstorms forecast with gale force gusts and potential waterspouts, in the Nassau area. This is the Nassau Meteorological office.'

Well we are already out, so not much we can do to heed that!

"Lets hope we make it in before the storm hits" says the skipper, he has given Gilbert and Sullivan a rest and is chewing his fingers. Nassau is in sight.

We don't. A very black sky ahead of us with thunder and lightning completely blocks out Nassau, so we turn tail and flee.

Brinsley sticks his head out. "Why have we turned around Dad?"

"We're running away from that storm." The skipper replies.

"Oh," says Brinsley phlegmatically and disappears down below again. It is starting to rain. Great big drops of heavy rain, flattening the water and bouncing off the deck. Visibility is down to a few feet.

Martin turns to me "Look at that." There is another storm approaching us and right now we are headed right into it. As we are now surrounded by storms or land it seems that our only option is to go bang through the centre of one of these storms. The radar, which we have only started to really use recently, shows up the rain storms clearly and even better we can see how big the storms are. We opt for the smallest one that will take us in the right direction towards Nassau.

We already have no sails up so we head through it and thankfully come out the other side intact, and the sun is shining on the red buildings of Nassau.

Go into Atlantis marina, which at $3 per foot, per night, is the most expensive marina we have been in yet. Two stone Marlin are silhouetted against the sky, they adorn the top of the huge hotel complex.

The boys are on deck. "Wow, look at that, and that." There are more super yachts here than normal ones like us, and no wonder. Atlantis is actually a big hotel cum resort into which we have 'free' entry whilst we are here. There is a bin for each yacht and a buggy that will transport you along the quay side if you feel you cannot walk the short distance. The boys think that it is wonderful.

We hope that we will meet Barry (from Penelope who came across the Atlantic the same time as us) here, but apparently he is actually in England at the moment seeing his daughters who are at boarding school there.

Our most important and pressing reason however for stopping off in the Bahamas is to get visas for the U.S.A. here.

In the marina office (which is air conditioned,) there is a television room with magazines and a pool table ostensibly for all the crews of these large yachts. And lovely showers, and washing machines and dryers. I think that we have hit civilisation and the American influence.

The boys are reading the brochure that we have been handed upon our arrival.

"Mum, can we go swimming there please?"

"Boys, it is pouring with rain, and besides right now we have to go and find out about getting visas for the States."

"The rain doesn't matter, we will get wet anyway."

"We'll go " I say, grabbing waterproofs for everybody and chivvying them outside, but not until we have found the American Embassy."

Perhaps here I should say that before we left home, we phoned the American Embassy in London, not once but twice to check if we need visas for the United States and both times were told that no we didn't as long as we were going to be there for less than three months, which is the case, and being British citizens we were part of the visa waiver program. However on getting out here to the Caribbean rumours begin to reach us that perhaps we will need visas after all. Never mind, a phone call to the U.S. Embassy in Nassau, and they tell us , that yes of course we can apply for visas here, and providing that there are no problems we should get one.

So here we are, waiting in the pouring rain, and it is coming down in torrents, waiting for a taxi to take us to the Embassy.

The Embassy is closed but we get the relevant forms and are told that we should try and be here at 6.30 a.m. the following morning if we want to get in the queue of people applying for visas.

The streets are flooded, rivers of now dirty water gushing and flowing down them looking for an escape route. Large drains and ditches are designed to cope with this so I doubt that the streets will stay flooded for very long, Our feet slip and slide inside the sandals that have become slimy and slippery with the wet.. The traffic is appalling and horns are hooting, as cars stop in the flooded streets.

Those lovely Caribbean Islands with hardly any traffic seem far away.

We decide to walk back to the marina as the rain has eased, stopping on the way to get photographs done of ourselves, for our visas which hopefully we will collect tomorrow.

"Mum, my feet hurt. Can we get a taxi?"

"No," I say, "My feet hurt too, but it is not far now."

"You always say it is not far when really it is miles and miles and miles." Comes the answer.

"Never mind," says their Dad, think how much more you are seeing by walking."

"What, houses and traffic?" comes the answer.

"Ah but it's different houses and traffic than you might see in Northwich."

The boys are unimpressed, and we all have sore feet. Walking in bare feet in soaking wet sandals is not to be recommended.

"Hey can we stop here? This looks like a shop that sells Pokemon," says David.

So we let them stop and look for Pokemon packs which they duly buy. I'm sure that once we reach the States, Pokemon will be in every shop and on every corner, so I am in no particular rush to get them now.

The following day we are up at 5.30 a.m. in order to get in the queue for visas early enough. It is not raining. Just as well really because when we get there, the gates are locked and we are by no means the first in the queue, so must sit on the pavement until the Embassy opens at eight o'clock.

Families and individuals of all nationalities join us. They sit on the pavement as we do or lean against the fence, faces bored and stressed. Will they or will they not get visas to enter the U.S.A?

There is a Macdonalds close by,(yes alas another sign of wealth and America)so Martin goes off and gets us all a Macdonalds breakfast to eat while we wait. We are frisked as we go in and sit on wooden benches waiting our turn to be seen by some official.

11.30 a.m. we are out but we have not got a visa and we are $225 poorer.

"No I am sorry sir, but we cannot issue you with a visa."

"Why not?"

"You are not Bahamian citizens."

"You told us on the phone that we could apply for a visa here."

"You can. You have just applied, but that does not mean that we have to grant you one."

The boys have found another boy sitting on the waiting bench, with his Pokemon cards and are chatting and thinking of trading cards.

We explain the whole story but it is no good. "You have to get someone to vouch for you, but even then it is unlikely that we can give you a visa. It is happening all the time that yachts people are coming here for visas because they have not been given one in their own country."

Angry, almost to the point of tears, at the misinformation we have been given, we look at the options. One is that Martin sails back from here. Not a very realistic option. Two is that we go to the States anyway and then take a risk that we can get one there, but it will cost us $180 per person, and we might not get it anyway, and the third is that we try the British Consulate and see if they can help us.

We opt for the third.

Thank goodness for our children. We rush into the British Consulate, children asked to be on their best behaviour...." We have to show them that they would like to have us in America." We say. They oblige and are quiet polite and charming. Without them I know that we would not have got our visas. The British Consulate are fantastic, and make us proud to be British (believe me that doesn't happen very often.)

"Just make sure that you tell every one you know that they need to get visas before they leave the country because we can't really do this, if for example you prove not to be bona fide citizens then we will be the ones to get the blame."

We thank them profusely and I wonder if the American citizens have as much trouble getting into Europe. Somehow I doubt it. They even issue Martin with a new passport as his old one American Embassy is still reluctant to issue us with our visas but he does. "That's OK." We answer, we are not planning to be in the states for longer than three months anyway." We have lost a lot of brain cells through stress, and have become experts at pleading our case, but our passports have visas in them and we can now set to enjoying the Bahamas. We have also learnt a lesson, that is whatever you are told, get a visa anyway before you leave home, then you can't go wrong. Back on the boat a cockroach greets us. I wonder when it came on board? Possibly along the warps in Antigua? And we have done so well so far. So we must buy some cockroach traps today.

"Mum NOW can we go to Atlantis and swim?"

"OK then, go and get a towel and trunks."

"We've got our trunks on.""

Well get everything else ready then."

"We ARE ready."

I can delay no longer. Tidying the boat can always wait. And actually they provide towels there. Just as well really. By now our towels are tatty and sunbleached. You drop into a large tank full of sharks, but don't worry to avoid getting eaten. You are protected inside a thick Perspex tube. From a middle aged mother's point of view, by far the worst is the Leap of Faith, which is a near vertical drop and as I stand watching it almost everybody screams as they descend, arms and legs crossed. "I am not going to do that!" I say adamantly. "Any of you boys coming with me?" However, by our second day there: "Mum, if I can do it then surely you can." This is from John who has just capitulated to his brothers entreaties and been down the 'leap of faith'. "You always tell us to try things before saying that we don't like them." I cannot argue with that so, full of trepidation, I follow the boys up the steps and at the top a young lad looks at me. "Don't worry, you'll be fine." I hadn't even said anything to him. Why are all these people so very fat?" This is from David, and he is right, we look positively skeletal compared to most of these American tourists staying at this resort. "They eat too much and do too little exercise." I respond, as a lady in front of us lowers her bulk which is overflowing from a tight swimming costume , into the chair in front of us. She has an ice cream in her hand. "Mum, can we have an ice cream?" asks Brinsley plonking himself down next to us, laying on the pristine fluffy blue and fresh. However, we do manage to buy cockroach traps here.

"I hope we will be able to get the generator fixed here," says the skipper as we approach Fort Lauderdale. Fort Lauderdale actually has agents for our Ferryman generator, so if they can't fix it here then where can they fix it. Well we are here, not much wind, so we had to motor most of the way, 'across the stream', as people say; that is, across the Gulf Stream which in bad weather can be quite hazardous to cross as it rushes with such force Northward. Get the fenders and warps ready, please."

The crew scurry around to do their skipper's bidding. But we have plenty of time, we must wait for another fifteen minutes before the bridge will open and let us through onto the Intra Coastal Waterway and thence into the Marina. Strictly speaking nobody but the skipper is supposed to leave the boat until it has cleared customs, but as the customs place is some way away we all decide to go. We take a taxi to the customs and immigration place. We didn't think that the visa problem could get any worse. "Ah but they are C3 visas; that means that they are crew's visas, and you can only stay for twenty nine consecutive days. You may leave after that and re-enter if you like." This is ridiculous, and we don't like. The skipper is not happy....neither am I for that matter. Martin continues to explain our problems so far.

"Why don't you ring up the Embassy in Nassau?" So it was done, but of course the Embassy in Nassau was closed. "You can pay $180."

The situation is getting desperate. The man behind the counter continues. "How do you expect us to issue you with a visa, if we have no proof that you are going to leave the country?"

"But someone coming in on a flight could easily decide to remain." bearing in mind that the U.S.A. has a visa waiver system meaning that if you are on a commercial flight or a cruise liner you don't need a visa. The boys meanwhile have got bored and have disappeared outside into the corridor, they can be are left to wait. The noise of the boys has disappeared. I wonder what they are up to. "Dr Cross!" A new face has appeared. Martin stands up. "Where are your children?" I go out to find them. They are sitting on the floor by a drinking fountain in some imaginary world. I return children in hand. He peers over his glasses at them, now sitting neatly on the chairs.

"OK, obviously there's been a mistake. I cannot believe that however good your boys might be as crew on your boat, they would be given crews visas. So I am willing to concede you were issued with the wrong visas."

Martin relaxes slightly. "And?"

"We can issue a six month temporary visa. And waive the fees."

I am ready to kiss him, but the counter and my reticence prevent this.

221

We walk out into hot sunshine, with a weight removed from our shoulders. Compared with immigration, customs is easy, and takes only ten minutes. Soon we are walking through the docklands. Shops are everywhere. What a consumer nation the USA is. Is it becoming as bad in the UK? I cannot remember.

We stop at an all American Diner which could almost be from a film set, where the food is good and cheap. If it is as cheap and good to eat out always here, I can see us going the way of some of those people we had seen in the Bahamas.

"Can I have burger and chips please?"

"Can I have sausage and chips please?"

"Will I get heart disease?" This last is from David.

As we stay here, we are gradually getting sucked back into the consumer culture. It is very easy to see something and then covet it, or think different.

Then to the marine chandlery. There is everything we have wanted all year. Things we have not found even in England. Here all measures are Imperial. They burn propane and not butane, and electrical power is very different. But we manage and get the engine functioning the American way.

"Wow, look at that rain!"

From inside the chandlery we stand and look. The heavens have opened and a thunderstorm is raging outside, almost overhead.

"We always get them at about three o'clock at this time of year," the checkout girl informs us, as she rings up our purchases on the till.

"You did of course shut the hatches didn't you?" Martin asks me.

"It was a gloriously sunny day when we left."

We head straight back to the boat. There does not appear to be an inch of dry anywhere. The skipper growls and stares at me. The boat is soaked; there are several inches in the heads. At least, two forward cabins are dry. It could be worse. It could be sea water. Needless to say, the first mate is not high in any popularity stakes.

We close the hatches and attempt to clean up. The sun will dry everything properly on the following day.

Next morning the boys call to me.

"Mum, come and look," they say. "We've caught two cockroaches this time."

Our single Bahamian cockroach was not single after all. We regularly catch them in the traps I have laid everywhere.

"What's for tea?"

"How about artichokes?"

"Yes please."

So we sit on deck eating our artichokes and watching and feeling a thunderstorm above us. We are not yet immune to the daily afternoon thunderstorms; they still provide a dramatic show. But we must finish eating down below when it starts to rain, and as it is still not dry, it is like eating in a sauna.

John's diary for the 8th June reads. 'Today we went to the internet café and the swimming pool.'

"What are you doing?" I ask. I have returned to the boat where we have got the professionals in to fix the generator. Martin and the two men are standing peering into the water. Martin is on the phone and one of the men is lying flat on the jetty with his head close to the water.

"He's dropped his phone overboard, we are seeing if we can hear it ring."

"And can you?" I ask.

"No."

The phone owner disappears, maybe in search of another phone and the remaining man squeezes himself back into the generator locker.

Martin comes out, mopping sweat from his brow.

"Is it fixed?" I ask.

"Not yet. It is in pieces."

The problem is solved however, and because Martin had helped in finding the phone, a compromise is reached on the amount we pay.

"Where are the boys?" he says wiping a drip of sweat that is rolling down his nose.

"In the pool diving for coins that one of them has to throw in."

There is a swimming pool on the roof of the hotel to which the marina is affiliated. We have this need to make the most use of everything for which we have paid!

Finally we leave Fort Lauderdale. We are definitely getting port rot here, and time is again pushing us northwards. We leave at 7a.m. The children are still. Before long we are in a forty five knot prolonged squall (that's a gale). Despite being well reefed down, we are still knocked fairly flat, but we have implicit faith in our skipper.....just as well some might say. Thank goodness I am drugged up.

"Are we in a gale?" Gopher one pops his head out of the hatch.

"Sort of."

"Ow!" comes a shout from down below. Gopher two has just got out of his bunk and been thrown across his cabin.

The wind and spray stop us from talking as we race along. *Brandamajo* has almost taken on a life of her own. It is quite a relief when the squall dies out.

At Forth Worth we find a muddy patch to anchor in the shelter of the Waterway. I tell the boys this is no place to swim.

A large man and a blonde women come close in their dinghy.

"We were wondering about the flags," she yells. "Where are you from?"

Not only do we have the Red Ensign but we are also flying a skull and crossbones and the flag of Budworth Sailing Club. "England!" we yell back, though they are coming in closer. "How did you get here?" is her next question as the dinghy slows down so that she can conduct this conversation. The boys have been attracted from down below and are all stood in the companionway listening. "Sailed." "You don't mean you *sailed* across the big one, that big patch of water?"

"Yes. Come aboard," we say. It is difficult not to match her shout level even if it is totally unnecessary.

"Houston we have a problem,......." Down below they are watching *Apollo 13*, one of our videos which not only the children but all of us could probably recite verbatim, we have watched it so often.

They climb aboard with not much grace. The silent husband can barely fit past the steering wheel

They have wine and cokes.

"These are not really cokes. We have already spiced them up with rum!" she laughs.

Later, after a succession of drinks (will I be fit to cook a meal?) and many questions, they declare it is time to return to their dinghy.

It is dark now but there is a surprising amount of light from the buildings and we shine a torch to help them back to their dinghy. The lady gets into the dinghy and the man follows suit, but he is no sooner seated on the edge of the rubber dinghy than he rolls off backwards into the water, with a surprisingly gentle splash, his hands come up and get hold of the edge of the dinghy and *Brandamajo*. (Remember those men you used to get that if you pushed them; they would bounce back upright.) The rubber dinghy where she is sitting rises high in the air. She balances precariously before regaining balance.

"I'm fine," he says showing remarkable dignity.

"He's fine, he's fine," she shouts, even though they are right next to us, "Just a little wet aren't you honey?"

And they motor off into the night, back to their motor launch anchored not far away.

CHAPTER TEN

THE INTRACOASTAL WATERWAY

We decide the next day to try the Intracoastal Waterway, more commonly known as the I.C.W. Now this is at least one thousand miles of waterway, sometimes river, sometimes canal and sometimes lagoon, stretching up the east coast of America. It crosses estuaries, has bridges and locks and we will not be using the sails up much of it. After my first initial disappointment of the high rises of Fort Lauderdale I am pleasantly surprised by the Waterway which makes us realise just how big America is.

"Mum, come and have a look at this!"

I shake my hands dry and kneel down on the floor where now all three boys are crouched.

"What am I looking at?"

"This, Mum, what has happened to this cockroach?"

I look at the glue trap the boys are examining, and there is a well stuck dead cockroach abdomen extended and all around lots of tiny baby cockroaches stuck onto the glue as well.

"That's a good haul," I say picking up the trap and putting it into the bin. We have obviously not got rid of the cockroaches yet. I always thought that cockroaches laid eggs.

So we set off up the waterway, past houses with their gardens stretching down to the water, each with their own private jetty, many with a motor boat hauled out on a pulley, or perhaps in the water. This is Florida, for the wealthy, we are cruising down its watery street, but the boys soon lose interest and are back down in the gopher hole, until I suggest work when all of a sudden the outside becomes more interesting again!

The first bridge we encounter is fixed and the gauge shows 62ft. We do not want to risk that so we anchor and wait for the tide to go down. The water is wide here and, apart from where it has been dredged, it is shallow. Our mast has been measured at 64ft including the aerials.

"What do you think?" the skipper has come to join me where I am sitting on the bow with a pair of binoculars looking at the gauge.

"It says 64ft now." I say.

"Shall we go?" he says.

"Well we'll only just hit the top of the aerials won't we?"

Neither of us wants to be the one who causes our mast to break, so we are reluctant to make the decision

"Go, on, get the anchor up and we'll take it very slowly.

Now if you have ever been under a bridge where you actually have quite a lot to spare, that looks scary. When you really only have inches to spare it looks VERY scary.

As we edge closer to it, I am lying on the side deck on my back holding a finger vertical in front of my nose trying to judge if we will make it or not, but to be quite honest it is impossible to tell until we are under the bridge.

The aerials bounce along the bridge. 'Thwack, thwack, thwack, thwack, thwack.'

That can't have been 64ft," says Martin. I agree with him.

"How many bridges do we have to go under today?"

"Eight. Most of them are opening ones though."

That's a relief.

The engine is running continuously, so the boys can play on the computer, and the fridge can be on so we can have COLD BEER.

I will never take power and water for granted again. George (the autohelm) can take a holiday as there are no straight lines in the waterway and we must manually steer her all the way.

"What was that!" a loud noise like a wet sneeze right by the boat, has us peering over the edge.

"It's a dolphin," shouts Martin. "Boys, there's a dolphin playing by the boat."

"Dolphin! Dolphin!" the call echoes around the boat, despite the frequency with which we have seen these, it never fails to be exciting, they are just such lovely animals, and come deliberately to play with us.

It is very strange seeing them in this riverine setting, surrounded by banks and trees, and not out at sea. . This one here is an old scarred bottlenosed dolphin and stays with us for some way playing in our bow wave until he gets bored. Or maybe until we move out of his territory. I don't know if in this environment dolphins are territorial or not.

Unlike the dolphins we see at sea, the water here is so very brown that you can only see then when they are very close to the surface.

'Beep, beep, beep, beep,' the depth alarm is going off almost continuously, we are learning to ignore the beeping, but it means that we must keep a close eye on the echo sounder, at 1.3 metre we go aground. (The alarm starts going off at 3m) Most of the time we have only one or two feet beneath the keel.

"I though this waterway was supposed to be ten feet," says David who has decided to forgo Pokemon and the computer and come on deck for a while.

"It is."

"Then why is the depth alarm going off all the time?"

"Because there seems to be a difference between 'supposed' and reality."

"Oh. Why?"

"It just is that's all."

"I'm hungry, when's lunch?"

We slow down as we wait for a bridge to open, and momentarily veer off the centre of the channel, resulting in us touching the bottom. "Whoops." We come to a sudden stop, but the skipper soon has her in reverse and luckily we are off soon enough.

Here in the States they have lots of marine and waterway rescue craft that will pull you off if you get stuck but as we declined to take up their insurance's. I hope that we will not need to use them, apparently it costs about $3000 to get pulled off the mud.

Pelicans with their velvety golden necks, and big heavy beaks folded downwards as if they are too heavy to hold up, sit and preen themselves on the Bridge fenders or fish in the Waterway. Dolphins are regular visitors and on about every third or fourth waterway marker is an osprey's nest, usually with an osprey in it and sometimes some very large chicks.

"Addison Point Bridge, Addison Point Bridge, this is sailing vessel *Brandamajo*, *Brandamajo* requesting opening please."

"Sailing vessel *Brandamajo*, we see you, we will open when you come a little closer."

Then just as we think that we are going to have to slow down before we hit the bridge we see the road barriers start to close and the bridge is opened in time for us to pass through.

Some of the bridges will open on request, and some of them will only open at preset times. But for us, the opening bridges are a welcome release from the stress of passing under the fixed bridges.

Well we have been under eight fixed bridges so far and we have hit every single one of them, so either American feet are shorter than English ones or we have measured the mast wrong. (And the first mate didn't measure the mast!). Sometimes we go under bridges with the depth alarm going off and the aerials whacking the underside of the bridge in a rhythmic sound as they bounce from girder to girder.

The severity of our hits are judged by a one aerial hit or a two aerial hit, as we have two radio aerials atop our mast. It will be quite a relief to drop anchor here for the night and let our adrenaline levels fall to normal for a while. Crossing the Atlantic was much more relaxing than coming up this waterway, where we are probably about the biggest boat, both depth and height wise, that it is possible to bring up.

Once through Addison Point Bridge we slowly edge our way through the shallow water so that we are off the dredged channel and drop our anchor in the lee of the bridge. A big hairy nose comes up quickly to look at the anchor as the chain goes down. It is a manatee.

"Manatee, manatee!" I shout back jumping up and down in excitement. The skipper is still trying to manoeuvre us in this very tight spot so has caught my excitement but can't possibly come up and have a look.

"I think we're dragging, he says after a while." I am still looking for manatees, but I dutifully go back to what I should be doing and that is helping make sure that we are well and truly anchored. It is difficult and every time the anchor comes up it is covered in thick, black, gooey mud.

Very bad holding ground, and after repeated attempts, we decided that as there is no wind we will drop all the chain and risk staying the night, hoping that the weight of the anchor plus all its chain will keep us stationary.

It is flat calm here, dolphins are playing in the calm waters breaking the mirror like surface as they surface, a pair of ospreys are nesting in the channel marker not far away and pelicans are preening themselves on the bridge.

The NASA space shuttle building is on the horizon and there is a life-sized space shuttle sticking up behind us at the Astronaut Hall of Fame. What more could we ask for to satisfy the whole Cross family?

In the morning there is still no wind so we row ashore and tie the dinghy under a bush so that it can't be seen from the road and walk to the Hall of Fame.

"Look boys, a 4G simulator, like the ones they use to train astronauts. Who's for a go?" The Astronaut hall of fame is totally empty. Apparently we are lucky there are no school parties today. Martin is standing by the simulator.

"What's it like Dad?" Both John and David are standing by it eager to go yet slightly hesitant.

"If you don't like it, there is always this button you can press." The attendant shows them inside.

John and David go on first, I am standing watching from the outside as the little tin can is spun faster and faster around, I have no intention whatsoever of going on that thing, it makes me feel quite sick even to look at it. "Whoops somebody has pressed the button," says the attendant.

"That'll be John," I reply. Sure enough when the thing stops, John steps out. "I was beginning to feel a bit sick," he says " I HAD to press the button".

Brinsley takes his place. He and David both emerge a few minutes later, David looking distinctly white.

"That was cool," says Brinsley grinning.

David declines to comment. "Are you all right?" I ask him.

"Yes," he says, but he looks far from all right. To say no would be to admit failure, but then I am not even going to try and go in the thing.

Thirty seconds later. "I think I'm going to be sick!" He promptly is, but someone manages to chuck us a plastic bag. "I don't think I want to be an astronaut," he says and walks rather woozily around the rest of the place, where we also see young future astronauts training to space walk during their summer school.

It is finally time to return to *Brandamajo*. With her dicky anchorage, we are not happy at leaving her for too long.

The dinghy is still under the scrubby bush and we carry her down to the water through thick squelchy rotting grass, before climbing in and pushing her off.

"Oh, look!" I say. There are manatees playing not far from the boat.

"Can we go over and see them?" ask the boys. We row quietly over to them and they look at us inquisitively, then we just let ourselves drift. It is not long before one of them comes up to investigate us. They are huge and you can understand why they are called 'sea cows'. They are exactly that, large herbivorous water animals grazing on the sea grass and as they stick their whiskered noses out, opening the nostrils to breathe in some air, and sniff us, they look remarkably similar.

One nudges the dinghy.

"I wouldn't like to be turned over by these," says Martin.

"Brin, Brin, come over here. It's this side of the dinghy," says David excitedly. The children all move across, and the great big lumbering animal dives down, scars visible on its back where it has been hit by propellers, the dinghy moves as it goes underneath us. Another one has appeared at out stern and is just watching the boys. They return the stares.

"Can we touch it?" asks Brinsley.

I am not sure, but "If you're gentle," I reply. The boys all touch the rough skin of the animal, and it doesn't seem to mind in the least.

Eventually the manatees get bored, and the boys have seen enough and we finish rowing back to the boat.

We go to a marina in Titusville. We are going to be tourists here for a couple of days, and if there is one thing the Americans know how to do it is be tourists. They have so much money and so much leisure time. We will be much happier leaving the boat at a marina than at anchor while we disappear for days at a time.

An osprey catches a fish and then eats it atop the mast of an adjacent yacht.

The skipper bags the hammock and falls asleep. The boys and their teacher must get some schoolwork done.

So the next two days we do Universal Studios, and the Kennedy Space centre: the former mostly for the boys, and the latter mostly for us adults.

But even for me, a confirmed theme park hater, Universal Studios was great fun. I even enjoy most of the 'rides'. Between rides and shows the boys cannot help ogling the obesity of the American people.

"Mum, why is that boy in a push chair?" asks John as another overweight seven year old is pushed along whilst he eats his ice cream.

"Too fat to walk," I say. "Now you understand why these people are so overweight?"

"Yuck, mum," says David, and we feel thinner by the minute.

However I have to admit that I am beginning to like the smile and 'have a nice day' attitude with which we are greeted in every shop or attraction. Even if they don't mean it, it still makes you feel good.

Two days solid sightseeing is quite wearing. We must catch up on laundry and jobs, and remeasure the mast.

Martin climbs up the ladder. We have two methods of getting him up the mast, one is for him to go in the bosun's chair and I will winch him up and the other is to hoist some canvas steps up which he will climb. The boson's chair is very hard work for me, but it does mean that he can work better whilst he is up there, and the ladder is hard work for him.

He takes a tape measure up with him and I hold the bottom, he marks off every two feet.

"I think you are two feet out!" I shout up. He is now at the top.

"I can't possibly be!" he yells back.

We measure it again on the way down, and then must do from the mast foot to the waterline.

The original measurements were indeed two feet out and as a result we now know that our mast is 64ft 9 in to the top of the hard bit, the aerials adding at least another three feet.

Now when the official height of the bridges is 65 ft, 3 inches is not a lot to spare!

He is down and we are in the cockpit, an osprey mewing overhead.

"So now what?" we both ask.

We have come under eight bridges so far, and neither one of us wants to go back. Also the water is getting more tidal, so being a bit cocky and having come thus far unscathed, we decide to continue.

"We could look on the bright side," he says. "If we had measured the mast correctly in the first place we would never have attempted to come up the waterway. No manatees, no ospreys, no inland dolphins."

That is true, and despite our misgivings and the stress of the bridges and the shallow water, the wildlife has been fantastic, and we have seen parts of the States that you wouldn't normally see.

Go under a bridge that the gauge says 68 ft, and guess what? We don't hit it. No familiar thwack, thwack, thwack. Cause for celebration.

Without the trade winds of the Caribbean, the weather is hot and sticky. At night when we are at anchor hundreds of midges, (yes just like Scotland) or 'noseeums' they call them here, invade us during twilight.

Anchor surrounded by marshland that night and then decide to have a day sailing outside. A group of pelicans gives us a fly by as we sail out and race up the coast of Florida in the Gulf Stream.

And so we work our way up North, sometimes anchoring and sometimes going in marinas. Big oaks with hanging moss, give way to days of green marsh land. Empty of people and houses and in the U.K. we would be past it in half a day; here it just goes on and on. It is quite beautiful. Posts mark the channel of the waterway, red triangles to port and green squares to starboard.

In our chart book of the Intracoastal Waterway the skipper has circled all of the fixed bridges and we know that until we are under them for the day we cannot relax.

Stop at a place called Jekyll Island in Georgia to refuel and decide to stay the night, the marina provides bicycles inclusive in their charges and there is a restaurant, small pool and in theory use of the marina car should we want to go shopping.

"It's lovely to stop for a bit" say the boys. And we agree with them.

"Who's coming for a cycle then?"

"Me, me, me." We all go. Baking hot.

"I'm thirsty."

"This bike's no good. The chain keeps coming off."

"Come here let me sort it." David brings his bike and we sit on the ground in the sweltering heat and fix the chain back on.

With oily fingers and sweaty backs we continue and try and catch up with the rest of the family who have gone head in frustration. We can hear them though so they can't be that far ahead.

" Look at that bird mum. It's bright red." A red cardinal, which is a crested bright red finch is perched on a bough ahead of us.

"It's nice going for a bike ride instead of walking isn't it?

Sweat is dribbling down between our shoulder blades as the afternoon thunderstorm builds up, and we return to the marina where we jump into the little pool shaded by the large oaks hanging with Spanish moss, a red cardinal watches as we cool off and the boys play diving for coins.

"That's enough fun. I must go and clean the boat," says the skipper. The river water has left a brown stain along the waterline and especially where the bow wave rides. Helpful locals suggest different remedies to get the stain off; none of them seem to work very well.

It's dark, but on the bikes again and armed with the torches and strobe lights from the boat, we set off round the island to see if we can see turtles coming in to lay their eggs, which apparently they do here.

We walk along the beach in the blackness, torches off now, and occasionally bump into other small groups of people also turtle hunting.

"Hey, look, they must have found one!" says Brinsley, pointing through the darkness to a family grouped together, round the dim light of a torch, on the beach. We go over to investigate, to discover that they must have got bored of hunting for the real thing and have now built a sand turtle!

Well at least we can't say that we haven't seen one." I say.

"That's not very funny Mum." Comes the reply. Turtle hunting is obviously losing its appeal.

We walk for a couple of hours and then sit down on the beach. Everybody starts to fall asleep.

"I'm tired."

"Shall we go back then?"

"We've seen turtles anyway."

"My legs hurt."

So we head back on our bikes, strobe lights flashing in our hands. (We have these on board for people on night watch to keep in their pockets in case they go overboard. It should help finding them.)

We leave as soon as the tide is right to get under the next bridge the following morning, and that night edge our way up a creek in the marshes called Cattle Pen Creek, in Georgia. After a day with the noise of the motor, the silence is blissful. Grassland marshes all around us and we can hear the waves of the sea breaking not far away across them.

Nobody is here except us and the wildlife. A dolphin is stirring up mud at the edge of the creek, it swims along the muddy edge of the creek snuffling, snorting and splashing, is it looking to stir up tasty morsels to eat? Or is it perhaps playing? As the tide goes out the mud and reeds crackle and pop with all sorts of noises that in the silence from anything manmade, are loud. It is very narrow here, but we have carefully anchored ourselves in the middle of the channel. I hope that we don't find ourselves high and dry in the morning.

"Can we go swimming here mum?"

The boys are looking at the cool water.

I peer into the water, thinking that it must be all right; doesn't look too polluted, despite the lack of clarity of those Caribbean waters.

"Look an alligator swimming past!" shouts Brinsley.

"Where? Where?"

"I don't believe you!"

We look and sure enough there is a baby alligator circling the boat. Guess what?

"Actually mum I don't think I want to go swimming any more!"

White egrets, elegant against the green reeds and brown mud, a spoonbill with its strange flattened bill and black ibis shiny and harder to see, all feed in the mud as the tide goes down and the boys go off alligator hunting in the dinghy. Another yacht comes and ends our solitude. He drops its anchor a little further down the creek.

The skipper looks up from his book, hearing the rattle of the strangers anchor chain going out. "He's doing the sensible thing, he's dropped his anchor so close to that bank, he must be going to put a kedge anchor down (an anchor from he stern as well as the bow). We should have done that; it would definitely keep us in the middle of the channel.

But we are too relaxed drinking our beers and reading to want to move.

"I'm sure we're central enough not to get too hard aground," he says and goes back to his book.

The other yacht does not in fact put a kedge anchor down.

The boys come rushing back in the dinghy. "We've just seen a HUGE alligator slide back into those grasses," they say, slightly out of breath.

"And this one wasn't a baby!" They point to where there is an obvious path of flattened grasses, as they tie the dinghy back on and clamber aboard.

When the following morning dawns our neighbour is high and dry at a most peculiar angle on the bank, there is nothing we can do except wish him a good morning as we pass, he must wait for the tide to come in and float him off. He will have about an eight-hour wait.

"Mu-um"

"Yes John." We have left our idyllic anchorage and are once more heading north through the Waterway.

The boys are appearing from their cabins. We have been on the go already for a few hours.

"My tooth still hurts."

"Come here and let me have a look." I peer into his mouth and cannot see much except that the tooth in question does look slightly inflamed.

"It's not getting better; it's getting worse," he says, obviously in pain.

I dose him up with painkillers and know that we must find a dentist at our next port of call.

Savannah, Georgia. The wife of one of the people who works here at the marina works in a dentist's and we can get an appointment for John almost straight away.

Public transport proves difficult so we order a taxi and head out to the dentist.

"I lurve yo accent," we are greeted as we enter the surgery.

"And you're the English family who are sailing around on a yacht? What a fantastic experience for y'all." The accent is a definite southern drawl. John has an abscess and they take his tooth out, (Not until I have filled in numerous forms and promised to pay) and before we leave we are all taken in and lined up for them to take a photo of!

"They all speak like Forrest Gump here," say the children. We are in central Forrest Gump territory and set of in Savannah to find the bench where he sat and recounted his tale. The bench of course is not there, much to the children's disappointment, but the square is.

We don't have many videos on the boat but Forrest Gump is one of them, and the boys can recite most of the film verbatim so keep coming out with quotes, all in unison. The skipper has also taken to speaking Forrest Gump lingo.

The shrimping boats are coming in, their long metal arms folding in like skeletal arms and when I ask he boys if they are ready to do some schoolwork their answer is in unison "My mama says life is like a box of chocolates..."

I get the books out anyway; perhaps in my teacher guise I will have more success. "Mum?"

"Mmmm"

Do you know that we have three Jennys on this boat?"

"No?"

"Yes, the Genoa (large foresail), the Wind generator, and the diesel generator."

"So we have." I point fiercely at the open books on the table.

The skipper emerges from the shower, padding wet footprints across the floor.

"Mum, the headmaster's naked again!"

It is obviously not going to be a very productive school day today.

As we head north, the bird life begins to change, and we start to see familiar oyster catchers as well as the pelicans, and still occasionally a large log that turns out to be an alligator.

Sometimes the pelicans give us a 'fly by' that is a long line of them flapping their ungainly wings almost in unison fly past the boat close and low to the water.

We leave the swamps and start travelling through thickly forested rivers, we have left Georgia and are in the Carolinas now.

The first of July arrives and we are still south of 35 degrees. Let's hope that a hurricane does not hit us now, as the insurance company would not pay up.

For a while the wild life gives way to American tourist life and horrible loud jetskis (I hate the things) powering up and down the waterway. Young men showing off to their loved ones. The motorbikes of the water. If not jet skis, then noisy motorboats, whizzing from one restaurant to another, their wash ripping the river bank away from the roots of the trees leaving gaunt roots sticking up, leaving the trees to die a slow death. Speed limit signs don't seem to be adhered to, and it is sad to see the banks getting destroyed.

It is the weekend, so perhaps it will be better tomorrow, but the banks will not heal themselves before the next onslaught next weekend.

If you play with fire you will eventually get burnt. "Thwack, thwack, thwack, we are still going under the fixed bridges and judging their height by whether it is a one or two aerial hit. One bridge too many, and one bridge too low.

We are in our usual positions, me lying on the side deck looking up at the mast, finger against my nose, and the skipper at the helm, with *Brandamajo* going as slowly as she will, we have got this down to a fine art now and are perhaps getting too cocky. Martin has stuck a piece of stick coming out horizontally from the top of the mast, pointing forward so that in theory, the piece of stick should hit the bridge first and give us enough warning to go into reverse and get out in time before any damage is done to the mast.

We have yet to put it into practise though.

We should have two feet of tide in our favour, so we are not particularly worried about this particular bridge. The gauge says 64.5 ft so we are cutting it close but so far none of the gauges have been at all accurate.

"Are we going to make it?"

I look up. "Very close this one," I answer, waiting for the point of the stick to go under the bridge so that I can give him the all clear to go ahead.

"In neutral !" I yell.

"Already am." we are drifting slowly forwards inch by inch. The stick goes under without touching. I give the thumbs up sign.

But before he puts the boat into gear there is a tearing crash and tinkle as glass falls to the deck.

"Stop, stop! We've hit." My comments are unnecessary as it is patently obvious that we have hit the bridge and we are now stationary but beginning to slew slightly sideways. These bridges are made of girders, either concrete or steel, and although we had gone under the first, the second must have been a centimetre or so lower, but low enough to catch the top of the navigation lights, which are now hanging down along with the radar reflector. As we are in the middle of the bridge we may as well carry on going and get out from under. Anyway we have now made our mast several inches smaller!

"Now what?" the skipper is chewing his thumbs, I remain silent for a while, comments are unnecessary at the moment.

We keep going.

I think that we will continue the rest of the way outside as soon as we can get out, there are limited places that we can exit from the waterway into the Atlantic beyond and looking a the charts it seems that there is some distance and several bridges to go before an exit recommended by the chart book. Need to stop for the night, but the marina that is deep enough has too many pieces of wood sticking out and is not safe. Finally find a place to anchor and the skipper can go up the mast and assess the damage.

The skipper is not smiling yet and the boys are sensibly remaining quietly down below.

"Are you ready to haul me up then?" he asks.
I reply by unattaching the topping lift (helps support the boom when we are not sailing) from the end of the boom, we attach this to the boson's chair in which I will then haul him up.

He is at the top now. "Hey look at that man up the mast darling?" A father is whizzing around in a motor boat showing his daughter the sights, he speeds past us turning sharply creating a wash and what as sea level is a mild movement, up at the top of the mast is magnified several times, the skipper holds on as the top of the mast sways violently from side to side. He is trying to detach the broken navigation light. I scowl at the passing boat and he I think gets the message for he moves away.

Martin finally comes back down with the broken navigation light and radar reflector, but thankfully the mast itself is undamaged.

Having made the decision to go out, (we are in a place called Swansborough at the moment) we look at the inlet on the chart, it is called the Bogue inlet and is described as unnavigable, but fishing boats are going out and if we can go under bridges we shouldn't be going under then just maybe we can go out of this inlet. We talk to all the locals (most of whom who advise us against going out.) However, after a lot of decision taking and examination of the weather, we decide that it is possible, and we will take the risk. Especially as the Marine Corps are dredging it at the moment. The weather is flat calm so we couldn't have better conditions. The skipper is keener than the first mate! And after seeing that the mast is not seriously damaged has regained his smile and Gilbert and Sullivan singing capabilities.

We are told that it will probably take us about an hour to get through the inlet, so we find out when high tide is and aim to be at the shallowest part at high tide.

Six a.m. and we get up, my heart churning much more than it did half way across the Atlantic. There are buoys to mark a channel of sorts, and these get moved as the channel changes with the shifting sands.

As we edge our way out, the boys are sleeping down below and we notice lots of small boats whizzing out, but they are all keeping within the channel. There is nothing with our sort of draught here, but then we lost other yachts a while back and have only met motor launches for some time now.

The shallow alarm is continuously going.

The skipper suddenly slows the boat down to almost dead slow.

"What?" I ask.

"We are about to go aground I think."

I peer over to look at the instruments, the depth is reading 1.4m. That means that we have 10 cm under the keel!

Slowly but surely though the depth starts to creep up again as we wend our way towards the dredger.

"Marine Corps dredger, Marine Corps dredger, this is Yacht *Brandamajo*, *Brandamajo*, over."

We call up the dredger that we can now see, as we have been advised to do.

"Yacht calling dredger, this is the Marine Corps." The boats here are not very strict at sticking to radio protocol.

""Hello there, this is the sailing vessel *Brandamajo*, we are at present coming out of the Bogue inlet, and wonder can you give us some advice on the navigable depth?"

"*Brandamajo*, what is your draught?"

"Six and a half feet."

You should be all right, stick to the port hand side of the channel as you are on your present heading and then when you reach the red buoy number eleven, head towards the starboard side, you should be OK. When you reach us we will move out of your way."

Either side of us we can see where the sand breaks the surface of the water, from a distance it would be hard to believe that there is a channel of any sorts through the sand.

"Thank you for that information, *Brandamajo* standing by,"

The dredger is sucking up huge mouthfuls of dirty sand through one end and spewing it out of the other. It stops its lumbering work and moves sideways as we pass, the men on deck giving us a cheery wave.

And so we make it out into the open sea and can relax. There is no wind at all so we motor all the way to Beaufort where we totally cock up getting into the marina and manage to puncture the dinghy on very sharp oyster shells, which are clinging to the harbour wall, whilst doing so.

"Mum, there's a bird out there, I think that it is drowning."

Martin looks up from where he is lashing some ropes and I pop up from down below. "We must rescue it, before it dies."

Brinsley is looking distraught. "Come on quickly, it's going to drown!"

John and David come up from down below and they all stare at the wet bird.

There is a very bedraggled looking pigeon floating in the water. Brinsley is already getting in the (now repaired) dinghy, and the other two walk around on the dockside as the flapping pigeon moves closer to the wall.

A few tourists lean over to see what it is we are rescuing from the water.

"I've got it!" Brin scoops up the bird triumphantly, and passes it up to his brothers on the quayside so he can row the dinghy back unhindered.

I am thinking: what on earth are we going to do with a half drowned manky pigeon on the boat?

But the bird comes back and is immediately placed in my hands the boys expecting a ready remedy.

"What shall we do with it?" asks David.
I hand them a tatty tea towel and wrap the bird in it and then the boys take it in turns holding it and laying it in the sun to warm it up.

"Let's call it Pidgeot."(A Pokemon card).

"Can we give it something to eat?" says Brinsley.

I hand them some breadcrumbs.

He's sort of pecking at them" say the boys watching the feeble bird as it looks around at the giant humans in whose hands it now is.

"Can we keep it?"

"I don't think it would like life on the boat very much," I say, hopefully. It doesn't look as though it will live for much longer. We must find somewhere to put it before it dies in the boys' hands.

The bird is warm and dry and with Martin they go ashore and find a nice safe place where they leave it with some bread and away from humans, so that it can recover or die in peace.

Next morning, as soon as they are up they are out of the boat and running to the place where Pidgeot was left. They are soon back "He's gone, Pidgeot has gone!" they shout. "He must have got better, because you can see where he has been pecking the bread.

"Fantastic," I say, meaning it but hoping that if a cat has taken it then there is no evidence.

"You have got something nice to write in your diaries today then."

We have good diary days and bad diary days, depending on what has happened the previous day, and their diaries are the one thing they are not allowed to slack on. Lets hope that it doesn't put them off diary writing forever.

"Whose are these black hairs?" David is cleaning the heads and holds up a little nest of hairs for me to see. It gives them great pleasure to be able to find fault with their parents!

I just smile sweetly at him.

Finally by the 6th of July we decide that we must leave and sail up to the Chesapeake.

It will only take us two days and two nights to get up to the Chesapeake now, but here are not really any more ways back into the waterway, and we are sailing round Cape Hatteras, which hereabouts people just call 'the Cape'. So lets hope that the weather stays fine.

The wind is against us but the Gulf Stream of course with us, so the seas are choppy, I am glad that I am drugged up!

"Our last sail together as a family until we are back in the U.K.," says Martin as we sit and eat out tea in the cockpit with the sun setting behind us.

"Our last sunset at sea for a long time." We sit and watch the golden sun sink below the horizon, full of emotion because back home we rarely have the time or the weather or even unbroken sea to just watch the sun go down.

"Our trip is nearly at an end isn't it?" asks David. "I wish we could keep on going for another year."

"So do I David, so do I. But what about your friends, and school, aren't you looking forward to those?" I ask him.

"My friends yes, school no."

David will be starting secondary school when we return so it is a big step for him and he is apprehensive.

"What is that over there?" one of the boys points and we peer through the binoculars, at a light coloured blob on the ocean.

"I think it's a rubber dinghy."

"Let me have a look?"

"No me first!"

The binoculars are passed from boy to boy and eventually the adults get to have a look.

"Is there anybody in it?"

"Don't think so."

"Maybe there's a dead person lying in the bottom of it that you can't see." Adds John.

"Mum, what will you do if there IS a dead person lying in the bottom of that dinghy?" asks David.

"I have no idea." I answer. By now the skipper has turned about and is heading towards it. Just in case.

"He might not be dead," says Brinsley. "Then we will have to resuscitate him."

We reach the dinghy, it is empty, nobody in it, dead or alive, much to the children's disappointment, but we attach it to our boat and hope that we will be able to return it to the rightful owner.

It is in perfect order and must just have come untied.

"Can we keep it?" asks Brinsley.

"Lets see if we can find the owner first." The dinghy has a registration number painted on the side, so we call up the coastguard and report our find.

"How about a fish for our last tea at sea?" I ask.

"We'll believe that when we see it," replies the skipper. Our fishing record is not that wonderful.

"I hope you've got something else planned?"

"Pasta in tomato sauce?" I say.

"A fish! A fish!" And we catch our fish for tea, a Spanish mackerel. Delicious.

We round Cape Hatteras during the night, the seas do get larger, as we go over the shallow ground, and then we head in towards the Chesapeake and safety from any hurricanes. If we do, we are now north of 35 degrees, so the insurance would pay up.

It is too hazy or too dark for us to see any of the lighthouses that abound along this coast, but during the night we can identify their lights.

The Chesapeake Bay is huge, I don't think I had realised just quite how big it is, but we sail up it towards Deltaville and meet the rightful owner of the dinghy en route, they are very pleased to have it back!

"Where exactly are we going?" I ask Martin who has an email in front of him giving details of how to get to the boat yard, which is a Bavaria dealer.

"There should be a green buoy up here, we turn in just there and keep to the right of the channel.

The depth alarm is going off, but we are fairly immune to that now and we see a white shed with Deltaville Yachts written on a signboard.

It is Sunday so there is nobody about; I stand holding the warps ready to leap ashore. Guess what though? I have forgotten to take the bottom guard rail off.

"Ouch, help! Stop! Splash!" My elegant leap ashore is an ungainly somersault overboard as we come alongside.

"Dad, stop! Mum's fallen overboard."

"Quick stop, don't crush her!" the boys are looking anxiously at me as I haul myself up onto the jetty, and out of the way of *Brandamajo* still slowly coming in, I am bruised and wet but mercifully uncrushed. Not a very seaman-like finale to our year away.

"You all right Bub?" calls the skipper. Then having ascertained that I am. "Well that wasn't the correct way to tie up was it?"

A couple of days later, the weekend over, we are getting lifted out, the anode on the sail drive needs replacing again as do the rudder bearings, The backstay is loosened, the bimini is down and the boat is hauled out and slowly moved into place where they begin to chock her up. The children and myself are running around looking on anxiously but we are getting more used to seeing our home be lifted out of the water.

"Why is she heeling Mum?" asks Brinsley.

"They're trying to balance her." I answer,

"I wouldn't be trying to balance it if I were them, I would be trying to figure out how to take the travel lift off," he says.

I look up, and it is apparent that the travel lift will not be able to be removed without ripping off the wind generator and radar.

"Oh dear."

So she has to be slowly put back in the water and then turned around so that we can try getting her out the other way round.

Then the next problem occurs, once she is back in the water, she won't move, she is fast aground, so we can not turn her around. Not only that, but neither can any other boat be taken out today, as we must wait until high tide before we can move her.

It is a small boat yard and we are now sitting stuck fast in the only place that can be used for hauling out any boats.

"Well so much for today's plan then!" says the skipper as we settle down to a days little jobs.

Two days later she is out, both forestays had to be removed, but she is out and safe. There is a swimming pool not far away. Nothing shop wise within walking distance.

I try running to the garage to buy some milk and orange juice. Fine running there but not quite so easy running back laden with two plastic bags. I don't think that anybody walks around here. Ken Parsons, part owner of the boat yard comes to our rescue and offers to lend us his pickup truck for the duration of our stay here. I can't imagine finding that sort of generosity back home.

Ken is not the only generous person here; we are made to feel extremely welcome by everyone. Dick appears at the bottom of the ladder with fresh herbs picked by his wife this morning with the dew still on them.

Ken invites us back to his family home to meet his wife Janet and two daughters, Kapi and Joanna. It is the first time we have slept in a bed for a year. Most strange not to have the lapping of water, or the gentle rocking. And the silence it quite unnerving, we have got so used to the life movements and sounds of our boat.

We go sightseeing in Williamsburg, the children catch lightning bugs (fireflies) and we learn about the colonisation of America.

The following morning Janet and Ken have prepared a full cooked breakfast for us. The boys are as usual starving and David has almost finished his plate, with the others not far behind, when Ken asks us to join hands and we all say Grace. "Were you hungry?" he asks David by way of mild rebuke. We are all shamefaced, but not made to feel so.

Included on the breakfast plate are grits.

"What is that Mum?" John whispers in my ear."

Those are grits John. Try them."

He takes a minuscule bite and decides that they are not for him. I can't say that I blame him. Brinsley is the only one who manages to eat them, us British are not used to having our porridge on the same plate as our eggs and bacon!

We barbecue, swim, get school work done, get jobs on the boat done and the month here is all to soon over, I must fly back with the

246

boys and Martin must wait here for his crew to arrive so that he can make the return journey. I am quite disappointed not to be going with him.

We still have cockroaches, so I buy traps in abundance and set them all over the boat. We are still high and dry, Martin has decided that he would rather antifoul the boat here in ninety degrees that at home in October in about ten degrees! Can't say I blame that decision.

Of course being out of the water has only one problem and that is going to the loo. There are two options, one is a Portaloo which the workers here at the yard use. It is precariously balanced on two planks of wood and wobbles as you use it. Added to which it is definitely smelly.

As I walk to it in the dark, loud croaking frogs leap out of my way, and I hope that there is not a snake lurking underneath it.

The other option is to go to the yacht club, which involves walking across a field, where especially at dusk, swarms of mosquitoes rise as you walk through the swampy bit. And there is a plank of wood which you walk on to avoid the puddle, unfortunately this plank of wood has a hole in one end and as you tread on the other end a fountain of, usually foul, water shoots up and if you are not careful hits you in the face!

For the boys the option is easier they have a disused water container which they use in the boat!

We also have a break by becoming tourists for the odd day, or going shopping, the boys love going to Wal Mart.

Busch Gardens, a theme park, for the boys, and it is not long before we are on the train bound for New York where we are going to spend a last family weekend before we part.

EPILOGUE

And so we leave the boat and take a train bound for New York.

"Isn't it sad?" The boys and myself leave with nostalgia, and sadness, but at least we have the weekend in New York to look forward to.

We have a seven and a half hour train journey to New York and the train has already been travelling for 24 hours!

Past swamps, wild roses forests, towns and a building which has 'Association for Aged Crows' painted on the side. "

"Do you really think that that has old crows in it?" ask the mystified boys.

"I have no idea." But lots of lovely images are conjured up.

The engine changes from diesel to electric which halts the increasing tardiness (it is now running an hour late.) and we finally arrive in New York. Here people have lost the smiles and the welcomes. We are just one of thousands of odd bods rushing around in the maelstrom of a city.

In the peace of the hotel we fight for the bath (The skipper wins!), watch telly and sleep.

Over the next couple of days we do all the true touristy bits, go up the Statue of Liberty, the Empire state building, see Jesus Christ Superstar on Broadway (actually just off Broadway) and go to the Guggenheim.

On the last day Martin, is leaving first to catch his train back to Deltaville, and we are heading off to the airport to catch a flight home. There are tears all around. It will be a long time before we see each other again.

In Gatwick we stand, a forlorn little tribe, with luggage all around us and the boys now struggling to keep their eyes open, having had great fun playing computer games and watching films on the flight.

Rebecca Pearse kindly meets us and we spend the first couple of nights with them. It will be the first of many nights with the hospitality of various friends, until we find someplace to live.

Back in Cheshire, I stay with Jane and her three boys, whilst Ian has flown across the Atlantic to sail the boat back with Martin and some other male friends. I am jealous, but the boys need to get back into school for the start of the school term.

Eventually I find a caravan, no running water and old musty mattresses, mildew on the ceiling, but very cheap and a place to call our own. Also it is in the boatyard to which eventually *Brandamajo* will come and we will live in her until we start getting a salary again and can find a house to rent.

Meanwhile back in Deltaville the skipper is antifouling the bottom of *Brandamajo*, watching the weather forecasts with increasing anxiety as hurricanes form down near the equator and head their way North or dissipate before getting anywhere.

"Well not the most advisable time to cross, but it has been done," says Herb, the weather routing guru from Canada, who has seen many yachts across the Atlantic.

We have left it so late because we bought the boat Vat free and cannot return into the EU until we have been out a year.

Hindsight becomes clearer and clearer as he waits for a spell to cross. His crew are Ian, mountaineer, father of three boys the same age as ours and husband of Jane, one of my best friends in Cheshire. Then there is Matt, of Matt and Kate, who has sailed with us several times. Chris Baldwin, Matthew Baldwin's father, business entrepreneur and sailor himself, Keith, classified landlubber, but always game to give anything a go, and great for keeping crew morale up. And last but not least, a friend of Matt's, Rob.

They have a fairly uneventful crossing to the Azores. Ian discovers that he would prefer to have his feet on dry land and tries out one of the best diets ever - a three week course of seasickness. Sharing a cabin with Keith, who likes cold curry for breakfast. He kisses the ground as they land in the Azores. But he never shirks his duties.

Keith cracks his head open on the cockpit door. He is the only one who manages to put on weight instead of taking it off

Keith, Matt and Ian must leave them in the Azores, as they have to get back to jobs. The three remaining bring her back to Liverpool. On this leg of the trip they encounter a whale, a Minke whale so close to the stern of the boat that they can see the fold of skin under its mouth and its little beady eye.

They get so tired that they start hallucinating, but they bring *Brandamajo* home safe and sound. We are all waiting for her at Liverpool docks, including Grandma and Grandad who have come down to welcome them back.

Now the crew and family have left, we have taken the mast down and taken the boat up the Manchester Ship Canal and the Weaver Navigation, to Northwich, where she will be our home for a while. We are still married, we are still a family and if anything we are a stronger family than we were before we left. We have no house, no money, and a boat that has turned from an asset into a liability. But even now we don't regret doing what we did. Perhaps the only regret is that we didn't manage to do it earlier.

THE END